THE ISRAEL–PALESTINE CONFLICT

The conflict between Israelis and their forebears, on the one hand, and Palestinians and theirs, on the other, has lasted more than a century and generated more than its share of commentaries and histories. James L. Gelvin's new account of that conflict offers a compelling, accessible, and up-to-the-moment introduction for students and general readers. Beginning in the mid-nineteenth century, when the inhabitants of Ottoman Palestine and the Jews of eastern Europe began to conceive of themselves as members of national communities, the book traces the evolution and interaction of these communities from their first encounters in Palestine through to the present, exploring the external pressures and internal logic that have propelled their conflict. The book, which places events in Palestine within the framework of global history, skillfully interweaves biographical sketches, eyewitness accounts, poetry, fiction, and official documentation into its narrative and includes photographs, maps, and an abundance of supplementary material.

James L. Gelvin is Associate Professor in History at the University of California, Los Angeles. His research focuses on nationalism and the social and cultural history of the modern Middle East during the late nineteenth and early twentieth centuries. He is the author of *Divided Loyalties: Nationalism and Mass Politics in Syria at the Close of Empire* (1998) and *The Modern Middle East: A History* (2004).

THE ISRAEL–PALESTINE CONFLICT

One Hundred Years of War

JAMES L. GELVIN
University of California, Los Angeles

CAMBRIDGE
UNIVERSITY PRESS

CAMBRIDGE UNIVERSITY PRESS
Cambridge, New York, Melbourne, Madrid, Cape Town, Singapore, São Paulo

Cambridge University Press
40 West 20th Street, New York, NY 10011-4211, USA

www.cambridge.org
Information on this title: www.cambridge.org/9780521852890

© Cambridge University Press 2005

First published 2005

Printed in the United States of America

A catalog record for this publication is available from the British Library.

Library of Congress Cataloging in Publication Data
Gelvin, James L., 1951–
The Israel–Palestine conflict : one hundred years of war / James L. Gelvin.
p. cm.
Includes bibliographical references and index.
ISBN-13: 978-0-521-85289-0 (hardback)
ISBN-10: 0-521-85289-7 (hardback)
ISBN-13: 978-0-521-61804-5 (paperback)
ISBN-10: 0-521-61804-5 (paperback)
1. Arab-Israeli conflict. 2. Arab-Israeli conflict – 1993 – Peace. 3. Jews – Israel –
Politics and government – 20th century. 4. Palestinian Arabs –
Politics and government – 20th century. 5. Jewish nationalism – Israel.
6. Arab nationalism – Gaza Strip. 7. Arab nationalism – West Bank.
8. Nationalism – Israel. 9. Nationalism – Gaza Strip. 10. Nationalism – West Bank.
I. Title.
DS119.7.G3895   2005
956.04′2 – dc22   2005012022

ISBN-13   978-0-521-85289-0 hardback
ISBN-10   0-521-85289-7 hardback

ISBN-13   978-0-521-61804-5 paperback
ISBN-10   0-521-61804-5 paperback

CONTENTS

LIST OF ILLUSTRATIONS
AND MAPS

ILLUSTRATIONS

MAPS

AUTHOR'S NOTE

This is a book about the creation, evolution, interaction, and mutual definition of two national communities. It is about the struggle between those two communities, the inner logic that has propelled that struggle, and the historical conditions that have delimited its course. If for no other reason than its persistence and its never-ending demand for attention, the Israeli–Palestinian struggle has earned its claim to uniqueness. By most other standards, however, it might be regarded as the quintessential struggle of the modern age. Either way, it is a story worth recounting.

Sometimes the struggle between the two national communities in Palestine has been submerged in wider struggles that embroiled outside powers. There was a time when it seemingly dropped off the radar screen altogether. For the forty-five years between 1948 and 1993, most of the world chose to regard the struggle for Palestine as an Arab-Israeli conflict, as if the claims of one of the principals in the struggle could be addressed by outside powers or simply written off. With the hindsight of history, we now know better. The Arab-Israeli conflict was but a phase in a struggle that has come full circle, and no peace between Israel and its sovereign neighbors will bring the struggle to an end. Only the principals can do that.

I have written this book for students and general readers who wish to understand the broad sweep of the history of the Israeli–Palestinian struggle and situate it in its global context. The book is not, nor was it intended to be, encyclopedic. It is interpretive. It is also concise and, hopefully, engaging. If I have neglected or been too cavalier with your favorite hero, event, or peace plan, I apologize in advance. You might want to take consolation from the fact that I have honed the narrative you are about to read with care. You might also want to take consolation from the fact that, in return for the sacrifice of a few details, you are getting the occasional pearl. Where else are you going to find Michel Foucault's theory of governmentality slimmed down to a couple of paragraphs and written as if it were meant to be understood?

True believers on both sides of the struggle are, of course, beyond consolation. As you will soon see, I regard Zionism as a – perhaps the – prototypical nineteenth-century nationalist movement. I do not regard it as the fulfillment of Jewish history (as many of its adherents maintain), nor do I regard it as a "particularly virulent form of racism" (as its opponents have written). As a national movement, it is, to paraphrase Henry Fielding, no better than it should be. And yes, the word "Palestinian" does refer to a real nation, albeit one whose ancient lineage is as spurious as the ancient lineage of any other nation, and the word "Palestinian" can be used as a noun, not just as an adjective modifying the word "terrorist." While it is the role of the true believer to believe, it is the role of the historian to treat the self-aggrandizing claims of any and all nationalist movements with skepticism. The same goes for the claims of their opponents. I only hope I have done so evenly and effectively.

Skeptics, like pioneers, get all the arrows. Thus, it is with a certain amount of trepidation that I list those who have contributed to my efforts. First off, there is Marigold Acland, my editor at Cambridge University Press, who suggested I write this book even though I had stiffed her on another one. This is my penance. I also wish to thank others on the editorial side of this book: Eric Crahan, Isabelle Dambricourt, Pauline Ireland, and Sue Nicholas. Then there are those friends and colleagues who have read this or earlier versions of the book, made suggestions, or contributed in other ways: Carol Bakhos, David Dean Commins, Michael Cooperson, Roya Klaidman, Ussama Makdisi, David N. Myers, A. Rantin Polemick, Manal Quota, and Jihad Turk. Finally, to this list I would like to add those undergraduates who read this book in its preliminary stages and graciously called my attention to every typo and misplaced comma, as well as those who raised questions that forced me to rewrite or rethink what I was trying to say. For the second time in as many years, I wish to dedicate a book to them.

THE LAND AND ITS LURE

The British short story writer Saki (H. H. Munro) once described the island of Crete as a place that has produced more history than could be consumed locally. The same might be said of Palestine, the region that includes the contemporary State of Israel, the West Bank, and the Gaza Strip. The area in question is quite small. It stretches from the Mediterranean Sea in the west to the Jordan River in the east and from Lebanon in the north to the Gulf of Aqaba and the Sinai Peninsula in the south. Israel in its commonly recognized borders is roughly the size of the state of New Jersey. And Israel comprises almost 80 percent of historic Palestine. (As with most everything else pertaining to Palestine, there are those who would challenge even these simple assertions. According to right-wing Revisionist Zionists, whom we shall meet again later in our story, and [ironically] the left-wing Popular Front for the Liberation of Palestine, which we shall also meet again, Palestine includes the territory of the Hashemite Kingdom of Jordan as well. Hence, the slogan of the latter group: "The road to Jerusalem begins in Amman.")

The population of Palestine is also small. Israel's population is about 6.5 million, smaller than the population of London or New York City. There are approximately 3 million to 3.5 million Palestinians in the occupied territories – roughly the population of Chicago. (Although the exact figure is unknown, estimates for total number of Palestinians in the world run as high as 9 million.) Since 1948, wars between Israel and its neighbors have claimed upwards of 150,000 casualties. These wars were certainly tragic, but they just as certainly pale in horror when compared with the most grievous squandering of lives in the region during its recent history. In the Iran-Iraq War, which lasted from 1980 to 1988, there were 500,000 to 1 million dead and 1 million to 2 million

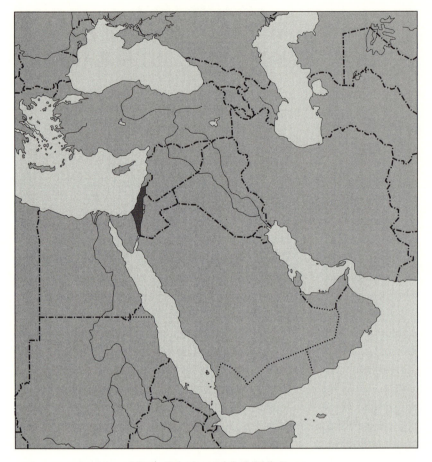

Map 1. Palestine and the Middle East.

wounded. Outside the region, there was the Bosnian war of 1992–5 (upwards of 250,000 dead), the 1994–5 genocide in Rwanda (500,000 to 850,000 dead), and the ongoing civil war in the Sudan (approximately 1.5 million dead from war and war-created famine).

The size of Palestine and the numbers directly affected by its political problems are thus minuscule in comparative terms. Nevertheless, the dispute between Israel, on the one hand, and the Palestinians and various Arab states, on the other, has been at the forefront of international attention for more than fifty years, and its roots stretch back more than a half century before that. Indeed, the dispute has gone on for such a long time and has been the subject of so much heated debate that it is easy to lose sight of the fundamental issue involved. The problem is, simply

1. Detail of 1892 topographic relief map of the "Holy Land," from the coastal plain (foreground) to the Jordan depression. (Source: From the collection of the author)

put, a dispute over real estate. Jewish immigrants and their descendants, guided by the nationalist ideology of Zionism, and the Palestinian Arab inhabitants among whom the Zionists settled both claim an exclusive right to inhabit and control some or all of Palestine.

Perhaps the best place to start, then, is with a brief look at the real estate in question. At the center of the territory of Palestine is a range of hills stretching from Lebanon in the north to the Negev desert in the south. The hills are interrupted in the northern Galilee region by the Valley of Jezreel (Plain of Esdraelon). For millennia the Valley of Jezreel was a major trade route linking the Mediterranean and Egypt with southwest Asia. It also provided the path for conquerors, from the Assyrians to the Persians.

South of the Valley of Jezreel is a hilly area that was the center of the ancient Jewish settlement and is the site of Jerusalem. Today the plateau forms what the Palestinians call "the occupied West Bank" and what the Israeli government calls "Judea and Samaria," after their Biblical names.

This area is mostly populated by Palestinians, many of whom live near or in the principal cities of the West Bank: Nablus, Ramallah, Hebron (al-Khalil), and Jericho, the original seat of the Palestinian Authority, the Palestinian government in the process of formation. Many of the Palestinians living on the West Bank can trace their ancestry back for generations, if not longer. Others fled to the West Bank from their homes in contemporary Israel as a result of the 1948 war.

Lowlands lie on either side of the plateau and to its south. To the west of the hilly area lies a coastal plain. The coastal plain provided two of the centers of Jewish immigration in the nineteenth century, one around Tel Aviv–Jaffa, the other about a third of the way up the coast to the port city of Haifa. To the east of the hilly area there is an area called the Jordan depression. This is not a psychological term – it refers to the fact that this area is low lying. The area is marked by the Dead Sea, which is below sea level – the lowest elevation of land on the planet. The Negev desert lies to the south of the hilly area. Until the establishment of the State of Israel, it was largely inhabited by bedouin. Further west, on the Mediterranean coast, lies the Gaza Strip, estimated to be the most densely populated territory on earth.

Although countless cities, towns, and villages dot this landscape, several in particular play an important role in our story. First, there are those that lie on the coastal plain. Furthest north is the port city of Acre. Acre was the principal harbor of the First Crusade, launched in 1096. The First Crusade was, for all intents and purposes, the only truly successful Crusade. It resulted in the capture of Jerusalem in 1099 and the establishment of the Kingdom of Jerusalem, which lasted about a century. Zionist historians of an earlier generation found comfort in the kingdom's longevity; Palestinian historians, in its eventual dislocation. Haifa, the principal seaport of Israel, lies to the south of Acre. It was originally built during the eighteenth century by an Ottoman vassal who sought to preserve his autonomy from the Ottomans by enriching himself and his principality by expanding trade with Europe. The port was modernized and enlarged during the British mandate period (1922–48), in part because it served as the terminus of an oil pipeline that stretched from Iraq to the Mediterranean. Further south still is Tel Aviv, which was founded in 1909 as a Jewish suburb of the Palestinian city of Jaffa. Tel Aviv is the largest city in contemporary Israel.

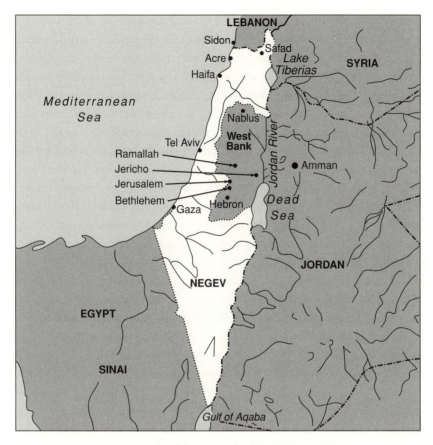

Map 2. Israel and the occupied Palestinian territories.

Jerusalem lies inland. The city was, according to the Bible, originally built by a people known as the Jebusites. Although "ownership" of the city is disputed, one untried solution would be to return the city to its original occupants, if any Jebusites can yet be found. For centuries, Jerusalem has been significant as a religious center and pilgrimage site. For Jews, it is the capital of David and Solomon's kingdom and the site of the Western (Wailing) Wall, which is the only remaining remnant of the second temple. For Muslims, it is the site from which Muhammad ascended to heaven on his famous night journey. For Christians, it is the site of the Passion and Crucifixion.

The struggle for control over some or all of the territory of Palestine pits two nationalist movements against each other. In spite of their claims to uniqueness, all nationalist movements bear a remarkable resemblance to one another. Each constructs a historical narrative that traces the unbroken lineage of a group – a nation – over time. Each endows the site of the nation's birth or greatest cultural or political moment with special meaning. Each uses its purported "special relationship" to some territory to justify its right to establish a sovereign state in that territory. This is where nationalism differs from mere nostalgia or collective memory: Whereas all sorts of religious and ethnic groups feel sentimental attachment to places, nationalism converts sentiment into politics. The adherents of a nationalist movement demand exclusive sovereignty over the designated territory and, for their nation, membership in the global order of nation-states. When it comes to connecting history and geography to political rights, neither Zionism nor Palestinian nationalism is a slacker.

Zionism views itself as the political expression of the Jewish nation. Indeed, it views itself as the fulfillment of Jewish history. In a manner analogous to most other nationalisms, Zionism has constructed a three-part narrative that traces the unbroken history of the Jewish nation from its birth and efflorescence in Palestine through a period of decay and degeneration in exile to a period of redemption at the hands of the modern Zionist movement and its return to its ancestral home in Palestine. For Zionists, the Jewish claim to Palestine can be found in the Bible and corroborative archaeological evidence. Most commonly, the Zionist narrative of Jewish history begins with Abraham and his descendants, who immigrated to Palestine in the second millennium BC, possibly from Iraq. The standard Zionist narrative considers the tenth-century BC reigns of King David and King Solomon the highpoint of the Jewish presence in Palestine. Theirs was a period of cultural and political glory, when the Jewish nation was politically united and religious authority radiated from the great temple in Jerusalem. But theirs was also a short-lived period, lasting a little less than seventy years, about half the length of the "golden age" of Greece.

Following the death of King Solomon, the Jewish community fragmented politically. In 63 BC, the Romans conquered Jerusalem, the capital of David and Solomon's kingdom, and in AD 135, after a series of revolts, they destroyed Jerusalem, enslaved or slaughtered its inhabitants, and dispersed most of the Jewish community. The Romans, drawing on the more extensive vocabulary of their Greek forerunners, renamed the reconquered province "Palestina" (from which we get the names "Palestine" and its Arabic equivalent, "Filastin"). Without a central cultic site, the hub of Jewish life shifted to the diaspora – Jewish communities outside Palestine, including some that had existed in such places as Babylon and Alexandria even before Roman times. The diaspora – later to include communities in Europe and the Americas – would remain the central site of Jewish life until the emergence of the Zionist movement. Zionists claim that Zionism saved the scattered Jewish nation from decay from within and corruption from without and redeemed it by restoring it to its rightful home in Palestine.

Zionists do not weave their narrative of Jewish history from whole cloth, of course. Nationalist movements – be they Russian, French, or American – never do. Palestine was, after all, recalled in Jewish texts and rituals for centuries, and for centuries Jews proclaimed at their yearly Passover seders, "Next year in Jerusalem." But there is a big difference between remembering Jerusalem and undertaking wholesale settlement activities in Palestine and eventually lodging a demand for Jewish self-determination in Palestine. What Zionists did, as all nationalist movements before and since have done, was to read their history selectively and draw conclusions from it that would not have been understandable to their ancestors before the advent of the modern era. The narrative of the Jewish people, as recounted by Zionists, situates periods of Jewish exile from Palestine (such as exile to Egypt and Babylon), dispersion (by the Assyrians), political division (most notably when the Jewish tribes divided themselves into two states, Israel and Judea), and wars with other inhabitants of the land (most notably the Philistines along the coast) within a framework that gives pride of place to ancient periods of political unity and dominance within Palestine. As the nineteenth-century French philosopher Ernest Renan once put it, "Getting history wrong is part of being a nation."

A good example of this getting history wrong can be found in the standard Israeli textbook accounts of the siege of Masada in AD 74. Masada was a fortress near the Dead Sea where Jewish rebels made their last stand against the Romans. According to one account, written by the Roman historian Josephus, the Jews of Masada

2. In an official ceremony, skeletons identified as belonging to second century Jewish rebels are reburied at Masada. (Source: David Rubinger/Corbis)

committed mass suicide rather than surrender to the Romans. The Romans, Josephus wrote, "encountering the mass of slain, instead of exulting as over enemies, admired the nobility of their resolve and the contempt of death displayed by so many in carrying it, unwavering, into execution."

The ruins of Masada, excavated in 1963–5, provide what one historian has called "an elaborate and persuasive stage scenery for a modern passion play of national rebirth."[1] The government of Israel considers Masada a historic monument. Maintained by the National Parks Authority, it is the site where members of the Israeli tank corps are sworn in. In 1968 (the year after the momentous and potentially cataclysmic Six-Day War), the Israeli government even organized a mass reburial of the skeletons found there. In the words of Israeli archaeologist Yigael Yadin,

Its scientific importance was known to be great. But more than that, Masada represents for all of us in Israel and for many elsewhere, archaeologists and

---

[1] Neil Asher Silberman, *Between Past and Present: Archaeology, Ideology, and Nationalism in the Modern Middle East* (New York: Doubleday, 1989), 88.

laymen, a symbol of courage, a monument of our great national figures, heroes who chose death over a life of physical and moral serfdom.[2]

The only problem with this rendition of the story of Masada is that it does not stand up to scrutiny. Our main source of the siege and mass suicide is Josephus's *The Jewish War*. Josephus was a Jewish turncoat who may have manufactured the entire story to slander a violent Jewish sect – either the better-known Zealots or the shadowy Sicarii (the "knife wielders"), one of which had control over the site during the period of the siege. By dwelling on the mass suicide, he very well may have been seeking to portray the barbarity of the besieged, not their heroism. After all, it was the same Masadans who apparently had raided a Jewish village nearby in AD 68, killing 700 Jewish men, women, and children. Hardly the stuff of national myth. Skeptics have also pointed out that archaeologists have found remains of pigs in kitchen areas (a clear violation of Jewish law that casts doubt on the very "Jewishness" of the site), that stories of mass suicide were as common in the classical period as serial killer movies are today, that in any event suicide is hardly condoned by Jewish law, and that no other Jewish text from the period recalls the incident. Yet, the slogan "Masada shall not fall again" still appears on coffee mugs and T-shirts on sale at souvenir shops near the site.

Investing sites such as Masada with special meaning reflects one way in which Zionists have used the Bible and archaeology to assert territorial claims. Another is through the act of naming. For Israelis, the West Bank town captured during the 1967 war is "Hebron," the Hebrew name for what is called in Arabic "al-Khalil." Hebron is mentioned in the Bible as one of the homes of the Jewish patriarch Abraham and as King David's first capital. Interestingly, both the Hebrew and Arabic names refer to the same individual. The Bible refers to Abraham as the "friend" (*haver*) of God. Muslims agree: Their prophet Abraham was also the "friend" (*al-khalil*) of God.

The town of Hebron lies in an area that most observers call "the occupied West Bank" but that Israelis officially designate "Judea and Samaria" after the territory's Biblical names. Calling the territory "the occupied West Bank," of course, presumes the Palestinianness of the

---

[2] Yigael Yadin, *Masada: Herod's Fortress and the Zealots' Last Stand* (New York: Random House, 1966), 13.

territory and the foreignness of the Israeli occupation. It thus serves to justify Palestinian aspirations to establish an independent entity there. On the other hand, by calling the territory "Judea and Samaria," Israelis are calling attention to their Biblical roots in the land and their right to inhabit or control it.

The problem of duelling names is not restricted to geography. Each side in the struggle for Palestine also seeks to buttress its historic narrative by naming events as well. Hence, what for Israelis is their War of Independence is for Palestinians the *nakba* (disaster). For the former, the name denotes the fulfillment of Zionist goals. For the latter, the name denotes a very different result of the 1948 war: the destruction of the Palestinian community in the territory of Israel and the expulsion or flight of almost three-quarters of a million Palestinians. (As in the case of geographic names, readers would be well advised not to read significance into the names used to designate events in this book. I use what I find comfortable, and for me "Hebron" is more comfortable than "al-Khalil," and "the occupied West Bank" is more comfortable than "Judea and Samaria.")

If this account seems a bit one-sided so far, it is merely because most Palestinians see their connection to the territory of Palestine as self-evident. According the 1968 version of the Charter of the Palestine Liberation Organization, for example,

The Palestinians are those Arab nationals who, until 1947, normally resided in Palestine, regardless of whether they were evicted from it or stayed there.... [That] there is a Palestinian community and that it has material, spiritual, and historical connections with Palestine are indisputable facts.

Archaeology has been called the national sport of Israel. On the other hand, the popularity of archaeology within the Palestinian community has never been as intense. The most important reason for the seeming lack of interest is that most Palestinians would wince at the idea that they have to establish a connection between themselves and the land. What Biblical narrative and archaeological evidence is to Zionism, their presence in Palestine at the time of Zionist immigration is to Palestinians.

Nevertheless, a historical narrative complete with elisions similar to those found in Zionist histories can be found in the writings of some Palestinian nationalists as well. Like the Zionist narrative, Palestinian narratives commonly begin in ancient times. Whereas Zionists begin their narratives with the migration of Abraham and his family to Palestine, the Palestinian narratives begin with the peoples he encountered there. Before the arrival of the Israelites, the ancient inhabitants of the land were of two types. First, there were the Canaanites, who spoke a northern Semitic language similar to Arabic and Hebrew. Another group, the Philistines, came to Palestine in the twelfth century BC. Many archaeologists associate the Philistines with the so-called Peoples of the Sea, who spread havoc among Phoenician, Egyptian, and Hittite habitations along the eastern Mediterranean coast. Palestinian histories assert that, unlike the Canaanites, the Philistines were never conquered by the Israelites.

The Philistines have gotten a bad rap from history. Contrary to Biblical accounts, traces of their civilization, recently dug up, indicate that they had established a flourishing urban civilization at a time when the tribes of the Biblical patriarchs were still pastoral. As a matter of fact, the Philistines united themselves into a "league of five cities" – Ashdod, Ashkelon, Ekron, Gath, and Gaza – in the territory of present-day Palestine. (The use of the term "Philistine" to mean an uncouth person came much later. Its first recorded use was by a chaplain at the University of Jena who, in 1694, claimed that the townsmen of Jena who beat up his students were no better than the Philistines of the Bible.)

Over time, according to the narrative, inhabitants of the region were joined by large numbers of Arabs from the Arabian peninsula, who had begun to drift north even before Muhammad's time and the first Islamic conquests. With those conquests, the inhabitants of Palestine became part of the great Islamic empire that stretched, at its height, from Spain to Afghanistan. Palestine played an important symbolic role in early Islam: The first Muslims prayed in the direction of Jerusalem, not Mecca and Medina, and, as previously mentioned, Jerusalem's Temple Mount (called by Muslims the "Haram al-Sharif" [the Noble Sanctuary]), the site of the great Dome of the Rock and al-Aqsa mosques, marks the spot of Muhammad's ascent to heaven during his night journey.

As in the case of the Zionist narrative, the Palestinian narrative asserts that a period of decline followed the period of glory. According to some accounts, it was Turkic invasions of Arab lands that first reduced the area to decay. As T. E. Lawrence would later put it in his *Seven Pillars of Wisdom,*

Early in the Middle Ages, the Turks found a footing in the Arab states, first as servants, then as helpers, and then as a parasitic growth which choked the life out of the old body politic. The last phase was of enmity, when the Hulagus or Timurs sated their blood lust, burning and destroying everything which irked them with a pretension of superiority.... By stages the Semites of Asia passed under their yoke, and found it a slow death.[3]

We shall see in the next chapter how far this assessment of "the Turk" misses the mark.

As in the Zionist narrative, worse was yet to come: European imperialism, eventually in its Zionist form. The Ottoman Empire and the Arab successor states that took its place were too weak or too compliant to withstand the European onslaught, setting the stage for the Palestinian national disaster of 1948. Again, to quote Renan, "Where national memories are concerned, griefs are of more value than triumphs, for they impose duties, and require a common effort." Now it was the Palestinians who faced the prospect of diaspora life. But just as the Zionist narrative ends with the self-glorification of modern Zionism as the means for the redemption of the Jewish nation, the Palestinian national narrative concludes in a similar manner, with the awakening of the Palestinian nation to self-consciousness and its struggle to achieve national fulfillment in a state of its own.

Like the Zionists, the Palestinians have not woven their national myth from whole cloth. And like the Zionist myth, the Palestinian national myth contains its own share of elisions and historically doubtful assertions. But also like the Zionist myth, the Palestinian national myth has to be taken seriously because it inspires belief and action among its adherents.

SUGGESTIONS FOR FURTHER READING

General Works

Abu-Lughud, Ibrahim, ed. *The Transformation of Palestine: Essays on the Origin and Development of the Arab-Israeli Conflict.* Evanston, IL: Northwestern

[3] T. E. Lawrence, *Seven Pillars of Wisdom: A Triumph* (New York: Anchor Books, 1991), 44.

University Press, 1971. Although by now a bit dated, a good anthology of articles on the social and political history of Palestine.

Gelvin, James L. *The Modern Middle East: A History*. New York: Oxford University Press, 2004. Puts the history of the Palestinian-Zionist/Israeli conflict in its Middle East and world historical contexts.

Laqueur, Walter, and Barry Rubin, eds. *The Israel-Arab Reader: A Documentary History of the Middle East Conflict*. New York: Penguin, 1995. Comprehensive compilation of documents relating to the conflict.

Owen, Roger. *The Middle East in the World Economy, 1800–1914*. London: I. B. Tauris, 1993. The gold standard for nineteenth-century Middle East political/ economic history.

Owen, Roger, and Sevket Pamuk. *A History of Middle East Economies in the Twentieth Century*. Cambridge, MA: Harvard University Press, 1999. Chronological supplement to *The Middle East in the World Economy*; uses a "national economy" approach to post–World War I economics of the region.

Smith, Charles D. *Palestine and the Arab-Israeli Conflict: A History with Documents*. Boston: Bedford/St. Martin's, 2001. One of the best comprehensive, blow-by-blow accounts of the Palestinian-Israeli conflict.

Smith, Pamela Ann. *Palestine and the Palestinians, 1876–1983*. New York: St. Martin's, 1984. Illustrated social history of Palestine and Palestinians; provides broad overview of over a century of Palestinian history.

Tessler, Mark. *A History of the Israeli–Palestinian Conflict*. Bloomington, IN: Indiana University Press, 1994. If not the most comprehensive one-volume account of the conflict, certainly the heaviest.

Specialized Works

Abu El-Haj, Nadia. *Facts on the Ground: Archeological Practice and Territorial Self-Fashioning in Israeli Society*. Chicago: University of Chicago Press, 2002. Probably the most sophisticated presentation of Israel's archaeological obsession and its relation to nationalism and "colonial knowledge."

Ben-Yehuda, Nachman. *The Masada Myth: Collective Memory and Mythmaking in Israel*. Madison: University of Wisconsin Press, 1995. Examination of how the fortress of Masada became a national monument in Israel.

Silberman, Neil Asher. *Between Past and Present: Archaeology, Ideology, and Nationalism in the Modern Middle East*. New York: Henry Holt, 1989. Series of essays examining the relationship between archaeology and nationalism in the region.

Slyomovics, Susan. *The Object of Memory: Arab and Jew Narrate the Palestinian Village*. Philadelphia: University of Pennsylvania Press, 1998. An anthropologist examines the attitudes and activities of the two communities with relation to a single site of no particular significance to anyone but those who contest its memory.

Zerubavel, Yael. *Recovered Roots: Collective Memory and the Making of Israeli National Tradition*. Chicago: University of Chicago Press, 1995. Traces several symbols central to the Israeli national mythos from the period of the Yishuv onwards.

2

CULTURES OF NATIONALISM

Nationalist narratives, such as those underlying Zionism and Palestinian nationalism, present us with a skewed and incomplete rendition of history. Two other factors further erode their usefulness. First, nationalist narratives assume that nations – such as the ones whose genealogy they describe – have existed throughout history. Nationalist movements, they assert, exist merely to bring those nations to a state of self-awareness. This assertion is far too modest. Nationalist movements do not bring preexisting nations to a state of self-awareness; nationalist movements create those nations. Second, nationalist narratives obscure or ignore the similarities between the nations whose history they claim to relate and other nations. This, of course, is done deliberately: By making it appear that its nation is distinctive, a nationalist narrative confirms the right of that nation to self-rule and sovereignty over a designated piece of real estate.

Zionism and Palestinian nationalism were cast in the same mold. Furthermore, while the advent of Zionism and the advent of a distinct Palestinian nationalism were never foregone conclusions, there can be no doubt that in a world in which nation-states provide the model for organizing political communities, Jews and the indigenous inhabitants of Palestine would claim to belong to some nation – either their own or someone else's – and espouse some nationalist creed. Again, this nationalist creed would be either their own or someone else's.

This last point is important and deserves to be underscored. As we shall see, Zionism emerged in the late nineteenth century for two reasons: Zionism was a reaction to European anti-Semitism and various nationalist movements that excluded Jews from political communities in the process of formation. But Zionism would have been impossible had Jews not been subjected to the same transformative processes that had equipped their neighbors with expectations about the proper ordering of political communities. That in a world of nation-states Jews would become nationalists was inevitable. That they would become *Jewish* nationalists was not. The same with Palestinian nationalism, which did not become a mass phenomenon until well into the period between World War I and World War II. That Palestinians would travel a nationalist path was also to be expected. But as we shall see, the path they travelled to *Palestinian* nationalism was laden with obstacles and detours.

The emergence of nations and nationalism is inextricably linked to the emergence of the modern state in western Europe. The diffusion of nations and nationalism throughout the world is linked as well to the global spread of the modern state system. Before the nineteenth century, the predominant form of political organization in most of the world was either smaller than the modern state (city-states, principalities, etc.) or much larger (empires). It is empires that concern us here. Empires have existed for all of recorded history. These empires were not like modern overseas empires where a "metropolitan" or "home" state ruled over peoples (usually of a darker skin color) far away. Rather, the empires of the premodern and early modern eras ruled over expanses of adjoining territory. Thus, when thinking about premodern or early modern empires, it is more helpful to think of the Roman Empire in ancient times rather than the British Empire of the nineteenth century.

Although premodern and early modern empires came in various shapes and sizes, they all shared three characteristics. First, these empires did not much interfere in the day-to-day lives of their citizens. Overall, imperial rulers expected two things from their populations: They expected the populations they ruled to behave themselves by not rebelling against imperial control and to pay taxes or tribute to the state. Empires used the taxes and tribute they collected to pay for imperial defense, a centralized bureaucracy, and the deliberately awe inspiring lifestyles of the rulers. As a matter of fact, it might be stated that empires were only as large as the territory from which they could extract taxes and tribute.

The second characteristic of empires was that they were governed by imperial elites who frequently were of a different religion, were of a different descent, and spoke a different language from those they ruled.

As any reader of Tolstoy knows, for example, the court language in imperial Russia was French, not the Russian spoken by peasants. In a similar vein, Turkish-speaking Muslim elites in the Ottoman Empire ruled over populations that spoke a variety of languages (Arabic, Greek, Armenian, etc.), practiced a variety of religions (Christianity in all its forms, Judaism, non-Sunni Islam), and included Slavs, Arabs, Kurds, and so on, as well as Turks.

Finally, premodern and early modern empires rarely attempted to impose any sort of uniformity on their populations. In other words, they did not attempt to standardize the language of their populations, nor did they attempt to impose on them cultural standards through a single educational system. There were two reasons for this. On the one hand, they could not. Before the advent of modern communications, transportation, and military technologies, central control was too weak. Commonly, imperial elites based in capital cities such as Istanbul relied on cooperative local leaders who acted as mediators with local populations in Baghdad or Damascus. On the other hand, imperial elites did not think of the state as we do. It never occurred to them that the population over which they ruled had to share common characteristics, had to have a common identity, or had to share the same culture as members of the imperial court. Such thinking would come later.

There were, of course, exceptions. Some empires, such as the Roman Empire, did attempt to promote a common "civic" religion. The Romans, for example, expected everyone to worship the Roman gods as a sign of loyalty to the empire, although they did not demand that the populations they governed abandon their local cults. This was why the Romans so brutally suppressed the Jewish revolt of the second century AD. Uniquely among Roman subjects, Jews refused to worship Roman gods alongside their own – an act that the Romans interpreted not so much as heresy but treason.

Because they were able to draw resources and manpower from vast expanses, empires were particularly powerful political units. And empires might have continued to be the most powerful political units had there not occurred a conceptual breakthrough among European statesmen and rulers during the sixteenth and seventeenth centuries. To gain advantage for their states in the highly competitive European environment, and to find a way out of the incessant religious wars that divided and weakened their states, these statesmen and rulers championed a novel approach to statecraft. They sought to make loyalty to the sovereign the ultimate object of loyalty for imperial subjects – one that transcended their subjects' loyalty to particular religious creeds. Rather than equating the strength of the state with the size of the territory from which they might extract taxes and tribute, statesmen and rulers came to believe that the strength of states lay in their "social power"– their ability to mobilize their populations and harness their energies for the common good. By inventing the notion that there existed something called a "population" that had a "common interest," statesmen and rulers imbued the inhabitants of their states with an identity and purpose. Statesmen and rulers made this common identity and purpose concrete to their newly established populations in two ways: they expanded the disciplinary reach of their states to more effectively police, coordinate, and direct the day-to-day activities of their subjects, and they engaged them in common practical activities that made them cogs in a "national" machine. Thus were born standardized legal codes and educational systems, conscript armies, and even rudimentary national economic planning.

Over time, the populations engaged by states in common activities internalized the notion that they were part of unified societies, that these societies had identities of their own, and that these societies compelled loyalty and placed obligations on their citizenry. They also came to believe that, much like themselves, the rest of humanity is also naturally divided into unified societies – nations – each of which can be identified by one or more characteristics (shared language, ethnicity, religion, history) its citizenry holds in common, that the only type of government that can promote the common interest is national self-government, and that nations are to be based in some territories that are the repository for the nations' history and memory. These beliefs form the basis of what might be called a "culture of nationalism." Some of these beliefs – the persistence of identities over time, the applicability of universal laws to human society – drew on ideas codified during the eighteenth-century European Enlightenment. Others – such as the belief in discrete communities rooted in specific territories – drew on ideas codified by the Romantic movement, which, ironically, arose in Europe in reaction to the Enlightenment.

Although originating in Europe, the new concept of statecraft diffused worldwide, leaving in its wake nations bound together by nationalism. This diffusion took place in three ways. Sometimes, Europeans imposed their conceptions of state directly through colonialism, as the British did in the Indian subcontinent. Sometimes, would-be national leaders, inspired by borrowed ideals or compelled by the requirements of the world system of nation-states (in which they sought membership for their purported nations), applied the new rules for state building. Such was the case in the Balkans, for example. Finally, sometimes imperial elites, seeking to enhance imperial power or to defend themselves against European imperialism by emulating their adversaries, adopted the European model. Such was the case in the Ottoman Empire, in which the territory of Palestine lay, and in the Austrian Empire (called the Austro-Hungarian Empire after 1867) and the Russian Empire, where the majority of Jews lived. The key to understanding the emergence of nationalism among both populations can be found in the transformation of these empires.

THE NATIONALIZATION OF OTTOMAN PALESTINE

The territory that is now called Palestine was one of the core areas of Islam. In other words, Palestine was one of the areas first conquered by Arab Muslims following the emergence of Islam in the seventh century. In the wake of the conquests, most of the population of Palestine adopted Arabic as its language and much of the population adopted Islam as well.

At first, the Islamic world was politically united under a caliph, literally, the "successor" to Muhammad. However, the political unity of the Islamic world did not hold for long. Although the initial fissures in the Islamic empire were generated by internal fragmentation, beginning in the tenth century invaders from outside the Middle East, attracted by the wealth or lack of political cohesion of the Islamic domains or impelled by troubles back home, began to enter the region. Among them were Turkish-speaking invaders from the north who carved out a number of independent principalities and even empires in the Middle East.

Sometimes, bands of Turkic warriors would form in frontier areas and raid the domains of other principalities or empires. One such band

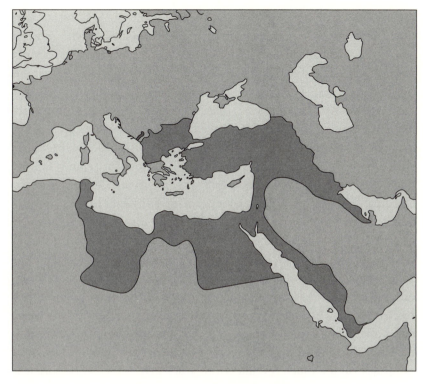

Map 3. Ottoman Empire, circa 1850.

formed adjacent to the frontier of the Byzantine Empire under the leadership of the legendary warrior Osman (1259–1326), the founder of the Ottoman dynasty. The Ottomans began their conquests in the far west of Anatolia (the site of the present-day Republic of Turkey) and in the Balkans. In 1453 the Ottomans captured Constantinople, the capital of the Byzantine Empire, and renamed it Istanbul. Since the Byzantine Empire was the successor to the Roman Empire, the Ottomans in effect put an end to an imperium that had ruled first from Rome, then from Constantinople, for over a millennium and a half. In 1516 the Ottomans began their conquest of the Middle East, establishing an empire that would last until 1918. At its height, the empire included much of the Balkans, the Middle East as far east as (but not including) Persia, parts of the Arabian peninsula, Egypt, and North Africa as far west as (but not including) Morocco.

The Ottoman Empire lasted for over four hundred years. During that time, its territorial expanse waxed and waned, as did the control exercised by Istanbul over often far-flung provinces. And during that time the relationship between the imperial government and the imperial subjects also changed dramatically, as the empire was forced to respond to both internal and external challenges. Thus, the Ottoman Empire of the sixteenth century was quite different from the empire of the nineteenth century. Suffice it to say that the Ottoman Empire of the early modern period – the period that stretched from the sixteenth century through at least the first half of the eighteenth – shared characteristics with other early modern empires. As in the case of other empires of the time, the principal external concerns of the Ottoman Empire were to expand the territory from which taxes and tribute might be collected and to defend its revenue-producing domains from rival empires. As in the case of other empires of the time, its principal internal concerns were to collect taxes and tribute from its population, protect the tax- and tribute-paying peasantry from the depredations of bedouin and bandits, ensure the safety and prosperity of commerce, deter urban unrest by ensuring urban areas were stocked with adequate supplies of goods, and prevent local notables and provincial functionaries, upon whom the empire depended for the collection of those taxes and tribute, from skimming off too much revenue for themselves or establishing independent power bases.

At the head of the Ottoman Empire stood the sultan, a descendent of Osman. As in the case of other early modern empires, religion provided one of the cornerstones of dynastic legitimacy in the Ottoman Empire. The empire was the preeminent (Sunni) Islamic empire of its time. Not only was *shari'a* – Islamic law – one of the sources for legal practice in the empire (the others being local customary law and *kanun*, or law derived from imperial pronouncements), and not only did the sultan occasionally lay claim to the title of caliph (although the occasions were rarer than one might expect), the empire included within its domains the two holy cities of Arabia, Mecca and Medina, and the holy city of Jerusalem.

Possession of the three holy cities increased the importance of Palestine in the minds of imperial elites. The Ottoman sultans invested great value in the annual *hajj* (pilgrimage) caravan that journeyed from Istanbul to Damascus to Egypt and Arabia. Supplying the caravan was a great economic boon to those who lived in areas, like Palestine, through which the caravan passed. Furthermore, when the government in Istanbul was strong and financially solvent, it set up military outposts in Palestine to protect the caravan from bedouin raids. Because the imperial military presence increased rural security during these times, both the area under cultivation and the rural population expanded. Ottoman sultans also sponsored public works in Jerusalem. Suleiman the Magnificent, who ruled from 1520 to 1566, for example, attempted to demonstrate his religiosity by reconstructing and refurbishing the city. He rebuilt the walls of the city (which exist to this day) and constructed aqueducts, fountains, hospitals, and schools.

(Although "high" Islam was an important source of legitimacy for the Ottoman state, popular belief and practice in Palestine varied widely – as they did for most religions in the early modern world. An eighteenth-century French traveller to Palestine describes the following incident:

"Why," asked a bedouin shaykh, "do you wish to return among the Franks? Since you have no aversion to our manners; since you know how to use the lance and manage a horse like a bedouin, why don't you stay among us? We shall give you cloaks, a tent, a virtuous and young bedouin girl, and a good blood mare. You shall live in our house."

"But do you not know," replied I, "that, born among the Franks, I have been educated in their religion? In what light will the Arabs view an infidel, or what will they think of an apostate?"

"And do not you yourself perceive," said he, "that the Arabs live without troubling themselves either about the Prophet, or the Qur'an? Every man with us follows the direction of his conscience. Men have a right to judge of actions, but religion itself must be left to God alone."

This tale is obviously as embroidered as the cloaks promised the traveller, but there is a grain of truth to it. As in much of the Islamic world, Islamic practice in Palestine varied widely. The attempt to impose a rigid Islamic orthodoxy and "Islamic lifestyle" in Palestine would come only with the arrival of the modern age.)

Whatever Palestine's religious significance, during the first centuries of Ottoman control the hand of the imperial government rested lightly on its population, as it did on the population in most of the empire. Not only was a vast majority of the population of Palestine rural – as late as 1922, 65 percent of the population lived in rural areas – it was heavily concentrated on or near the hilly spine of inland Palestine. Living on the coastal plain or eastern lowlands would have placed peasants at the mercy of bedouin, whose depredations the imperial government was powerless to prevent. Without modern communications and military technology, the early modern Ottomans found it difficult to control areas in which the terrain was rough. Up to the end of the eighteenth century, for example, the imperial government could only collect taxes in the region of Nablus through a process called a *dawra* (circuit). Rather than maintaining a permanent presence in the area, the Ottoman governor or his deputy personally led a contingent of troops on an annual tour through the countryside to show the flag and remind the population of their financial obligations to the Ottoman state.

It has been estimated that at the beginning of the nineteenth century there were more than one thousand villages in the territory that is now Palestine. In her wanderings around Palestine in 1855, a British traveller, Mary Eliza Rogers, described one such village as follows:

When I went out on the 11th of February, I saw labourers busy in the plain, at the foot of the Carmel Hills. Large patches of land were being ploughed. The rich brown earth was thrown up by clumsy-looking ploughshares, dragged by oxen. Boys were employed in gathering out stones from tracts of land, round which men were building low rough stone walls. New hedges of prickly pears were being planted round gardens and orchards. The gardens and orchards looked very beautiful. Almond trees were full of blossom. Lemon and shad-dock trees were laden with fruit. [Suddenly], two little girls of the Sakhali family came to me. I invited my friendly little guests to remain with me to breakfast. They wore dark cotton trousers, made very full and long, and cloth jackets, closely fitting and fastened up to the throat. Their mundils, or bright coloured muslin kerchiefs, were put on like shawls over the head, crossed under the chin, and the ends tied on the top of the head. They were amused to hear about English children, and laughed heartily when I told them that in England a few camels are kept as curiosities, in a beautiful garden. They could not understand how we could live in a land where there are no camels to carry burdens. I tried to explain to them the use of carts and railed roads; but as they had never seen a wheeled carriage of any kind, it was very diffi-cult to convey the idea, even with the help of pictures. They were very clever, quick children; and though only eight and nine years old, they could already make bread and prepare many simple dishes. They were surprised that I had not been taught how to cook; it is the chief point in the education of an Arab girl.[1]

---

[1] Mary Eliza Rogers, *Domestic Life in Palestine* (London: Kegan Paul International, 1989), 169–70.

Although Rogers's comments are useful for getting a feel of Palestinian village life, it would be wrong to give them too much credence. Like many Western travellers, Mary Eliza Rogers found in Palestine what she had come to find: the Holy Land, unchanged since the time of Jesus. Little did she realize that her travels coincided with a period of profound change in Palestinian society. This change affected both the material and the mental experiences of the population she encountered. Two factors contributed to this change.

The first of these two factors was the expansion of market relations in Palestine and the integration of Palestine into the world economy. The Palestine that Mary Eliza Rogers thought she encountered was a Palestine in which self-sufficient villagers produced almost all of what they needed. When confronted by the few needs they could not themselves meet, they went to market and exchanged their surplus for commodities they could not fashion themselves. The sort of economy Mary Eliza Rogers expected to find in Palestine is called a marketplace economy, and although many of the villagers she met would have felt at home in such an economy, an increasing number of villages in Palestine were being integrated into a market economy – an economy in which people produced not just for consumption but for exchange. This meant that, rather than raising a variety of crops to meet their immediate needs, over time more and more farmers were specializing in a single crop – cotton, for example – which they could then sell. They would then take the proceeds from the sale and exchange them for the goods they needed.

The emergence of market economies throughout the world coincided with the expansion of a global economy based on an unequal exchange between a few "core" countries, which produced finished products and exported them to lesser developed, "peripheral" countries, which produced raw materials to feed the factories of the core. The expansion of this global economy into the Middle East coincided with the onset of the Industrial Revolution in western Europe and accelerated with the reestablishment of peace and stability during the post-Napoleonic (post-1815) period.

The expansion of the global economy into the Middle East sparked the emergence of the so-called cotton principalities in Palestine. During the eighteenth century, the power of the central Ottoman government was in one of its "waning" periods, and the government's authority throughout the empire was increasingly challenged by local warlords. Two warlords of note emerged in Palestine. A warlord of bedouin origin, Zahir al-ʿUmar, took control over the Galilee region and established a principality with its capital at Acre. Further north, a former slave from Egypt, Ahmad Pasha al-Jazzar, took control over the port of Sidon (in present-day Lebanon) and established a principality that stretched into southern Syria. The legendary exploits of al-Jazzar, whose disposition can be seen from his nickname, *al-saffah* (the butcher), are still recounted in Palestine. According to one tale, al-Jazzar's servants were so afraid of him that when he died they waited for three days before entering his chamber. Only when his decomposing body began to stink did they know for sure that their intrusion would not incur his wrath.

That both Zahir al-ʿUmar and Ahmad Pasha al-Jazzar chose to establish their capitals on the coast is indicative of the growing importance of international commerce during this period. The Industrial Revolution began with advances in textile manufacture, and the best-quality cotton in the Ottoman Empire came from the Galilee region. In the early eighteenth century, French traders had established themselves in Sidon and Acre. Traders from other nations soon followed. As European competition increased for a limited amount of cotton, prices rose and landlords expanded the acreage under cultivation. Hence, the availability of cotton for the Sakhali daughters' outfits, which, unbeknownst to Mary Eliza Rogers, would probably have been made from wool a century earlier. Zahir al-ʿUmar traded cotton grown in his domains for European weapons and used his profits to rebuild Acre and found another port city, Haifa. For the Ottomans, enough was enough. In 1775, the Ottoman government sent a naval force against Zahir al-ʿUmar's capital and recognized al-Jazzar as governor of the region. Warlords being warlords, al-Jazzar quickly dealt with the Zahir al-ʿUmar problem.

As governor, al-Jazzar maintained his province's dependence on cotton. This dependence sometimes had disastrous consequences. When Eli Whitney invented the cotton gin in 1793, the area of cotton cultivation in the American south expanded, and American cotton glutted the market. By 1852 the price of cotton exported from the Galilee had dropped 90 percent, driving many of the farmers who grew it into bankruptcy. Nevertheless, hope sprang eternal. With the onset of the Crimean War (1853–6), the demand for cotton among European states increased, as it did during the American Civil War, which took American cotton

3. Jaffa market in the nineteenth century. (Source: From the collection of the author)

temporarily off the market. During this period, Palestinian farmers once again turned to cotton cultivation. And when American cotton came back on the market in 1865, they suffered from the same misfortune they had a decade and a half before.

Overall, the cultivation of cash crops in Palestine expanded during the nineteenth century. In 1850, the estimated value of agricultural exports from the port of Jaffa was £24,000; in 1881, it was £336,000; on the eve of World War I, the highpoint of what some historians call the "first era of globalization," it was £750,000. Although the bulk of these exports consisted of cereals, after 1873 they came to include the famous Jaffa orange, whose thick skin allowed it to be buffeted in the cargo hold of a steamship without bruising.

As we have seen, the increasing dependence of Palestinian farmers on exports during the "long nineteenth century" trapped them in the boom-and-bust cycle of the international market. But the integration of Palestine into the world economy and the expansion of a market economy inside Palestine had other effects as well. The expansion of a market economy in Palestine enlarged what one historian calls the "social space" of its inhabitants, in effect changing their perception of their lived world as links between cities and countryside, and between inhabitants of the region and inhabitants of the world beyond, increased in number and importance.

The second factor that contributed to the transformation of Palestine in the nineteenth, century was the restructuring of the governmental apparatus so that the state could more effectively undertake a broader range of activities, more effectively intervene into the lives of its citizens, and more effectively police and regiment their endeavors. Ironically, it was not the Ottoman Empire that initiated these efforts in Palestine. Rather, it was the obstreperous warlord of Egypt, Mehmet Ali, who introduced Palestinians to the techniques of modern statecraft during the decade-long (1831–41) Egyptian occupation of Palestine.

Mehmet Ali was the son of an Albanian pirate. After Napoleon's invasion of Egypt in 1798, Mehmet Ali led a contingent of troops attached to a joint Anglo-Ottoman force sent to oust the diminutive general from what was, after all, a province of the Ottoman Empire. In the wake of the campaign, Mehmet Ali seized control of Egypt and, to secure his position against Ottoman retribution, began a concerted effort to restructure the government, military, and economy of the province. But Mehmet Ali's ambitions were not so easily satisfied. Claiming that the Ottomans had promised him the territory that is now Palestine, Syria, and Lebanon in exchange for his assistance in putting down a rebellion in the Ottoman province of Greece, Mehmet Ali sent his son, Ibrahim Pasha, north at the head of an army. For Mehmet Ali, this territory – also known as "Greater Syria" – was a prize worth fighting for. Occupying this territory would enable the Egyptians to control the commerce passing through the eastern Mediterranean. It would also gain for Egypt access to raw materials such as lumber, silk, and cotton to supply the factories and shipyards Mehmet Ali envisioned for his domains. Finally, by occupying Greater Syria the Egyptians would be able to secure the escape route that Egyptian peasants, who did not relish conscription into the military or the labor gangs organized by the Egyptian government, all too often used to flee from their newly imposed obligations.

As his father had done in Egypt, Ibrahim Pasha introduced into Palestine many of the institutions and structures associated with modern states. He disarmed the peasantry and introduced military conscription to ensure the state's monopoly on violence and safeguard his newly acquired territory. He imposed direct taxation on the population so that intermediaries would not siphon off revenues intended for the state, and to assist Egyptian governors in extracting revenues from an often recalcitrant population, he appointed advisory councils made up of local notables who knew the lay of the land. He encouraged the cultivation of cash crops that could be sold abroad to earn foreign exchange, and he invested in public works such as roads and irrigation canals to expand the acreage of land under cultivation, allow cash crops to be transported to market quickly, and strengthen central control.

As might be expected, the population of Palestine was rarely enthusiastic about what we take for granted as signs of modernity. Mary Eliza Rogers tells the following story in her memoirs:

My acquaintance, Muhammad, had lost the use of one eye. In answer to my inquiry, he told me that his mother had purposely destroyed the sight by application of poisonous leaves when he was young, to render him unfit for service in the army. This practice was very common in Egypt until Ibrahim Pasha put an effectual stop to it by ordering a regiment to be formed entirely of one-eyed men, and every one who had lost the sight of an eye, either by accident or design, was compelled to join it. Muhammad, among others, was enrolled, and their Cyclopean regiment became the most formidable in Egyptian service.[2]

Nevertheless, the clock was not to be turned back. After the Ottomans, with British assistance, expelled the Egyptian army and administration from Palestine, not only did they retain many of the innovations introduced by the Egyptians, they expanded them. Although many of the programs introduced by the Ottoman government stumbled in the provinces or produced effects that differed from their intention, the expansion of Ottoman state capabilities, like the integration of Palestine into the world economy, continued unabated for the remainder of the century and into the next. How, then, did the expansion of state control affect life in Palestine?

First, the reassertion of Ottoman power over Palestine ensured that there would be greater security for agriculture and agriculturalists. Guaranteed by the presence of an occupying army, security in Palestine had been tight during the Egyptian period. With the withdrawal of Egyptian troops in 1841, an intense struggle broke out among powerful local leaders, particularly in the Jerusalem area. In the early 1850s, fearing

---

[2] Mary Eliza Rogers, *Domestic Life in Palestine* (London: Kegan Paul International, 1989), 175.

that a dispute among rival Christian sects over access to holy places in Jerusalem would provoke European intervention, the Ottomans posted a garrison in the city and placed Jerusalem under direct Ottoman control. The Ottomans soon subdued the immediate countryside and, as revenues from the pacified areas increased, brought district after district under their control. Wherever they were able to assert their authority, the Ottomans imposed conscription, reimposed tax collection, and broke the military power of local families. Once Ottoman control was established in the mountains, the Ottomans turned their attention to the plains. The Ottomans established new garrisons, built new railroads (including the famous Hijaz Railway and a rail link that connected Jerusalem to Jaffa on the coast), and settled the bedouin. By the 1870s, most of the Jezreel Valley was planted with wheat, barley, millet, sesame, cotton, tobacco, and the castor oil plant. On the coast between Haifa and Jaffa, the process of recultivation was slower but still irreversible.

A number of groups participated in the recultivation of the plains. There were, for example, bedouin. Although the Ottoman army forcibly settled the more reluctant bedouin, other tribes settled voluntarily, obviously believing discretion to be the better part of valor. Some even embraced settlement because the worldwide increase in agricultural prices made the cultivation of cash crops more lucrative and secure than plundering their neighbors. The relative security of the plains also attracted religious settlers from Europe, such as the latter-day Templars, a group of German Protestant settlers who came to Palestine beginning in the late 1860s and established colonies as far inland as the Galilee. Perhaps the most important group to recultivate the coastal plain, however, consisted of farmers from nearby hill villages who established satellite settlements called *khirab* (sing. *khirba*) in the lowlands. *Khirba* literally means "ruins." Since villagers resided in their home villages for most of the year and only went down to the plains for the planting and harvest, their temporary quarters often appeared abandoned and ramshackle.

The forsaken state of these satellite villages created an impression of Palestine among Western visitors and Zionist settlers far removed from reality. For example, Mark Twain, who visited Palestine in 1867, described Palestine as follows in *Innocents Abroad*:

[Palestine is] a desolate country, whose soil is rich enough, but is given over wholly to weeds – a silent, mournful expanse.... A desolation is here that

4. Palestinian peasants harvesting olives, 1886. (Source: From the collection of the author)

not even imagination can grace with the pomp of life and action. . . . We never saw a human being on the whole route. . . . There was hardly a tree or a shrub anywhere. Even the olive and cactus, those fast friends of worthless soil, had almost deserted the country.

And then there were those among the early Zionists, ensconced in Europe, who invented the slogan "A land without a people for a people [Jews] without a land." Little did tourists like Twain or advocates of settlement like the early Zionists comprehend that the seemingly abandoned and ramshackle villages on the plain indicated an increase in security and prosperity, not an absence of habitation. As a matter of fact, statistics belie the illusion of an empty land awaiting reclamation: From 1880 to 1913 there was steady demographic growth in Palestine. During this period, the overall population of Palestine increased by approximately 50 percent, and the population of the largest towns doubled. Although the influx of 50,000 European Jews certainly pushed up these numbers, Jewish immigrants made up only 7 percent of the total population of 750,000. Palestine was hardly a "land without a people."

Increased security and the lure of profits were not the only reasons for the reclamation of agricultural land. Nor were they the only reasons why land in Palestine became such an attractive investment during the second half of the nineteenth century. Desperate to increase revenue, the Ottoman government changed the rules of the real estate game in midcentury. In 1858, the government promulgated a new land code that gave legal sanction to what in effect was private ownership of most land in the empire.

To understand just how revolutionary the 1858 land code was, it is important to understand that before its announcement most of the land in the empire was legally in the hands of the state. This land was known as *miri* land. Although Ottoman peasants were free and not bound to this land, they did not have unconditional rights to the soil they tilled. For the most part, peasants had the right to live on, work, and enjoy the fruits of their lands, but they did not own them as "freehold," they could not legally sell them, nor could they legally pass them on as property to their descendants. (And here one must differentiate between actual practice and legal niceties. In legal terms, land ownership was unusual in the Ottoman Empire; in practice, it was not.)

In Palestine, village organization made land tenure even more complicated. If the fundamental building block of Palestinian society was the village, the fundamental building block of the Palestinian village was the family. A typical village was composed of four or five clans (*hama'il*, sing. *hamula*). At the head of each clan was an elder (*shaykh*), and a village shaykh was chosen from among them. The village shaykh represented his village to the outside world, which in this case meant neighboring villages, bedouin bands, and the government; the other shaykhs arbitrated intravillage disputes and regulated access to land. Each clan was entitled to cultivate a fixed proportion of land, and each family of each clan received an allotment during a periodic redivision of land-use rights. That redivision commonly occurred every two years. Grazing lands, woodlands, and water were held in common by the entire village.

This entire system raised a perplexing question for Ottoman tax collectors: Who, exactly, was responsible for the payment of what to the central government? The purpose of the 1858 land code was to resolve this question and, by doing so, ensure a steady stream of tax revenue to the government. The law allowed individuals to register the miri lands they cultivated in their names, and by so doing they automatically assumed the tax burden of their property. It also allowed individuals to transfer title to others. The key word here is "individuals": Because collective ownership of land would have made it impossible to determine tax liability, the state did not allow whole villages to register the land they had managed by custom. Although those who registered land did not have absolute rights over it – the state reserved for itself the right to regulate land transfer and land usage – the effect of the law rendered state land closer to an ideal "freehold" than it had ever been before.

At least on paper. In fact, the 1858 land code ran into problems unforeseen by bureaucrats in Istanbul and led to unintended consequences that no one could have predicted. Because the law did not recognize collective ownership of land, village shaykhs and bedouin chieftains frequently registered land in their own name. This, of course, created a system of rigid social and economic stratification where none had existed previously. In addition, peasants who cultivated the land often could not afford the registration fee, lost their land to usurers who had advanced them money for seed or supplies and charged them up to 40 percent interest for the privilege, or simply transferred the land to urban notables who were more than willing to take it off their hands. Peasants well understood that it was not generosity that motivated the Ottoman government to grant them the right to register their lands in their own names; rather, many justifiably believed that registering the lands they cultivated in their own names would enable the government to tax them more efficiently and ferret out their sons for military service.

Urban notables did not benefit just from the suspicions of Palestinian peasants. Often, they would use their position to gain access to land. After it had retaken control of Palestine, the Ottoman government authorized the formation of elected councils to assist Ottoman functionaries appointed from Istanbul. Since the councils had responsibility for enforcing the 1858 land code, their most enterprising members were able to get first dibs on unregistered property through a process the Tammany Hall politicians of New York liked to call "honest graft" – that is, by using knowledge and access only available to insiders for personal enrichment. The opportunities for honest graft expanded in Palestine in the mid to late nineteenth century when the Ottoman government empowered cities to tax their residents, draw up their own budgets, and offer contracts for municipal services for the first time in their history. Jerusalem obtained these rights in 1863, Jaffa in 1872. For urban notables, as for New York's Democratic Party bosses, position begat wealth, wealth begat power, and power begat position. Urban notables would continue to play a central role in local Palestinian politics, in one form or another, through the late interwar period. As we shall see, their continued competition for position and status only served to hinder the emergence of a unified Palestinian national movement.

The fact that lands often ended up in the hands of absentee landowners affected the future history of Palestine in another way as well. Landowners who acquired land because it was a safe or lucrative investment frequently lived in cities distant from their holdings and had little attachment to them or to the people who resided on them. Sometimes their holdings were extensive: The Sursoq family of Beirut, for example, was able to accumulate over seventy square miles of prime real estate in the Jezreel Valley. When representatives of the Jewish National Fund came around offering top dollar for land on which to establish Jewish settlements, many did not hesitate to sell. The differentiation between those families that sold land to Zionists and those that refused to do so still holds a place in Palestinian collective memory.

If elected councils, municipal charters, and land registration enabled a thin stratum of urban notables to consolidate their power and influence within Palestinian society, other policies had a very different effect. During the nineteenth century, the Ottoman government issued two decrees that redefined the relations among imperial subjects and between those subjects and the state that governed them: the Hatt-i Sharif of Gulhane (1839) and the Islahat Fermani (1856). The documents promised all Ottoman subjects "perfect security for life, honor, and property" and religious liberty and equality for the non-Muslim inhabitants of the empire. In other words, the Hatt-i Sharif of Gulhane and the Islahat Fermani redefined imperial subjects as citizens who were bound to each other because of their residence in a common territory, their commitment to a common set of legal norms, and their common loyalty to the Ottoman state.

It should be clear by now what the Ottoman government hoped to achieve by issuing these decrees. What is surprising, however, is the speed with which the new Ottoman citizens took to the promises the government made. According to historian Beshara Doumani, as early as the 1840s peasants in Palestine addressed petitions to the government in Istanbul that mimicked the language of the Hatt-i Sharif. In those petitions, peasants pledged their loyalty, complained about the misdeeds of their social and economic betters, and beseeched the sultan to make good on his commitment to establish justice and equal rights under the law. The petitions offer us a clear indication that, despite signs of increasing social and economic stratification within Palestinian society, the "nationalization" of the inhabitants of Palestine – the adoption of a worldview compatible with the principles of the nation-state system – was on its way.

THE NATIONALIZATION OF EUROPE'S JEWS

Joseph Roth was a Jew born in the Austrian crownland of Galicia in 1894. More cosmopolitan subjects of the Austro-Hungarian Empire, including its German-speaking Jews, considered Galicia an imperial backwater. Acquired by the Austrians in 1772 during one of the periodic divisions of Poland that took place in the eighteenth century, the crownland bordered the Russian Empire and was inhabited by a mix of mostly poor Ukrainians, Poles, and Jews. Yet the small city of Roth's birth, Brody, was one of the centers of the Jewish Enlightenment (about which more later), and many of its Jewish residents aspired to the sort of Western-style culture then fashionable in German-speaking parts of the empire. Roth himself attended a German-language secondary school in Brody before completing his studies in Vienna, the capital of the vast

Austro-Hungarian Empire. Nevertheless, he remained conscious of his provincial Jewish roots: "There is no harder fate," he once wrote, "than being an *Ostjude* [eastern European Jew] outsider in Vienna."[3]

The youthful Roth thus journeyed between two worlds, and this gave him a unique vantage point when he became a journalist and writer. His novels and short stories, written after World War I, are filled with nostalgia for the old world of the Austro-Hungarian Empire and the shock of the new world in which empires had given way to their nation-state successors. In one of his best short stories, "The Bust of the Emperor," he describes this change through the eyes of a minor Austrian aristocrat, Franz Xaver Morstin. Roth introduces Morstin in the following way:

Well now, in the village of Lopatyny lived a Count Franz Xaver Morstin, the scion of an old Polish family – a family which, by the way, had originally come from Italy, and moved to Poland in the course of the sixteenth century. As a young man, Count Morstin had served with the Ninth Dragoons. He thought of himself neither as Polish nor Italian, neither as a member of the Polish aristocracy nor as an aristocrat of Italian descent. No, along with so many others like him in the former Crownlands of Austria-Hungary, he belonged to the noblest and purest type of Austrian there can be, which is to say: he was a man beyond nationality and therefore an aristocrat in the true sense. If one had asked him, for instance – but who would have wanted to ask such a nonsensical question? – to which "nationality" or people he felt he belonged, the Count would have looked blankly and uncomprehendingly at the questioner, or perhaps even with a measure of irritation. By what criteria should he have had to nominate his allegiance to this nation or that? He spoke most of the European languages with equal fluency, he knew his way around most European countries, he had friends and relatives scattered all over the wide and colorful world. Now, the Dual Monarchy was like this colorful world *in parvo*, and that was why it was the only possible homeland for the Count.[4]

Count Morstin was truly of the old school. He believed that there was no greater love than the love that he felt for his empire and its emperor, whose bust adorned the entrance to the count's castle, and no greater duty than to serve that empire and emperor in a manner befitting his rank. Others within the empire, however, felt differently, for as the

[3] J. M. Coetzee, "Emperor of Nostalgia," *New York Review of Books*, February 2002.

[4] All quotes from Joseph Roth, "The Bust of the Emperor," in *The Collected Stories of Joseph Roth*, trans. Michael Hofmann (New York: W. W. Norton, 2003), 227–47.

sympathetic narrator of the story puts it, "It had been discovered in the course of the nineteenth century that every individual had to be a member of a particular race or nation, if he wanted to be a fully rounded bourgeois individual."

This the count just could not fathom. The count was in the habit of going to the Jewish publican Solomon Piniowsky, the only man far and wide who he thought showed a bit of commonsense, and saying: "Listen to me, Solomon! That hateful Darwin fellow who says people are descended from apes, well, he seems to be right after all. They are no longer content to be divided into peoples. No! It seems they're hell bent on belonging to different nations. Nationalism – get this, Solomon! – not even monkeys could have come up with that one. The only thing wrong with Darwin's theory is that he's got it back to front. In my book, it's the monkeys that are descended from the nationalists, because they're a step up from them. You know your Bible, Solomon, you know it's written there that on the sixth day God created man, but where does it say anything about the nationalist? Isn't that right, Solomon?"

"Quite right, Count!" replied the Jew, Solomon.

Needless to say, the count and his Jewish friend are sadly behind the times. Rather than the passing fancy Count Morstin takes it to be, nationalism proves to be the undoing of the count's beloved empire. Returning home after fulfilling his imperial duties in World War I, the count comes to a melancholy realization:

My former home...was a large house with many doors and many rooms for many different kinds of people. This house has been divided, broken up, ruined. I have no business with what is there now. I am used to living in a house, not in cabins.

Unable to adjust to a world that requires passports but has little use for emperors, Count Morstin dies a broken man. His final request is to be buried alongside the interred bust of the emperor who represented for him all that was right with the world.

"The Bust of the Emperor" is, of course, a parable, and Roth clearly felt that the "dreadful nightmare" of nationalism from which the count could not awaken was a form of mass psychosis to which all of Europe – including its Jews – had fallen victim. Like Morstin, Roth is dumbfounded by the fact that, as he puts it, "all those people who had never been anything other than Austrians in Tarnopol, in Sarajevo, in Vienna, in Brünn, in Prague, in Czernowitz, in Oderburg, in Troppau...began, in compliance with the 'order of the day,' to call themselves part of the Polish, the Czech, the Ukrainian, the German, the Romanian, the Slovenian, the Croatian [and, we might add, Jewish] 'nation.'" But for all one might sympathize with Count Morstin's predicament, Roth's treatment of nationalism and its roots is shallow and unsatisfying. Nationalism did not spread throughout imperial Europe because impulsive and short-sighted imperial subjects made foolish decisions or because it "was the fitting expression of the meanest instincts of all those who constitute the meanest castes of a recently created nation." The diffusion of nationalism throughout imperial Europe came about as a natural reaction to the same conditions that prompted its diffusion throughout the Ottoman Empire: the spread of the international state system and state consolidation, on the one hand, and the extension of the international economic system throughout the globe and the spread of market relations within imperial domains, on the other. Both these conditions affected the Jews of Europe, home to about 90 percent of the world's Jews.

From the Middle Ages through the beginning of the modern period, many of Europe's Jews lived in specially designated urban areas, known as ghettos, in which the community itself regulated much of daily life. In other words, in most of Europe states ceded to the Jewish community responsibility for a wide range of activities, including social rites (circumcision, marriage, burial), provisioning, education, charity and welfare, and the adjudication of disputes and business transactions within the community.

The first cracks in this system began to occur with the emergence of what historians call the absolutist state. During the eighteenth century, a number of energetic rulers – Louis XIV of France (r. 1643–1715), Frederick the Great of Prussia (r. 1740–86), Catherine the Great of Russia (r. 1762–96) and Maria Theresa (r. 1740–80) and Joseph II of Austria (r. 1780–90) – asserted the primacy of the ruler over both subjects and the territory those subjects inhabited. While the states they constructed did not possess the efficacy, regularity, and breadth of activity possessed by modern states, the model of statecraft rulers adopted led them to attempt to dismantle all structures that mediated between the ruler and ruled. Among those structures were the corporate structures that gave to groups of their subjects, such as Jews, whatever local autonomy they enjoyed. This process was uneven both within states and from state to state, and since the modern state emerged from the absolutist state in western and central Europe before it did in eastern Europe, the subsequent history of the two regions and their Jewish communities began to diverge. Nevertheless, the year 1791 marks a watershed in the history of Jews in both regions.

In western and central Europe, the destruction of corporate structures and the legal distinctions that separated Jews from their compatriots is called "Jewish emancipation." The highpoint of Jewish emancipation occurred in France in 1791 during the time of the French Revolution, when the promise of "liberty, equality, fraternity" came to replace (at least in theory) aristocratic privilege and rigid social hierarchies. One member of the French National Assembly argued the case for granting Jews full rights of French citizenship in the following way:

The Jews should be denied everything as a nation, but granted everything as individuals. They must be citizens. It is claimed that they do not want to be citizens, [but] there cannot be one nation within another nation. It is intolerable that the Jews should become a separate political formation or class in the country. Every one of them must individually become a citizen.[5]

After France, other nations of western and central Europe granted full emancipation to their Jews: Great Britain (1858), Switzerland (1866), Austria (1867), Italy (1870), and Germany (1871). In all, the process of legal emancipation was largely completed in western and central Europe by the 1870s, although it was not without its setbacks. By becoming attuned to the ideas of citizenship, by experiencing the rights and obligations of citizens, by engaging in practical activity side by side with their co-nationals, the Jews of western and central Europe increasingly became nationalized, much in the same way that the inhabitants of the Ottoman Empire were becoming nationalized during the same period. But though much of the Jewish population of western and central Europe welcomed Jewish emancipation – among the holdouts were "traditional" community leaders who naturally feared for their position and status under the new system – and though the Jews of eastern Europe often kept abreast of the progress of Jewish emancipation, the emancipation of the Jews of eastern Europe would have to wait. Russia, for example, did not emancipate its Jews until 1915.

---

[5] Paul Mendes-Flohr and Jehuda Reinharz, *The Jew in the Modern World: A Documentary History* (New York: Oxford University Press, 1995), 115.

5. A Jewish shtetl (village) in Poland, date unknown. (Source: The Jewish Museum, London)

About 75 percent of the world's Jews lived in eastern Europe during the nineteenth century, and most of those Jews lived within the boundaries of the Russian Empire. These Jews will be the focus of our story because it was among them that Zionism would achieve its most notable success. The presence of so many Jews in the Russian Empire was a relatively new phenomenon. Before the eighteenth century, Russian tsars had attempted to keep Jews outside their domains. However, the consolidation of the state under Peter the Great and Catherine the Great, as well as Russia's seeming unquenchable appetite for territorial expansion, soon rendered that policy futile. In 1772, Russia, Austria, and Prussia divided Poland among themselves, then redivided it in 1793 and again in 1795. The territories annexed by Russia (and, for that matter, by Austria and Prussia) contained large numbers of Jews who had lived there for centuries.

The sudden appearance of large numbers of Jews within their empire was a matter of concern to Russian imperial elites. In 1791, Catherine the Great hit upon a novel plan to deal with them: Henceforth, Jews living within the empire were to reside in a specially designated area on the empire's western fringes. The Jewish Pale of Settlement, as this area was called, stretched from the Baltic Sea

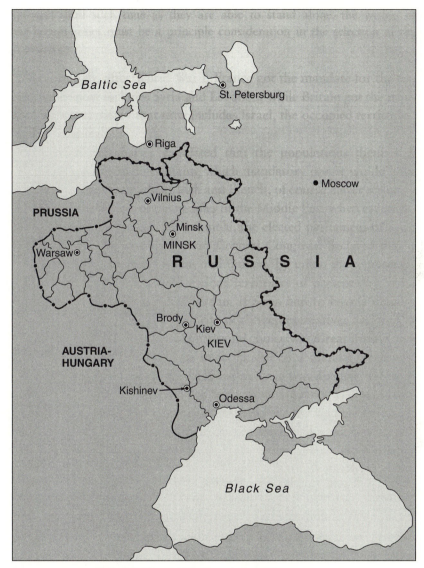

–•—•—•—•—•– Pale of Settlement. The boundaries of the
Pale of Settlement were intermittently altered.

Map 4. The Jewish Pale of Settlement.

in the north to the Black Sea in the south and included within its
boundaries territories that make up the contemporary states of Latvia,
Lithuania, Belarus, and Ukraine and parts of Poland. The Russian government permitted Jews to live outside the pale only under special

circumstances and only with special permission. Most Jews of the pale lived in poverty in small towns and villages (*shtetls*), the targets of periodic violence inflicted by their non-Jewish neighbors. Culturally segregated from those neighbors, they used Yiddish – a blend of mostly German and Hebrew with a smattering of Slavic and even Old French – as their lingua franca.

A number of factors motivated Catherine to establish the pale. Although Russian merchants in St. Petersburg and Moscow feared Jewish competition, many within the Russian government believed that the empire's underpopulated and underdeveloped western borderlands could only benefit by the presence of a Jewish commercial class. Furthermore, Russian political elites feared that the integration of large numbers of Jews into Russia proper would have deleterious effects on the body politic. Some argued that Jews should be kept separate until they had been "Russified." To further this project, the Russian government enacted legislation regulating all aspects of pale life. The legislation it proposed was designed to undermine traditional community structures, direct Jews into "useful occupations" so they would not compete with non-Jews, and encourage assimilation (and conversion) by integrating Jews as individual citizens into the empire.

Starting in 1827, for example, the Russian government began conscripting Jews into the tsar's army alongside the non-Jewish population of Russia. Unlike non-Jews, however, Jews faced conscription at an earlier age and had to remain in the military for a longer duration – twenty-five years. The memo that accompanied the conscription law bore an absurdly long title that made explicit its ostensible purpose: "Memorandum on Turning the Jews to the Advantage of the Empire by Gradually Drawing Them to Profess the Christian Faith, Bringing Them Closer to, and Ultimately Completely Fusing Them with, the Other Subjects of the Empire." With the same purpose in mind, the Russian government began sponsoring state schools for the Jews of the empire in 1841.

Overall, the attempt to remove the barriers that inhibited direct imperial control over the Jewish communities in the Russian Empire had two seemingly contradictory effects. On the one hand, the structures and institutions that had dominated Jewish life for centuries did crumble and the traditional leadership did lose its privileged status within the Jewish community. But on the other hand, the assimilation of Jews into Russian society did not occur. Much of the reason for this can be laid at the doorstep of anti-Semitism, which was not infrequently fanned by groups within the Russian government itself. It was the tsar's own secret police, for example, that concocted that most infamous of anti-Semitic tracts, "The Protocols of the Elders of Zion," in the early twentieth century. Anti-Semitism rendered Jews an inassimilable "other." Because anti-Semitism did not distinguish between observant and nonobservant Jews, it had the effect of strengthening the belief within the Jewish community that shared history and culture, not religious belief or practice, made their community a community. Although this transformation of Judaism into a cultural or historical marker did not make the emergence of Jewish nationalism inevitable (some Jews, for example, advocated a form of cultural autonomy for the Jewish community within the Russian and Austrian Empires), it certainly made it possible.

Not only did Jews within the Russian Empire have to deal with the political and social fallout from life in the pale and the government's Russification policy, they had to contend with a shifting and often hostile economic environment. Sometimes, it was the conditions in the pale that created this environment; sometimes, it was economic developments within Russia itself. In 1882, in the wake of anti-Jewish riots (pogroms), the Russian government passed legislation limiting Jewish rights to own and lease land and even reside in the countryside of the pale. According to the authorities, the pogroms demonstrated that, despite the best government efforts, "abnormal relations between the Jewish race and the rest of the population were continuing as before." Restricted to towns and forbidden to pursue certain occupations, Jews were forced to carve out an economic and demographic niche for themselves based on the opportunities available. For example, the construction of the Russian rail system between 1850 and 1870 created new opportunities for Jews as agents, assistants, and suppliers. At the same time, the freeing of the serfs (in 1861) and the founding of non-Jewish rural cooperatives reduced the need for Jews to act as intermediaries between town and countryside.

Restrictions on land ownership and dwindling opportunities in the rural economy also changed the demographic profile of the Jewish community in eastern Europe. Although most Jews continued to live in shtetls, over the course of the nineteenth century the profile of the Jewish community became increasingly urban, and large urban centers came to include larger and larger proportions of Jews. In 1860, the Jewish population of Warsaw was 41,000 (about one quarter of the population); in 1900, Warsaw contained 220,000 Jews (about one third). During the same period, the Jewish population of Odessa expanded from 25,000 to 140,000. By 1929, only 4 percent of Jews worldwide practiced agriculture, while about 75 percent were involved in commerce, the professions, and industry. The urbanization of the Jewish population ensured that large numbers of Jews would be exposed to urban-based social and political movements, such as trade unionism, socialism, and nationalism. It also provided future Zionists with proof positive that life in exile had made the Jewish nation aberrant and in need of redemption through the love of a good nationalism.

In a way, the Zionists were correct: By the last decades of the nineteenth century, the Jewish community in Russia was, in comparison with the non-Jewish community, disproportionately urbanized, middle-class, and, if not Russified, at least more likely to have been exposed to the social and political questions that dominated public discourse than the typical Russian peasant. Urbanization and restrictions on life in the pale guided the choices made by many in the community while limiting the options available to them. In normal circumstances, urbanized artisans would have constituted the cream of Russian or any other nineteenth-century society. However, since Jews found themselves at the mercy of unpredictable eruptions of violence and the often debilitating restraints of imperial diktat, a disproportionate number of Jews decided simply to leave.

The decades preceding the onset of World War I was the great period of international migration. Spurred on by population increases that were placing a burden on available resources, cheap steamship travel, relatively open borders, a quarter century of international depression that ended only in 1896, and labor-poor settler colonies in North America, southern Africa, Latin America, and Australasia, many Europeans simply decamped elsewhere. Eastern European Jews were no exception. Between 1881 and 1914, more than 2.5 million Jews – about 20 percent of the total Jewish population of eastern Europe – left their homes for

6. Between 1881 and 1914, between 1.5 million and 2 million Jews emigrated from eastern Europe to the United States. The steamship *T.S.S. Polonia* sets sail from Poland with Jewish immigrants bound for America. (Source: From the collection of the author)

good. But unlike emigrants from southern Europe, for example, a larger proportion of Jewish emigrants were skilled (50 percent as opposed to 20 percent) and acculturated to the norms of urban life.

The abilities and background of most Jewish emigrants naturally affected their choice of destination. Much to the consternation of the Zionist movement, a vast majority – between 1.5 million and 2 million – made the United States, not Palestine, their destination of choice (another 350,000 or so went to western Europe), and there is no telling what the future of Jewish settlement in Palestine would have been had America not restricted immigration from Europe in 1921. The reason for the choice of America is not difficult to discern. As the East Prussian socialist and poet Judah Leib Levin argued in 1881,

In the Holy Land, our dream would be far from realized; there we would be slaves to the Sultan and the Pasha; there, as here, we would bear a heavy burden in the midst of a wild desert people, sustaining ourselves with the distant hope that if our numbers increased sufficiently we might perhaps, after many years, become another small principality that will, finally, in some ultimate utopia, achieve its destiny. But in America our dream is closer to fulfillment ... and our hope of attaining our independence and leading our lives in accordance with our beliefs and inclinations would not be long deferred.... The eloquence of the Bible, the piteous spectacle of the bereaved daughter of Zion, the emotion aroused by our ancient memories, all these speak for the Land of Israel. The good life recommends America. You know, my friend, that many will yearn for the Holy Land, and I know that even more will stream to America.[6]

As unsympathetic to the lure of Palestine as he was, however, even Levin understood its appeal. It was to that appeal that the dominant strain within the Zionist movement spoke. The novelty of Zionism was its ability to integrate the lure of Palestine within what might be regarded as a quintessential nineteenth-century nationalism. How this came about, and how Zionism was able to acquire its constituency among an often skeptical Jewish population, is the subject of the next chapter.

SUGGESTIONS FOR FURTHER READING

Cohen, Amnon. *Palestine in the 18th Century: Patterns of Government and Administration.* Jerusalem: Magnes Press, 1973. Institutional history of Palestine during a particularly turbulent century.

Doumani, Beshara. *Rediscovering Palestine: Merchants and Peasants in Jabal Nablus, 1700–1900.* Berkeley: University of California Press, 1995. Pathbreaking social, economic, and cultural history of central Palestine over two centuries.

Kushner, David, ed. *Palestine in the Late Ottoman Period: Political, Social, and Economic Transformation.* Jerusalem: Yad Izhak Ben Zvi, 1986. Excellent collection of essays on all aspects of Palestinian history during the nineteenth and early twentieth centuries.

Ma'oz, Moshe. *Ottoman Reform in Syria and Palestine, 1840–1861: The Impact of the Tanzimat on Politics and Society.* Oxford: Clarendon Press, 1975. History of Palestine during the first years of the Ottoman "reform" period.

———, ed. *Studies on Palestine during the Ottoman Period.* Jerusalem: Magnes Press, 1975. Contains essays on the social, cultural, economic, and political history of all eras of Ottoman Palestine.

Mendes-Flohr, Paul R., and Jehuda Reinharz, eds. *The Jew in the Modern World: A Documentary History.* New York: Oxford University Press, 1980. Marvelous collection of texts describing Jewish life throughout the modern period.

Reilly, James. "Peasantry of Late Ottoman Palestine." *Journal of Palestine Studies* 40 (Summer 1981): 82–97. Good introduction to the social and economic history of nineteenth-century Palestine.

Rogers, Mary Eliza. *Domestic Life in Palestine.* London: Kegan Paul International, 1989. Nineteenth-century account of the travels of an upper-class British woman in Palestine.

---

[6] Paul Mendes-Flohr and Jehuda Reinharz, *The Jew in the Modern World: A Documentary History* (New York: Oxford University Press, 1995), 413–14.

Schölch, Alexander. "Economic Development of Palestine, 1856–1882." *Journal of Palestine Studies* 10 (Spring 1981): 35–58. The changing nature of the nineteenth-century Palestinian economy, told by a leading scholar of Palestine.

Taylor, Alan R. "Zionism and Jewish History." *Journal of Palestine Studies* 2 (Winter 1972): 35–51. Overview of the origins and role of Zionism in Jewish thought and how Zionism redefined the Jewish past.

3

ZIONISM AND THE COLONIZATION OF PALESTINE

The Jews of eighteenth- and nineteenth-century Europe were hardly unaffected by the intellectual currents that coursed through the territories in which they lived. As a matter of fact, by breaking down the walls of ghettos and reconstituting Jews as citizens, the process of Jewish emancipation in western and central Europe not only exposed more and more Jews to those currents, it made those currents vital to their lives. Even in eastern Europe, where the process of Jewish emancipation was stillborn, constantly increasing numbers of Jews embraced the same ideas that attracted their brethren to the west.

Three factors contributed to the spread of new intellectual currents east. First, the pale and the restrictions it imposed on the lives of Jews appeared relatively late in Jewish history and were thus unsanctified by long-standing tradition. It was not strange that many Jews living in this "unnatural" state would heed the siren song of new ideas, just as it was not strange that many would seek out the West as a place of refuge. Furthermore, conditions intruding on the pale made these ideas relevant to its Jewish inhabitants. In the last chapter, we saw how urbanization, the expansion of state capabilities and demands, and the spread of market relations affected pale life. Ideas originating in the West and imported to the pale were not just coherent with the new social and economic dispensation, they provided its underlying principles. Finally, the Russian government itself promoted the spread of new ideas in the pale through its Russification program. As we have seen, during the 1840s the imperial government began building Russian-language secular schools in the pale. Because the number of qualified Jewish teachers was inadequate to meet the government's needs, these schools came to employ non-Jewish instructors, who, if not entirely sympathetic to western European ideas, provided their pupils with the linguistic training necessary to master them.

The granddaddy of modern western European intellectual movements that worked their way eastward was the Haskala, the Jewish Enlightenment. The Haskala provided its followers and their intellectual heirs with the tools and conceptual apparatus that made other movements, such as nationalism and socialism, comprehensible. The Haskala began in Germany during the final quarter of the eighteenth century. From there, it spread to the Austrian Empire and the pale. Like the European Enlightenment, from which it derived its principles, the Haskala asserted the primacy of science and rationality over religion and tradition. And like their Enlightenment counterparts, the devotees of the Haskala – the *maskilim* – believed that the laws governing human society were just as discernable by reason as the natural laws that governed the physical universe.

To discover those laws and to participate in the universal march of progress, the maskilim advocated immersion in both Biblical Hebrew and the languages of Europe. By mastering Biblical Hebrew, the maskilim hoped to bring to Biblical scholarship the critical tools their non-Jewish counterparts were using in the analysis of classical texts. This, they believed, would end the stranglehold of traditionalist rabbis over the cultural life of the Jewish community. And with Jewish emancipation and even the prospect of assimilation on the horizon, the celebration of Biblical texts and the Hebrew language served another purpose as well: It enabled the Jews of western Europe to assimilate into the societies in which they lived without the fear of losing their Jewish cultural identity. But as the Haskala spread eastward to Yiddish-speaking communities isolated from the original sites of the European Enlightenment, the focus of the maskilim shifted, and the study of Western languages eclipsed the study of Hebrew. From the third decade of the nineteenth century onward, maskilim active in such cities as Odessa, Vilnius, Riga, and Joseph Roth's Brody established schools to teach modern European languages and spread the gospel of science and progress among the younger generation.

And many of that generation responded to Enlightenment ideas with enthusiasm. Take the case of Solomon Maimon, a Polish Jew who wrote his intellectual biography in 1793. For Maimon,

The subjects of the Talmud, with the exception of those relating to jurispru-
dence, are dry and mostly unintelligible to a child – the laws of sacrifice,
of purification, of forbidden meats, of feasts and so forth.... For example, how many white hairs a red cow may have, and yet remain a *red
cow*; what sorts of scabs require this or that sort of purification; whether
a louse or a flea may be killed on the Sabbath.... Compare these glo-
rious disputations, which are served up to young people and forced on
them even to their disgust, with history, in which natural events are related
in an instructive and agreeable manner, and with a knowledge of the
world's structure, by which the outlook into nature is widened, and the vast
whole is brought into a well-ordered system; surely my preference will be
justified.[1]

Maimon goes on to describe how he painstakingly learned Latin and
German and the world these languages opened up to him:

I pocketed the few books, and returned home in rapture. After I had studied
these books thoroughly, my eyes were opened. I believed that I had found a
key to all the secrets of nature, as I now knew the origin of storms, of dew,
of rain, and such phenomena. I looked down with pride on all others who
did not yet know these things, laughed at their prejudices and superstitions,
and proposed to clear up their ideas on these subjects and to enlighten their
understanding.

One can only sympathize with Solomon's long-suffering parents.

Acting in concert with the social, political, and economic transformation of Jewish life during the nineteenth century, the cultural transformation inspired by the Haskala provided fertile ground for a number
of modern ideologies to take root among the Jews of Europe. One of
these ideologies was Zionism. But even though there is a direct line
connecting the ideas and skills promoted by the Haskala and Zionism,
Zionism cannot be viewed simply as a spontaneous outgrowth of the
Haskala. Before Zionism or any nationalism can emerge, someone has
to take the ideas pioneered by Enlightenment thinkers – that historical processes are susceptible to reason and obey generalizable principles, that historical time marches on in a linear manner, that there

---

[1] Paul Mendes-Flohr and Jehuda Reinharz, *The Jew in the Modern World: A Documentary
History* (New York: Oxford University Press, 1995), 250–3.

is progress in history, that individual entities (such as nations) retain their essential characteristics over time even though their attributes may change – and not only translate them into a nationalist idiom but put them in service of a nationalist program. In other words, nationalism is impossible without nationalists.

Among Zionists, no figure commands greater regard than Theodor Herzl (1860–1904). This is not because he was the first Zionist. There were Zionists whose activities predated those of Herzl. Nor is it because of any particular ideas Herzl brought to the Zionist movement. There were a number of Zionist thinkers who contributed more ideas to the movement than Herzl, and Herzl had to compromise his own beliefs more than once. Herzl's centrality derives from his unique organizational talents. These talents proved essential for the success of the Zionist cause.

Herzl was the son of a Hungarian merchant whose family had moved to Vienna at a time when that city seemed to promise so much to upwardly mobile Jews who wished to assimilate into mainstream European society and culture. Herzl received a secular education and acquired a doctorate in law. After practicing law and entering the civil service, Herzl went on to become the French correspondent for a prestigious Viennese newspaper. It was while he was in Paris that Herzl became a Zionist.

Historians are a quarrelsome lot when it comes to attributing motivations to historical personalities. Nevertheless, most concur that what became known as the "Dreyfus Affair" played a role – perhaps the key role – in inspiring Herzl's embrace of Zionism. In 1894 Alfred Dreyfus, a French army captain, was accused of spying for Germany. Dreyfus was, like Herzl, an assimilated Jew. His trial became a *cause célèbre* in France and the rest of Europe. For many, it was clear that Dreyfus had been guilty of little more than being a successful Jew in Catholic France. Among these was the French novelist Emile Zola, who condemned those who accused Dreyfus in the following words:

It is a crime to poison the minds of the small and simple and to excite the passions of reaction and intolerance while seeking refuge behind that hateful anti-Semitism of which great liberal France – France of the rights of man – will die, unless she is cured of her disease. It is a crime to exploit patriotism for works of hatred, and, finally, it is a crime to make of the sword a modern

God when all human science is labouring for the coming work of truth and justice.[2]

Herzl agreed with Zola. Even more, the Dreyfus Affair demonstrated to Herzl that if France could play host to virulent anti-Semitism, Jews could not be secure anywhere. What the Jews needed was a homeland of their own in which they would form a majority of citizens. Herzl thus became an outspoken advocate of the Zionist cause, publishing books and tracts to popularize the movement. Two years after the Dreyfus Affair, he published *The Jewish State*, a straightforward rendition of his ideas, and when the book went mostly unread, Herzl published it in the form of a didactic novel entitled *Old New Land*.

Around the time he published *The Jewish State*, Herzl submitted an article to a London weekly, *The Jewish Chronicle*, in which he presented his arguments in abbreviated form. In the article, Herzl defines the problem confronting Jews – what nineteenth-century intellectuals and politicians called the "Jewish Question" – as follows:

The Jewish Question still exists. It would be foolish to deny it. It exists wherever Jews live in perceptible numbers. Where it does not yet exist, it will be brought by Jews in the course of their migrations. We naturally move to those places where we are not persecuted, and there our presence soon produces persecution. This is true in every country, and will remain true even in those most highly civilised – France itself is no exception – till the Jewish Question finds a solution on a political basis.[3]

For Herzl, the promise of Jewish emancipation had proved empty:

When civilised nations awoke to the inhumanity of exclusive legislation, and enfranchised us – our enfranchisement came too late. For we had, curiously enough, developed while in the Ghetto into bourgeois people, and we stepped out of it only to enter into fierce competition with the middle classes. . . . We have honestly striven everywhere to merge ourselves in the social life of surrounding communities, and to preserve only the faith of our fathers. It has not been permitted to us.

---

[2] Paul Mendes-Flohr and Jehuda Reinharz, *The Jew in the Modern World: A Documentary History* (New York: Oxford University Press, 1995), 353.

[3] Theodor Herzl, from the *Jewish Chronicle*, in *The Jew in the Modern World: A Documentary History*, ed. Paul Mendes-Flohr and Jehuda Reinharz (New York: Oxford University Press, 1995), 533–7.

Jews throughout the world must therefore embrace the idea that they constitute a single nation, united, as in the case of all nations, by the ties and travails of history:

We are one people – our enemies have made us one in our despite, as repeatedly happens in history. Distress binds us together, and thus united, we suddenly discover our strength. Yes, we are strong enough to form a state, and a model state.

Herzl therefore proposed that representatives of the Jewish community approach the leaders of Europe who would grant Jews "sovereignty...over a portion of the globe large enough to satisfy the requirements of the nation." And those leaders would be sure to listen, for "the governments of all countries, scourged by anti-Semitism, will serve their own interests in assisting us to obtain the sovereignty we want." But Herzl did not appeal to self-interest alone. Should Jews decide to establish their state in Palestine, "we should also form a portion of the rampart of Europe against Asia, an outpost of civilization as opposed to barbarism." For Herzl, as for many of his contemporaries, it was but a small, unreflexive step that led from the Enlightenment to imperialism.

Palestine was but one option Herzl toyed with in this and other articles. Others included Argentina and the western United States, both of which contained sizable areas that were fertile and sparsely populated. But even Herzl was forced to acknowledge that "Palestine is our ever-memorable historic home" and "would attract our people with a force of extraordinary potency." And so he was willing to leave the question open, to be decided by Jewish popular opinion.

In spite of this appeal to popular opinion, Herzl brought to Zionism many of the prejudices of the upper crust of Viennese society, to which he aspired. These, too, were reflected in his *Jewish Chronicle* article. Herzl was suspicious of unbridled democracy, writing that his ideal form of government for a Jewish state would be "an aristocratic republic, although I am an ardent monarchist in my own country." He could be patronizing, as when he called on "men of practical judgment and of modern culture...to seek out the less favoured, to teach and to inspire them." And like other heirs to Enlightenment traditions, he could be obtuse and inflexible when it came to questions of religion: "[Our clergy] must clearly understand from the outset that we do not mean to found a theocracy, but a tolerant modern civil state."

But Herzl was also a practical man who understood that to succeed Zionism needed a permanent institutional structure that could speak in the name of the movement and move its diverse adherents toward consensus. "We need a 'gestor' [manager] to direct this Jewish political cause," he wrote.

This "gestor" cannot, of course, be a single individual, for an individual who would undertake this giant work alone, would probably be either a madman or an impostor. . . . The "gestor" of the Jews must be a union of several persons for the purpose, a body corporate.

It did not take long for Herzl to organize his "body corporate." In 1897 Herzl issued a call for a Zionist congress to meet in Basel, Switzerland. The First Zionist Congress, held that same year, brought together about two hundred Zionists to create a permanent association and agree on a common program. The First Zionist Congress thus founded the World Zionist Organization and approved what came to be known as the "Basel Program." The program, in its entirety, reads as follows:

The aim of Zionism is to create for the Jewish people a home in Palestine secured by public law.
The Congress contemplates the following means to the attainment of this end:
    1. The promotion, on suitable lines, of the colonization of Palestine by Jewish agricultural and industrial workers.
    2. The organization and binding together of the whole Jewry by means of appropriate institutions, local and international in accordance with the laws of each country.
    3. The strengthening and fostering of Jewish national sentiment and consciousness.
    4. Preparatory steps towards obtaining government consent, where necessary, to the attainment of the aim of Zionism.[4]

Three aspects of the program are worth emphasizing. First, although the World Zionist Organization endorsed the idea of founding a "Jewish home," not a "Jewish state," it would be a mistake to read too much into this. After all, Herzl had used the word "state" throughout his

[4] Paul Mendes-Flohr and Jehuda Reinharz, *The Jew in the Modern World: A Documentary History* (New York: Oxford University Press, 1995), 540.

writings and even entitled his most important work *The Jewish State*. Furthermore, if Zionism is to be defined as "Jewish nationalism," it has the word "state" encoded into its DNA just like all other nationalisms. This is why skeptics object to the idea that the so-called cultural Zionists – Jews who wanted to incubate a Jewish spiritual renaissance by maintaining a limited, non-political presence in Palestine – can be considered part of the Zionist movement at all. It is probable the delegates used the word "home" to dispel the concerns of an Ottoman government unlikely to look favorably on any movement with designs on its territory. Those concerns could derail the plans of the World Zionist Organization for two reasons: Not only did the Basel Program stipulate that the Jewish home should be in Palestine, it resolved that the Jewish home should be "secured by public law," that is, through diplomacy. This was the very tactic advocated by Herzl in *The Jewish Chronicle*.

Unfortunately for the Zionists, Ottoman authorities were already aware of both their aspirations and the conditions in eastern Europe. As early as 1882, after the worst pogroms to date in Russia, the Ottoman sultan issued a *firman* (ruling) granting Jews permission to immigrate to the empire. There were just two small conditions: The Jews who immigrated to the Ottoman Empire would have to renounce their European citizenships and become Ottoman subjects, and the Jews could immigrate to any place in the empire except Palestine. Thus, if Jewish immigration to Palestine did occur, it would have to occur secretly, and land purchases would have to be made through phantom agents. Fortunately for the Zionists, Ottoman inefficiency made the *firman* irrelevant.

Under Herzl's leadership, the World Zionist Organization became the premier organization working for the Zionist cause. But because the World Zionist Organization was a coalition representing diverse groups and interests, its meetings could become contentious. At the 1903 meeting, for example, delegates split on whether the Zionist movement should continue negotiating with the British liberal imperialist (Limp) colonial secretary, Joseph Chamberlain, who offered the Zionists the British colony of Uganda as a Jewish homeland. Most delegates sided with Herzl, who argued that accepting the Uganda proposal did not mean abandoning the Palestine project. To the contrary: Herzl argued that the road to Palestine began in Uganda. The Russian delegates to the congress were not convinced. They walked out and the Uganda project eventually faded away.

Disputes within the ranks were but one problem facing the early Zionist movement. Convincing Jews who remained outside the movement proved daunting as well. The World Zionist Organization and the Basel Program hardly met with universal approval among the Jews of Europe and North America. Indeed, the entire Zionist enterprise provoked controversy. To take one example, Herzl had intended to hold the founding meeting of the World Zionist Organization in Munich but was forced to change venues when the German Union of Rabbis circulated a letter of protest. "The efforts of the so-called Zionists to create a Jewish National State in Palestine are antagonistic to the messianic promises of Judaism as contained in Holy Writ and in later religious sources," the rabbis wrote. "Judaism obliges its followers to serve the country to which they belong with the utmost devotion, and to further its interest with their whole heart and all their strength."[5] Although the German rabbis did leave the door open for the establishment of Jewish agricultural colonies in Palestine, they made known their opposition to using those colonies as stepping stones to founding a state.

Other Jews attacked the Zionist program from the Left, asserting that the Jewish Question could only be resolved when the exploited viewed the world from the vantage point of their class interests, not national interests. Among them was Rosa Luxemburg, who became a leader of the Communist Party of Germany. In a letter written in 1916 Luxemburg stated,

I feel equally close to the wretched victims of the rubber plantations in Putumayo, or to the Negroes in Africa with whose bodies the Europeans play catch-ball. Do you remember the words elicited by the General Staff's work...in the Kalahari desert: "The rattling in the throats of the dying, and the mad screams of those who were withering from thirst, faded away into the sublime stillness of the infinite." Oh, this "sublime stillness of the infinite" in which so many screams fade away unheard – it reverberates within me so strongly that I have no separate corner in my heart for the ghetto. I feel at home in the entire world wherever there are clouds and birds and human tears.[6]

It is, of course, Marxism, not nationalism, that has been relegated to "the dustbin of history," to use Karl Marx's poignant expression. The appeal of nationalism has never been comprehensible to Marxists.

---

[5] Paul Mendes-Flohr and Jehuda Reinharz, *The Jew in the Modern World: A Documentary History* (New York: Oxford University Press, 1995), 539.

[6] Paul Mendes-Flohr and Jehuda Reinharz: *The Jew in the Modern World: A Documentary History* (New York: Oxford University Press, 1995), 261–2.

7. Theodor Herzl as Zionist icon: detail from 1948 Israeli postage stamp showing Herzl gazing on Zionist pioneers before the walls of Jerusalem. (Source: From the collection of the author)

Herzl devoted the remainder of his life to the sort of diplomatic activity endorsed by the First Zionist Congress. Not only did he court foreign leaders, including the Ottoman sultan, Abdulhamid II, he literally became the public face of the mainstream Zionist movement. As early as 1903, Herzl's bust adorned cigarette boxes, tea kettles, pocket watches, wall carpets, ash trays, pencils, and decorative lamps. The nationalist hagiolatry did not end there. Over the years, Herzl gave his name to Herzliyya, a suburban town north of Tel Aviv, and to hundreds of streets throughout Israel – an example of the sort of appropriation of space through renaming described in Chapter 1. And in a particularly symbolic gesture, Herzl's very body took on iconic stature through reburial in Israel.

Herzl was originally buried in his hometown of Vienna. From the 1930s on, Zionists supported the idea of bringing Herzl's body to Palestine. In 1935 a committee appointed by the leaders of the World Zionist Organization concluded that "Herzl's last resting place should be in Jerusalem, the capital of Palestine, and that, furthermore, both national sentiment and the political, national, and historical moment make Jerusalem the only choice." On 18 August 1949, Herzl was reburied on a hill redesignated Mt. Herzl in the first state funeral in Israeli history. Representatives of various settlements poured bags of earth they had brought with them into the open grave as a symbol of the success achieved by the Zionist movement Herzl had organized.

THE BEGINNINGS OF ZIONIST COLONIZATION

The founding of the World Zionist Organization was a seminal event in the history of Zionism. Now, the Zionist movement had an organization to speak in its name and an institutional structure to plan and coordinate its activities. But Herzl would not have been able to bring the World Zionist Organization into existence unless there had already been support for Zionism. In other words, the World Zionist organization was both a manifestation of the emergence of Zionism and a stimulus for its further development.

Most members of the World Zionist Organization believed they had to secure the support of a Great Power before undertaking the colonization of Palestine, and they opposed the colonization of Palestine without prior political guarantees. Hence, Herzl's never-ending diplomatic efforts. Other Jews, however, felt they could not wait. In fact, Jewish colonization of Palestine began even before the founding of the World Zionist Organization and, of course, continued long afterward.

The history of Jewish settlement is commonly divided into periods corresponding to waves of immigration. These waves of immigration are known as *aliyot*, and each one is known as an *aliyah*. The term "aliyah" comes from a Hebrew word meaning "to ascend." In other words, Zionists believed that Jewish settlers coming from Europe would ascend from their diaspora condition and be reborn in Palestine.

Between 1882 – the year of the beginning of the first aliyah – and the onset of World War II there were five aliyot. In general, historians have used four criteria when dividing Jewish immigration into separate waves: place of origin of the immigrants; destinations in Palestine to which the immigrants went (urban or rural, coastal or inland); the social and economic system by which the immigrants organized their communities; and the ideology that united the immigrants (or, in the case of economic refugees, the lack thereof), common experiences, and subsequent mythology built around those common experiences.

The first aliyah was triggered by the anti-Jewish pogroms that broke out in Russia in the wake of the assassination of Tsar Alexander II. Pogroms were not new to the Russian Empire, or indeed to other places in Europe. They commonly took place around Easter when rumors spread that Jews were killing Christian children for ritualistic purposes during the feast of Passover. But the pogroms of 1881 took place at a particularly inauspicious time for the Jews of Russia: Unlike his father, who had enjoyed a liberal reputation (Alexander II had freed the Russian serfs in 1861, two years before Abraham Lincoln issued his Emancipation Proclamation freeing American slaves), Alexander III used his father's assassination to roll back the process of liberalization. Alexander III persecuted non–Russian Orthodox religious minorities (including Jews), restored to local notables many of the privileges his predecessor had taken away, and decreed "temporary laws" that expanded the authority of local officials. Under Alexander III, the government was no friend of the Jews and did little to discourage (and may have even assisted in) attacks on them.

The number of those killed in the pogroms pale in comparison with the number of victims of twentieth-century and twenty-first–century atrocities. In Srebenica, Bosnia, for example, Bosnian Serbs massacred more than seven thousand civilians during a five-month period in 1995. Compare that with the toll of the worst of the pogroms: In Kishinev, in the contemporary state of Moldova (yes, there is a contemporary state of Moldova), mobs killed 118 Jews during two days of rioting in 1903. But the Kishinev pogrom took place at the dawn of the twentieth century, a time when the world had not yet grown inured to the horrors of the twentieth century and when educated Europeans flattered themselves with the belief that their continent was a place of civilization and progress. For many Jews who had come to believe in the same ideals, the pogroms acted as a wake-up call. From 1881 to the end of the century, Jewish emigration from Russia to the United States reached close to 450,000 – nearly double that of the previous eighty years.

Other Jews took away a different lesson from the pogroms. For them, the ease with which the Jewish communities of Russia could be victimized proved that the Zionists were correct when they complained that the Jewish nation had degenerated as a result of life in the diaspora. Take, for example, the following poem by Haim Nahman Bialik, whom many consider the godfather of modern Hebrew letters. Bialik grew up in the pale, yet like many others he was inspired by the culture of the Haskala. In the wake of the massacre, the Jewish Historical Commission sent him to Kishinev to interview survivors. Bialik's reaction to the Kishinev pogrom can be seen in this poem, which indicts not only the perpetrators of the massacre but the Jewish passivity that enabled them to commit their crime:

> Arise and go now to the city of slaughter;
> Into its courtyard wind thy way;
> There with thine own hand touch, and with the eyes of thine head,
> Behold on tree, on stone, on fence, on mural clay,
> The spattered blood and dried brains of the dead....
>
> Note also, do not fail to note,
> In that dark corner, and behind that cask
> Crouched husbands, bridegrooms, brothers, peering from the cracks...
> They saw it all;
> They did not stir nor move;
> They did not pluck their eyes out; they
> Beat not their brains against the wall!
>
> ... Come, now, and I will bring thee to their lairs
> The privies, jakes, and pigpens where the heirs of the Hasmoneans lay,
>   with trembling knees,
> Concealed and cowering – the sons of the Maccabees!
> The seed of saints, the scions of the lions!
> Who, crammed by scores in all the sanctuaries of their shame,
> So sanctified My name!
> It was the flight of mice they fled,
> The scurrying of roaches was their flight;
> They died like dogs, and they were dead![7]

Bialik emigrated to Palestine in 1924.

---

[7] Paul Mendes-Flohr and Jehuda Reinharz, *The Jew in the Modern World: A Documentary History* (New York: Oxford University Press, 1995), 410–11.

In the immediate aftermath of the pogroms of 1881, Jews in Russia and Romania began establishing committees for the purpose of assisting emigration to Palestine. Known as "Lovers of Zion" committees, they attracted at first students, then began to pull in nonstudent members from among the most Russified layers of the Jewish population. One observer described them as follows:

The men wear neither sidelocks nor caftans; they are handsome, tall, clean, intelligent. The women are almost elegant. I saw one the other day who expressed herself decently in French. The usual language of the people is Russian. When they speak German, they speak it with a Russian accent. Few of them employ Yiddish. Among the young people there are many, perhaps half, who were students expelled from the gymnasiums with the excuse that there was no more room. First, they were reproached with not wanting to assimilate, now it has been found that they are assimilating all too well. A quarter of the young are craftsmen sent away from their work-shops by their Christian masters or by other workmen or by Jewish masters who were ruined in April. I have porters on my list who were chased away from the port of Odessa by Greek porters. Among the refugees are old soldiers decorated for heroism.... One greybeard who came to me, who had won three decorations on the battlefield in his twenty-one years of service, had been expelled from Kiev for failing to be in the authorized category of residents.

In 1884, local Lovers of Zion groups united into a centralized organization. They elected Leo Pinsker their president. Pinsker was an assimilated Russian Jew who had served as a doctor in the Crimean War. The 1881 pogroms were for Pinsker what the Dreyfus Affair was to Herzl. In 1882 he wrote a pamphlet entitled *Autoemancipation*, which caused quite a stir. According to Pinsker,

The eternal problem presented by the Jewish question stirs men today as it did ages ago. The essence of the problem, as we see it, lies in the fact that, in the midst of nations among whom the Jews reside, they form a distinctive element which cannot be assimilated, which cannot be readily digested by any nation. Hence the problem is to find means of so adjusting the relations of this exclusive element to the whole body of the nations that there shall never be any further basis for the Jewish question....

We must prove that the misfortunes of the Jews are due, above all, to their lack of desire for national independence; and that this desire must be aroused and maintained in them if they do not wish to exist forever in a disgraceful state – in a word, we must prove that they must become a nation.[8]

The Lovers of Zion solicited contributions for their project and established an executive committee in Jaffa to coordinate what they anticipated would be a flow of immigrants to Palestine. About twenty-five thousand Jews emigrated in the first aliyah. Although a vast majority settled in Jaffa, Haifa, and Jerusalem, a few stalwarts established agricultural settlements called *moshavot* (sing. *moshava*) along the coast and around Lake Tiberias in the Galilee. Lacking experience in agriculture, they came to adopt agricultural techniques (subsistence farming and the field-crop system, or the planting of multiple crops to supply all needs) and even forms of organization (collective ownership of land and tools, for example) from the indigenous inhabitants of Palestine. Here we see one example of how the colonized affect the plans and arrangements of their colonizers, a phenomenon all too frequently ignored by historians of colonialism, who tend to ascribe to the colonizer and colonized an active and passive role, respectively.

(A brief word about the use of the words "colony," "colonizer," and "colonization": Since the end of World War II and the decolonization of areas previously held as European possessions, these words have rarely been used in a context in which they are not meant to be derogatory. In a more innocent, or perhaps more naive, age, these words had positive connotations, designating the expansion of European civilization and enlightenment – the white man's burden – into benighted regions of the globe. Hence, Herzl's unselfconscious declaration that Zionists would "form a portion of the rampart of Europe against Asia, an outpost of civilization as opposed to barbarism." It is within this context that the early Zionist "pioneers" – to use another word fraught with meaning – spoke of their project as colonization and their settlements as colonies.)

Threatened with a collapse of their agricultural colonies, settlers appealed to Baron Edmond de Rothschild, scion of the French branch of the famous banking dynasty, for assistance. From 1882 to 1900, Rothschild invested £1.5 million in the agricultural settlements. But Rothschild had a vision of his own that did not leave much room for

---

[8] Arthur Hertzberg, ed., *The Zionist Idea: A Historical Analysis and Reader* (New York: Atheneum, 1981), 181.

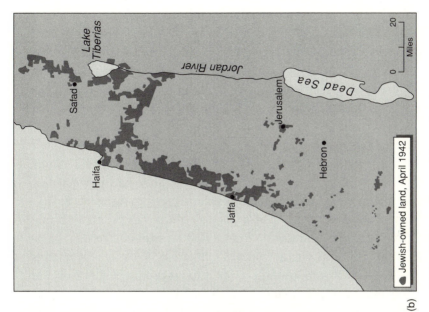

(b)

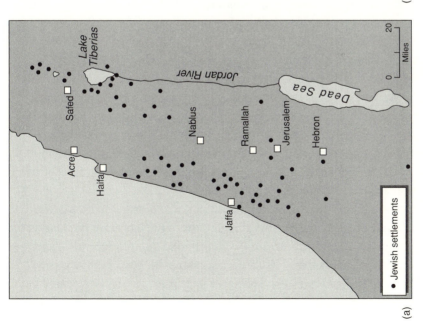

(a)

Map 5. (a) Jewish Settlements in Palestine, 1881–1914. (b) The Yishuv on the eve of the 1948 war.

subsistence farming. Rothschild introduced the plantation system into Palestine. He consolidated and expanded the land under cultivation, had the farmers who worked his lands plant cash crops instead of subsistence crops, and streamlined production by replacing the field-crop system with monoculture (specialization in a single crop). As a result, the fortunes of once independent settlements became entangled with the vagaries of the international market, and farmers who had originally envisioned themselves as independent producers became hired labor.

Many of the administrators brought in by Rothschild had cut their teeth in Algeria, where the French had established a plantation colony beginning in 1830. Borrowing from practices they had pioneered in North Africa, they expanded the cultivation of grapes for wine. Viticulture seemed a good investment in the late nineteenth century: During the 1870s, the wine industry in France had been decimated by a parasite that ate the roots of grapevines. Speculators and entrepreneurs thus began looking for opportunities abroad to make up the shortfall. But as good an investment as viticulture seemed at the time, it changed the social landscape of the Zionist colonies: To be profitable, the plantations required a plentiful supply of cheap labor. Rothschild's overseers found that labor among the indigenous inhabitants. Over time, the plantations came to employ five to ten times the number of Arabs as Jews. This hardly fit the Zionist ideal, which even at this early stage of settlement activity stressed the redemptive power of Jewish labor, particularly agricultural labor. And it was economically disastrous for the Zionist cause: Jews unable to find employment among the ranks of the overseers left the countryside for the cities of Palestine or emigrated abroad. By 1902, in the wake of a precipitous decline of wages, 65 percent of Jewish agricultural laborers had left Palestine.

Rothschild felt burned by his investment in Palestine. Not only were his plantations exposed to price fluctuations of the international market (and the late nineteenth century was a period of agricultural depression), land purchases were risky and development costs high. By 1900, Rothschild had had it. Frustrated by the lack of return on his investment, he transferred control of settlements to the Jewish Colonization Association, the brainchild of German financier Baron Maurice de Hirsch. While enthusiastic about establishing Jewish agricultural settlements worldwide, which he felt provided an ideal solution to the problems encountered by Russian Jews, Hirsch had no illusions about Palestine. The Jewish Colonization Association restructured Rothschild's plantation system to make it pay. The association stopped subsidizing unprofitable plantations, subdivided them, and transferred their ownership to others. The first aliyah had ended not so much with a bang as with a whimper.

Whatever its shortcomings, the first aliyah doubled the number of Jews living in Palestine, providing a viable nucleus for future settlement activities. In addition, it provided later Zionists with a powerful lesson of how things should not be done. The first aliyah demonstrated that a plantation system modelled on the Algerian example was incompatible with their project, not only because it was economically ill-suited for Palestine but because it fostered a social system that conflicted with their goal of Jewish national revival. Furthermore, the experience of dealing with Rothschild and Hirsch made many question the wisdom of relying so heavily on private interests to further Zionist aims. Central to their concerns was an issue that lay at the heart of the entire Zionist project: land acquisition and ownership. As early as the First Zionist Congress, delegates had decided to set up a Jewish National Fund to purchase land and hold it in trust for the Jewish nation. The fund came into existence in 1901 and is the reason why private ownership of land is so rare in Israel to this day.

The first aliyah also raises the always intriguing question of what might have been. During the aliyah, there was an intimate economic relationship between Jews and Arabs. In the beginning, Arab agricultural techniques provided the model for inexperienced Jewish farmers to follow, and Arabs even profited by selling provisions to the immigrants. The moshavot alone employed close to four thousand Arab laborers. After Rothschild stepped in, Arabs again provided labor for Jewish-owned and -managed plantations. Beginning with the second aliyah, however, Zionist settlers made the conscious decision to sever their economy from that of their neighbors. Although that severance oftentimes was more theoretical than actual (as late as the early 1930s, Arabs still provided more than one-third of the labor of Jewish agricultural settlements), the intimate economic relations between the two communities during the first aliyah would never exist again.

THE CHANGING FACE OF ZIONIST COLONIZATION

Horace M. Kallen was a German Jew who emigrated to the United States in 1887. In 1919 he joined a small group of like-minded academics who founded the New School for Social Research in New York City. The founders of the New School intended their institution to be a bastion of progressivism during a period marked by American isolationism, antiradicalism, and Republican Party ascendancy. During the interwar period, Kallen travelled to Palestine. Impressed by what he saw there, he wrote *Frontiers of Hope*, which contains the following passage:

The [Zionist pioneer] is naturally a laborite and a doctrinaire socialist. He is a pacifist with the passions of the greatest war in his past. He is passionate about education. He has the modernist preoccupation with the arts as special branches of life. He seeks in Palestine no simple personal salvation nor even the healing of the children of Israel. His aspiration is the prophetic one. . . . He believes in the mission of Israel and in Jewry's duty and destiny to be light unto the nations. His Kibbutzim and his Moshavot, his labor organization and his cooperative societies, are endeavors to kindle that light. His vision of a future counterweighs the orthodox Judaist's security of the past. His experiments, with all their grime and negligence, have the spark of life in them. They more than offset the black and unhappy repetitions that wring the heart here and there in this shining Palestinian countryside.[9]

This is, of course, a highly sanitized view of the second and third waves of immigration. Nevertheless, the passage captures the hold the second and third aliyot – and, in many respects, the entire Zionist endeavor – has had on the progressive imagination ever since.

Although the first aliyah did not provide viable economic and social structures that would support the Jewish colonization of Palestine, the second and third aliyot, which took place in the periods 1904–1914 and 1918–1923 respectively, did. These two waves of immigration brought approximately seventy-five thousand new settlers to Palestine. As in the first aliyah, a vast majority of the immigrants of the second and third aliyot came from Russia. The Jews who launched these two waves of immigration – which might be seen as a single wave temporarily suspended by World War I – did so in the wake of events that further demoralized and imperiled the Jews of Russia: the Kishinev

[9] Horace M. Kallen, *Frontiers of Hope* (New York: Horace Liveright, 1929), 91.

pogrom of 1903, discussed above; the Russo-Japanese War of 1904–5; and the failed Russian Revolution of 1905. For Jews who wished to forgo the opportunity to travel thousands of miles across Asian tundra at the tsar's expense to fight the Japanese, emigration seemed a good bet. It also seemed a good bet for those who had signed on to the losing side in the revolution that followed the war. This explains the inordinate number of young, unmarried men among the new immigrants to Palestine.

Much of the reason the second and third aliyot have seemed so alluring to progressive observers such as Kallen is the distinctive doctrines to which many of the immigrants adhered. Zionism, like all nationalist movements, might be best viewed as a house of many mansions. All Zionists, of course, believe in the nationness of Jews. Almost all came to believe that Palestine should be the site for the realization of their national destiny. Yet it is possible to discern a number of distinct intellectual currents within the Zionist movement. These currents derive their ideas both from a logic internal to the Zionist movement and from borrowed ideas popular in the times and places of their first expression. There is perhaps no clearer example of this than the ideas that bound together the immigrants in the second and third aliyot.

Many historians regard the second and third aliyot as "more ideological" than the aliyot that preceded and followed them. In part, this has to do with the mythology that has arisen about these two aliyot – a mythology propagated by members of the two aliyot and their descendants who (particularly in the case of the second aliyah) have formed the aristocracy of postindependence Israeli society. In part, it has to do with the fact that the ideology of the second and third aliyot left an indelible stamp on Jewish institutions of the Yishuv (the prestate Jewish community in Palestine) and the state that succeeded it. Two of these ideas are of particular importance for understanding the evolution of Zionist colonies in Palestine: the "conquest of land" and the "conquest of labor." Although these ideas were not entirely new to the Zionist movement, they were never so well articulated or so thoroughly inscribed in institutions as they were during the second and third aliyot.

The conquest of land is easy to understand. Zionists proposed to spread colonies throughout Palestine and make an indelible imprint on the land. Indeed, a cult developed around bringing land under cultivation, draining swamps, and "making the desert bloom." As one prominent Zionist put it,

Before the coming of the first Jewish pioneers to Palestine wells and springs had been allowed to dry up, the land had been denuded of trees, nothing prevented the sand dunes from encroaching. Only malarial swamps flourished in that once fruitful country. To this desolation came the pioneers. They drained swamps, built roads, removed stones and rocks from the good earth. They sowed and reaped, fought disease and hostile neighbors, established a new homeland for themselves and their children.

Zionists were not the only ones involved in a conquest-of-land movement at this time, nor were they the only ones involved in such a movement in Palestine. A similar back-to-the-land movement, called the Artamenan movement, had emerged in Germany at around the same time. German youths, also infused with Romantic notions of living close to nature in "authentic" village settings, established agricultural colonies in the frontier area of East Prussia, a territory inhabited largely by Poles. The German government naturally encouraged a movement that would strengthen German claims to the territory. Likewise, many of the same ideas that animated the Zionists of the second and third aliyot could be found in the German Templar movement, which, as we have seen, established religiously inspired agricultural colonies in Palestine. The conquest of land was very much of its time.

So was the conquest of labor. The conquest of labor was a logical extension of another central Zionist idea, the negation of exile. According to many Zionists, the experience of life in the diaspora had made Jews incapable of acting like a real nation. David Ben-Gurion, a second-aliyah immigrant and the first prime minister of Israel, wrote, for example,

The diaspora means dependence – material, political, cultural, and intellectual dependence – because we are aliens, a minority, bereft of a homeland, rootless and separated from the soil, from labor, and from basic industry. Our task is to break radically with this dependence and to become masters of our own fate – in a word, to achieve independence.[10]

For Ben-Gurion, Jews could only end their dependence by becoming economically autonomous; that is, by venturing beyond the narrow set

---

[10] Arthur Hertzberg, ed., *The Zionist Idea: A Historical Analysis and Reader* (New York: Atheneum, 1981), 609.

of occupations to which they had been consigned and filling all occupations – by conquering labor. Only then could they become a true nation. Ben-Gurion once put it another way: He said he would not be satisfied that the conquest of labor had been completed until he saw Jewish prostitutes plying their trade on the streets of Tel Aviv.

The roots of the conquest of labor and the institutions the immigrants of the second and third aliyot constructed in its name might be traced back to the doctrines and experiments of nineteenth-century utopian socialists. The utopian socialists were a diffuse group of social theorists and reformers who dreamed of creating a harmonious and egalitarian society free of the exploitation, competition, and class divisions spawned by the Industrial Revolution. Some, like the British industrialist and philanthropist Robert Owen, even established model communities to test their theories. It is hardly surprising that the immigrants of the second and third aliyot, exposed to many of the same conditions that gave rise to utopian socialism in the West and free to give rein to their visions in Palestine, would adopt borrowed or homegrown utopian socialist ideas to guide their endeavors.

But if utopian socialism provided the immigrants of the second and third aliyot with a set of guidelines, economic imperative provided them with the incentive to apply them. As we have seen in the case of the first aliyah, it was all to easy for Zionists to grow dependent on Arab labor, which was both cheap and plentiful. But employing Arabs could only undercut the Zionist project. Not only would it inhibit the emergence of an autonomous, self-sufficient Jewish nation in Palestine, it would expand the pool of available labor, depress wages in the Yishuv, and discourage Jewish workers and artisans from immigrating to Palestine. With the future of the Zionist project at stake, ideology reinforced sound economic policy and vice versa. And even though the complete severance of the Yishuv and Arab economies turned out to be a practical impossibility, it nonetheless remained an avowed goal of Yishuv leaders, one that would affect the interrelationship and evolution of the two communities.

Ideas endure when they become institutionalized or when they find expression in concrete policies. The immigrants of the second and third aliyot built the institutions and promoted the practices that became hallmarks of Yishuv society. After Israel declared its independence in 1948, many of these institutions and practices were directly adopted by the new state. Others were modified so that they might fit the new circumstances of statehood.

Take the policy regarding language. Like many other early Zionists, Theodor Herzl believed that no good would come from prescribing the language to be used in the Yishuv. Although Hebrew was the language of the ancient Israelites, most Jews Herzl hoped to recruit to the Zionist cause spoke Yiddish as their native language. Prescribing the language of the Yishuv would only divide and weaken the movement. So he temporized. "Every man can preserve the language in which his thoughts are at home," he proposed. "Switzerland offers us an example of the possibility of a federation of tongues."[11] The immigrants of the second and third aliyot would have none of that. Like their Romantic forebears, they believed that the spirit of a nation was embodied in its language. Besides, prescribing Hebrew as the language of national rebirth negated exile in a tangible way. So Hebrew it was.

Other policies and institutions likewise gave substance to the ideals of the second and third aliyot. In line with the cooperative principles of utopian socialism, for example, the settlers founded a labor federation, the Histadrut, that represented the social and economic interests of its members and provided them with credit, health care, and education. It did not hurt that the Histadrut was able to regulate the size of the labor market by pressuring Jewish employers to hire its members exclusively. After the establishment of the State of Israel, the Histadrut surrendered some functions to the state but maintained many of its responsibilities in the field of social welfare. The settlers also founded political parties to represent their political interests and articulate the principles of "Labor Zionism": Poale Zion (Workers of Zion; its creed, taken from the first line of the Communist Manifesto and rendered suitable for a national movement was "the history of mankind is a history of class and national [!] struggles") and Hapoel Hatzair (Young Worker). Since there was more uniting than dividing them – both parties were committed to the conquest-of-labor idea and to fostering Hebrew culture – they merged in 1930 to form the Mapai, the Labor Party of Israel. The Labor Party became the dominant party of the new state and provided Israel with every prime minister until 1977. And since real nations depend on no

---

[11] Paul Mendes-Flohr and Jehuda Reinharz, *The Jew in the Modern World: A Documentary History* (New York: Oxford University Press, 1995), 533–7.

one but themselves for defense, Labor Zionists were instrumental in organizing the first real militia in the Yishuv, the Haganah. The Haganah would become the core of the postindependence army, the Israel Defense Forces.

Perhaps no undertaking of the second and third aliyot carried as much symbolic weight as the immigrants' experiments in agricultural settlement. This is to be expected: Agricultural settlement combined the social laboratory so dear to utopian socialists with the Romantic obsession with nature and territoriality. It also connected the conquest of land and the conquest of labor within the framework of a single symbol. The second and third aliyot are often identified with two types of agricultural settlements: *kibbutzim* (sing. *kibbutz*) and *moshavim* (sing. *moshav*, not to be confused with the *moshava* [*moshavot*]). Unlike the plantations established during the first aliyah, these settlements engaged in "mixed farming." In other words, instead of specializing in a single cash crop, these settlements combined the cultivation of fruits and crops with animal husbandry and dairy farming. The kibbutzim were communal farms. They allowed no private property, no permanent hierarchy of position, no employment of outside labor, and very little privacy (*kibbutzniks* ate in communal dining halls, and child rearing was a community responsibility, with kibbutznik children raised in communal childcare facilities). Decision making was, for the most part, done collectively. The first kibbutz was established in 1909 in Degania on the southern tip of Lake Tiberias. Moshavim – cooperative farms that permitted individual landholdings and individual marketing of crops – emerged out of the kibbutz movement a little more than a decade later.

National symbols may not accurately portray history, but they certainly tell us something about a nation's self-conception. The kibbutz is such a national symbol, equivalent in Israel to what the cowboy is in America. The kibbutz thus came to symbolize the cooperative and egalitarian ethos and the pioneering spirit Labor Zionists imputed to the entirety of the Zionist movement. But just as the cowboy was a rarity in the America of the late nineteenth century, so was the kibbutznik. Out of a total Jewish population of 85,000, only about 12,000 (14 percent) belonged to either kibbutzim or moshavim. And just as the purportedly individualistic cowboy was actually a company man who worked for the cattle barons of the Old West, the kibbutz movement was not all that legend has made it out to be either. According to sociologist

8. The kibbutz became a national symbol of Israel. Top: the image. Below: the reality. (Source: From the collection of the author)

Gershon Shafir, rather than being the product of unalloyed idealism or utopian fancy, the kibbutzim served the very practical purpose of disengaging Jewish agriculture from the pool of Arab labor that threatened to dilute it. But great anxieties breed great symbols: Just as the legend of the American cowboy arose at a time when consumers of dime novels feared for the loss of the individualistic pioneering ethos at the hands of mass urbanized society in America, the celebration of the "kibbutz spirit" arose as early as the third aliyah, when a kindred uneasiness afflicted the Labor Zionist movement.

All told, the contributions made by the second and third aliyot to the future of Zionism in Palestine were substantial. That Israel became a Hebrew-speaking social democracy whose economic development followed the path that it did can be attributed to these two waves of immigration. Although an estimated 90 percent of the immigrants of the two aliyot left Palestine after only a brief sojourn there, as early as the onset of World War I the Jewish population of Palestine had reached what one historian calls a "critical demographic mass." In other words, it had reached a size that made its institutions and structures workable and, given the right circumstances, long-lived. As we shall see, the right circumstances occurred during World War I.

THE DOPPELGÄNGERS

If Zionist immigration had ended with the third aliyah, or if the dominance of the ideas and institutions of the second and third aliyot were uncontested, or if those ideas and institutions remained unaffected by changing circumstances, we might simply trace back the institutions and attitudes of the contemporary State of Israel to those forged by the second and third aliyot and call it a day. And because the settlers of the second and third aliyot and their descendants dominated the institutions of the Yishuv and the State of Israel for three quarters of a century, it is all too easy to identify their brand of Zionism and the institutions they created with Zionism as a whole. But their brand of Zionism was not unchallenged, nor did immigration end with the third aliyah. From the beginnings of the Zionist movement, for example, religious Zionists challenged the secularism of the dominant groupings in the Zionist movement. One party, the Mizrahi, summed up their philosophy in the slogan, "The land of Israel for the people of Israel according to the Torah of Israel." The Mizrahi was one of the forebears of the contemporary National Religious Party in Israel, a party that has wrung concessions on a variety of social and educational issues from Labor Zionists when they needed its parliamentary support. And religious Zionism was not the only challenge that Labor Zionism faced.

The fourth aliyah (1924–8) brought roughly 82,000 new immigrants to Palestine. These immigrants were quite different from the immigrants who participated in the previous two aliyot. About half of the new immigrants were Jews from Poland who chose emigration in the wake of anti-Jewish legislation in that country. They were more akin to refugees than their ideologically inspired predecessors. Furthermore, most were not young, idealistic, middle-class student-types. Many were small businessmen and shopowners. As a result, most did not subscribe to the socialist principles of the second and third aliyot, and the conquest of land held little allure for them. About four-fifths settled in cities, particularly Tel Aviv and Haifa, not in rural areas. From 1923 to 1926, the population of Tel Aviv alone rose from 16,000 to 40,000.

Many of these refugees found their spokesman in Vladimir Jabotinsky, the architect of what came to be known as Revisionist Zionism. Jabotinsky was born in Odessa in 1880 and received training as a journalist. Journalism was not the only attribute Jabotinsky holds in common with Theodor Herzl. As in the case of Herzl, the conventional narrative of Jabotinsky's life reduces the undoubtedly complex motivations behind his conversion to Zionism to a single event. In this case, it was the Kishinev pogrom. According to the narrative, Jabotinsky, like Bialik, was horrified at Jewish passivity during the pogrom. Unlike Bialik, he decided to do more than write about it. He thus began organizing Jewish self-defense groups. Whatever the source or sources of Jabotinsky's Zionism, militarism would remain the touchstone of his ideology for the remainder of his life. In 1923 he founded a youth group, Betar, which had all the trappings of the fascist youth groups being founded throughout Europe, down to the uniforms, drills, and fervent, unalloyed nationalism. Betar played an important role in sending recruits from eastern Europe to Palestine.

In 1931 Jabotinsky's followers in Palestine organized the Irgun Zvai Leumi, an underground militia. Along with the Stern Gang, an Irgun spin-off, the Irgun perpetrated some of the most appalling terrorist atrocities committed in modern Palestine, including a campaign of "reprisal" bombings in 1937 in Arab markets (during which close to 80 Arabs were killed) and the wholesale massacre of upwards of 250 innocents in the village of Dayr Yassin in 1948. "The programme [of the Revisionists] is not complicated," Jabotinsky once wrote. "The aim of Zionism is a Jewish state.... Hence the commandment of the

9. "The commandment of the hour: a new political campaign and the militarization of Jewish youth." Jabotinsky's Betar in full military regalia. (Source: Courtesy of the Jabotinsky Institute in Israel)

hour: a new political campaign and the militarization of Jewish youth in Eretz Israel and the Jewish diaspora."

Jabotinsky believed that Zionism had taken a wrong turn by burdening the movement with socialist claptrap. This created ideological divisions that weakened the Zionist movement and distracted it from its one and only goal: the establishment of an independent Jewish state in (all of) historic Palestine. Thus, for Jabotinsky it was necessary to "revise" the Zionist movement so that it might effect "the gradual transformation of Palestine (including Trans-Jordan) into a self-governing commonwealth under the auspices of an established Jewish majority." In line with his distaste for Labor Zionism, Jabotinsky even ordered his followers to break strikes called by the Histadrut. This only endeared him more to the petit bourgeois immigrants of the fourth aliyah, already attracted to his movement by its monomaniacal nationalism, territorial assertiveness, and populist, antielitist (anti-Labor Zionist) rhetoric.

The fourth aliyah embodied a different source for contemporary Israeli political thought than that represented by the second and third aliyot. Just as the Mapai Party might be seen as the ideological descendant of the parties established during the second and third aliyot, the rival Likud Party might be seen as the ideological descendant of Jabotinsky's Revisionists. The first Likud prime minister, Menachem Begin, took power in 1977. Since then, three other Likud prime ministers – Yitzhak Shamir, Benjamin Netanyahu, and Ariel Sharon – have governed Israel. As we shall see, on the questions of land and the fate of the indigenous inhabitants of Palestine, none strayed too far from the legacy of Vladimir Jabotinsky.

A postscript: In July 1964, the body of Vladimir Jabotinsky was disinterred from its grave in New York and reburied in Israel. The reburial – a reenactment of Theodor Herzl's reburial – was done at the request of the followers of Jabotinsky, including Menachem Begin. According to one Israeli historian, "This ceremony symbolized both the normalization of relations between Labor and the political descendants of the Revisionist movement, and the beginning of the latter's political rehabilitation and legitimization."[12] However reluctantly at first, the Revisionists and their heirs were finally acknowledged as full members of the Zionist club.

---

[12] Myron Aronoff, "Myths, Symbols, and Rituals of the Emerging State," in *New Perspectives on Israeli History: The Early Years of the State*, ed. Laurence J. Silberstein (New York: New York University Press, 1991), 183.

SUGGESTIONS FOR FURTHER READING

Aaronsohn, Ran. "Baron Rothschild and the Initial Stage of Jewish Settlement in Palestine (1882–1890): A Different Type of Colonization?" *Journal of Historical Geography* 19 (1993): 142–56. History of first aliyah related by a sympathetic observer.

Berkowitz, Michael. *Zionist Culture and West European Jewry before the First World War*. Cambridge: Cambridge University Press, 1993. Comprehensive history of early years of Zionism outside eastern Europe.

Brenner, Lenni. *Zionism in the Age of Dictators*. London: Croom Helm, 1983. Excellent account of the rise of Vladimir Jabotinsky and Revisionist Zionism.

Elon, Amos. *Herzl*. New York: Schocken Books, 1975. Readable account of the life and thought of the Zionist pioneer.

Hertzberg, Arthur, ed. *The Zionist Idea: A Historical Analysis and Reader*. New York: Atheneum, 1981. Introduction and selection of readings. Excerpts from a broad sweep of Zionist authors, with an excellent introduction on the intellectual history of Zionism.

Herzl, Theodor. *Old-New Land*. Translated by Lotta Levensohn. New York: Marcus Wiener, 1960. Because his *The Jewish State* did not reach a mass audience, Herzl wrote this novel to make his case.

Kurzman, Dan. *Ben-Gurion, Prophet of Fire*. New York: Simon and Schuster, 1983. Popular biography of first prime minister of Israel, who was also a symbol of the second and third aliyot.

Shafir, Gershon. *Land, Labor, and the Origins of the Israeli–Palestinian Conflict,1882–1914*. Cambridge: Cambridge University Press, 1989. Revisionist account of the origins and evolution of the Zionist "conquest of labor" strategy.

———. "Zionism and Colonialism: A Comparative Approach." In *Israel in Comparative Perspective: Challenging the Conventional Wisdom*, ed. Michael N. Barnett, 227–44. Albany: State University of New York Press, 1996. A less sympathetic comparison between Zionist settlement in Palestine and contemporaneous movements in other parts of the world.

Sternhell, Zeev. *The Founding Myths of Israel: Nationalism, Socialism, and the Making of the Jewish State*. Translated by David Maisel. Princeton, NJ: Princeton University Press, 1998. Analysis of cultural currents that went into the making of Israeli political culture.

4

WORLD WAR I AND THE
PALESTINE MANDATE

On 28 June 1914, the heir to the Austrian throne, Archduke Franz Ferdinand, was shot by a Serbian nationalist while visiting the city of Sarajevo. With the backing of its ally, Germany, Austria presented an ultimatum to Serbia. The Austrians demanded that the Serbs rein in the nationalist and anti-Austrian movements hatching plots in their territory. Then, even after the Serbian government agreed to the ultimatum, the Austrians declared war.

While Germany was allied with Austria, Russia was allied with Serbia. The Russians feared that they would be at a disadvantage if war broke out and Germany had completed its military preparations before them. The Russian tsar thus ordered a general mobilization. Germany also mobilized and, to avoid fighting Russia and France at the same time, decided to launch a knockout blow against France by striking west through Belgium. Because Britain was committed by treaty to Belgian independence, it declared war on Germany. World War I had started.

When we think of World War I, we generally think of trench warfare on the western front in France. It is important to understand, however, that World War I was truly a world war. As a matter of fact, although the British and French referred to the war as "the Great War" until World War II, the Germans coined the phrase "world war" early on to describe the conflict. German strategists understood that the war was being waged among rival empires with worldwide interests. These empires depended on their colonial possessions to maintain their strategic position and economic well-being. Colonies were also indispensable for the French and British military effort, since both powers depended on them for manpower to replenish the depleted ranks of their armies. As a result, much of the globe, including the Ottoman Empire, was dragged into a war that had begun in Europe.

World War I had both immediate and long-term effects on the Middle East. During the war, the Ottoman Empire suffered among the greatest number of casualties per capita of all combatants. Whereas Germany and France lost, respectively, about 9 and 11 percent of their populations as a result of the war, estimates for Ottoman losses run almost as high as 25 percent – approximately 5 million out of a population of 21 million. These casualties occurred both on and off the battlefield. As a matter of fact, four out of every five Ottoman citizens who died were noncombatants. Many succumbed to famine and disease, which spread to various parts of the empire because of the coastal blockade imposed by the British and French navies and also because of Ottoman requisitioning policies. Others died as a consequence of population transfer (the Ottomans attempted to move their coastal populations inland) and ethnic cleansing (which resulted in the deaths of about 1.5 million Armenians). All these factors affected the inhabitants of Palestine, both indigenous and Zionist. Although reliable data are lacking, it has been estimated that, in spite of an influx of Armenian refugees into the territory, there was an overall population decline in Palestine.

However tragic the wartime suffering of the population, it is the long-term effects of the war that concern us here. World War I was the most important political event in the history of the modern Middle East, and the political changes engendered by the war would have profound consequences for Palestine and the two communities living there.

Four effects of the war are particularly noteworthy. First, the war brought about the destruction of the Ottoman Empire and the division of the empire into a number of smaller political units. Over time, these units would become the independent states of the contemporary Middle East. Second, with the destruction of the Ottoman Empire, two of the victorious powers, Britain and France, assumed direct administrative responsibility for the territories that are now Palestine/Israel, Jordan, Iraq, Lebanon, and Syria. Britain and France managed these territories through a new form of rule that lay midway between colonial annexation and complete sovereignty: the mandate. Third, the Zionist movement received from a Great Power – Great Britain – support for its principle aim, "the [creation] for the Jewish people a home in

Palestine secured by public law." This support virtually guaranteed that the Zionist movement would not go the way of hundreds of other nationalist movements that had appeared briefly during the nineteenth and twentieth centuries, then faded into obscurity. Finally, the destruction of the Ottoman Empire destroyed the political framework that had united Turks and Arabs within a single state for four centuries. This encouraged the emergence or spread of a variety of nationalist movements that offered former Ottoman citizens alternative blueprints for reconstructing their political identities and their political communities. Among these movements were those that claimed to represent the national aspirations of the indigenous inhabitants of Palestine.

World War I has been called the graveyard of empires because three continental empires – the Ottoman, the Russian, and the Austro-Hungarian – succumbed as a result of the hostilities. Although European powers had nibbled at the edges of the Ottoman Empire during the nineteenth century and had left it with just a foothold on the European continent, the "sick man of Europe" (as Tsar Nicholas II called it) had entered the twentieth century geographically truncated but intact. The concert of European powers that had emerged in the wake of the Napoleonic wars had managed both to protect the interests of the individual European nations in the Ottoman Empire and to diffuse crisis after crisis through diplomacy. Only once during the century – in the Crimean War – did European nations go to war to resolve a dispute originating in the Middle East. But the rise of Germany disrupted the European balance of power and crippled the ability of European states to act together on issues of common interest. By the beginning of the twentieth century, the concert of Europe no longer existed. Instead, on the eve of World War I, European states divided themselves into two alliances. Britain, France, and Russia (and, in 1917, the United States) formed the core of the entente powers. Germany, the Austro-Hungarian Empire, and the Ottoman Empire formed the core of the Central Powers. Other states in Europe and elsewhere also signed on to one alliance or the other.

The Ottoman Empire joined the Central Powers for several reasons. Germany enjoyed extensive political and economic influence in the empire. The Austro-Hungarian Empire was anxious to control Ottoman ambitions in the Balkans and thus actively solicited the empire's participation in the war on its side. And for their part, the Ottomans were unlikely to join any alliance that included their traditional enemy, Russia, which had, over the course of the nineteenth century, made war on the Ottomans and conspired time and again to dismantle their empire. At the same time, the entente powers did not try very hard to attract the Ottomans to their side. Their governments believed that the war would be over before the Ottomans could make their presence on the battlefield felt, that even if the war lasted longer than expected Ottoman participation would not affect its outcome, and that the Ottomans would decide which side to join based on the progress of the war anyway. The entente powers also sought to attract Greece and Italy – two countries with territorial ambitions in the Ottoman Empire – to their ranks and believed that the promise of Ottoman territory was just the bait with which they might be snared. And so the Ottoman Empire joined the Central Powers.

As soon as it became clear that the war would not be over quickly, each of the entente powers began to maneuver to be in a position to claim the spoils it desired in the Middle East in the event of victory. The Russians, hoping to realize their long-standing dream of acquiring a warm-water port that could remain open all year round, laid claim to the Turkish Straits and Istanbul. In addition, because the tsars perceived themselves to be the guardians of Orthodoxy and Orthodox Christians the world over, the Russians sought to ensure that their coreligionists would have access to the holy places in Jerusalem should control of Palestine change hands. Because Orthodoxy was one of the foundations upon which their dynastic legitimacy rested, the Romanovs did not take their religious obligations lightly: Throughout the nineteenth century they feuded endlessly with the Catholic French over control of Jerusalem's holy sites and even came to blows with their rival over this (and other issues) in the Crimean War. For their part, the French laid claim to "historic rights" in "Syria" – an area of vague geographic boundaries that, when intoned by a Gallic voice, usually included Palestine. The French based their claims on their special relationship with the Catholic and near-Catholic minorities (such as the Maronite Christians of Lebanon) who lived there and on their investments in and trade with the region. The British were none too anxious for either the Russians or French to gain advantage or aggrandize themselves at British expense. As the world's dominant economic power, the British were fixated on free trade and security for investments in the region. Then, of course, there was the paramount imperial concern: protecting the route to India.

Beginning in 1915, the entente powers began negotiating secret treaties that pledged mutual support for the territorial claims made by themselves or their would-be allies. By negotiating these treaties, the entente powers hoped to confirm those claims, attract to their alliance outlying states such as Italy and Greece, and, as the war went on, keep the alliance intact by promising active combatants a payoff at the close of hostilities. For example, the British assumed that continued Russian pressure on Germany was the key to entente victory in Europe. To prevent Russia from signing a separate peace with the Central Powers and withdrawing from the war, the British and French negotiated a deal with the Russians. According to what became known as the "Constantinople Agreement," Britain and France recognized Russia's claims to the Turkish Straits and the city that overlooked them, Istanbul. In return for their generosity, France got recognition for its claims to Syria (whatever that meant), and Britain got recognition for its claims to territory elsewhere.

What makes the Constantinople Agreement important is not what it promised. Russia never got the straits, nor did it remain in the war until the bitter end. France and Britain enjoyed only temporary control of the territories promised them. What makes the agreement important is that it established the principle that the entente powers had a right to compensation for fighting their enemies and that at least part of this compensation should come in the form of territory carved out of the Middle East. Other secret treaties soon followed: the Treaty of London, the Sykes-Picot Agreement, the Treaty of Saint-Jean-de-Maurienne. All these treaties applied the principle of compensation. And many of these treaties dealt with the territory of Palestine – although, more often than not, not in any way that paid heed to previously negotiated treaties. Thus, by the end of the war, each of the entente powers had promised itself or one or more of its allies control over Palestine more than once.

To make matters worse, Great Britain not only signed secret treaties with its allies and would-be allies, it made pledges to a number of local warlords and nationalist groups, promising to support them if those warlords and groups aligned themselves with the entente side. For example, in 1915 the British made contact with an Arabian warlord based in Mecca, Sharif Husayn. Husayn promised to delegate his son,

Amir Faysal, to launch a revolt against the Ottoman Empire. In exchange, the British promised Husayn gold and guns and, once the war ended, the right to establish an Arab "state or states" with ambiguously defined borders in the predominantly Arab territories of the Ottoman Empire. Hence, the famous Arab Revolt, guided by the even more famous British colonel T. E. Lawrence (Lawrence of Arabia). Unfortunately for Sharif Husayn and Amir Faysal, neither was able to get the British to clarify exactly what they meant by an Arab state or states or what territory would be included in such an arrangement. Both the sharif and his son were confident that the territory of Palestine would be part of the package. The British, however, added so many qualifiers and circumlocutions to their pledge that they were able to demur after hostilities had ended and still credit themselves with upholding the British reputation for fair play. Although having little practical effect, the British pledge to Sharif Husayn and his son did yield one tangible result: The story of the pledge was picked up by later chroniclers of Arab nationalism and used as the basis of a narrative that recounted the Arab story as one of sacrifice, betrayal, and tragedy.

Another pledge made by the British during the war would have far greater consequences. In July 1917, Baron Lionel Walter Rothschild, a member of the British branch of the same banking family that produced Baron Edmond de Rothschild, submitted to the British Foreign Office a draft resolution on behalf of the British Zionist Federation. After tinkering with the wording of the original draft, the British foreign secretary, Alfred Balfour, placed the following notice in the *Times* (London):

I have much pleasure in conveying to you, on behalf of his Majesty's Government, the following declaration of sympathy with Jewish Zionist aspirations which has been submitted to and approved by the Cabinet: –

His Majesty's Government view with favour the establishment in Palestine of a national home for the Jewish people, and will use their best endeavours to facilitate the achievement of this object, it being clearly understood that nothing shall be done which may prejudice the civil and religious rights of existing non-Jewish communities in Palestine, or the rights and political status enjoyed by Jews in any other country.

I should be grateful if you would bring this declaration to the knowledge of the Zionist Federation.

This notice became known as the "Balfour Declaration."

The words of the Balfour Declaration were carefully chosen. It was no accident that the declaration contains the phrase "in Palestine" rather than "of Palestine," nor was it an accident that the foreign office would use the words "national home" rather than the more precise "state" – in spite of the fact that "national home" has no precedent or standing in international law. And what exactly do "view with favour" and "use their best endeavours" mean? The seeming ambiguities of the declaration reflect debates not only within the British government but within the British Zionist and Jewish communities as well. For example, the Jewish anti-Zionist secretary of state for India, Edwin Montagu, opposed the declaration altogether, fearing that support for the Zionist cause would threaten the status of Jews in their home countries. He was not alone in his disquiet: Even some Zionists counseled restraint. Thus it was that the British government put its imprimatur on a pledge whose carefully chosen evasions would bring it no end of grief.

This, of course, raises another question: Why would the British government choose to support Zionist aspirations at all? Historians list a number of possible reasons. Some have emphasized the strategic benefits the British thought they might derive from Jewish settlement in Palestine. Central to the British strategic imagination was protecting the route to India, and central to protecting the route to India was safeguarding the British position in the Suez Canal. A Jewish national home in Palestine, surrounded by a predominantly Muslim population and dependent on British goodwill and support, would provide such a safeguard.

Other historians argue that the British government was influenced by an overestimation of Jewish power in the United States and Russia – a sort of a patrician anti-Semitism. Although the United States had entered World War I on the side of the entente powers in April 1917, the British war effort was not embraced by many Americans, particularly not those of Irish and German descent. Furthermore, the British did not know quite what to make of President Woodrow Wilson and his conviction (before America's entrance into the war) that the way to end hostilities was for both sides to accept "peace without victory." Two of Wilson's closest advisors, Louis Brandeis and Felix Frankfurter, were avid Zionists. How better to shore up an uncertain ally than by endorsing Zionist aims? The British adopted similar thinking when it came to the Russians, who were in the midst of their revolution. Several of the most prominent revolutionaries, including Leon Trotsky, were of

Jewish descent. Why not see if they could be persuaded to keep Russia in the war by appealing to their latent Jewishness and giving them another reason to continue the fight?

For his part, David Lloyd George, the British prime minister at the time, lists in his memoirs at least nine reasons for announcing the Balfour Declaration. These include not only those already mentioned but also Britain's desire to attract Jewish financial resources, its worry that Germany would "capture the Zionist movement," his own "Christian Zionist" beliefs (Palestine "was a historic and sacred land, throbbing from Dan to Beersheba with immortal traditions"), the lobbying of Chaim Weizmann (a Zionist and celebrated chemist who figured out how to synthesize acetone, an ingredient in naval munitions), and sympathy with the worldwide plight of the Jews. Least convincing is his declaration that "the democratic Powers of Europe had always advocated emancipation of the subject races held down by Great empires." Sure, except perhaps in India. Most convincing is his assertion that "it was part of our propagandist strategy for mobilizing every opinion and force throughout the world which would weaken the enemy and improve the Allied chances." In other words, it couldn't hurt – and might even help.

Whatever the reasons behind the British decision to endorse the Zionist project, the announcement of the Balfour Declaration marked a milestone in the history of the Zionist movement. Nationalisms like Zionism do not succeed or fail because of the intrinsic truth or falsity of their doctrines. Inasmuch as all nationalisms create nations where no nations had been before, they are all false. Inasmuch as all nationalisms inspire belief in their citizens or would be citizens and provide them with identities and communities, they are true. Nationalisms succeed or fail not because they are true or false but because of factors extrinsic to the nationalisms themselves: the adversaries against whom they are arrayed, the resources available to them and their supporters, the support they receive from the international community. Thus, it might be stated without exaggeration that if it were not for the Balfour Declaration, Zionism might very well have gone the way of Confederate nationalism.

THE MANDATE

By the time the Great Powers arrived in Paris at the end of World War I, their wartime plans were in disarray. As we have seen, during the war the entente powers had negotiated a number of agreements dividing up Ottoman territory among themselves, and the British had made a number of pledges promising to support various warlords and national movements in the region. While the British and French continued to hold to the principle that the territories formerly governed by the Ottoman Empire should be treated as the spoils of war, they found they could not hold to all the agreements and pledges they had made.

In part, they had only themselves to blame. True, they had worked out the postwar distribution of Ottoman lands through their treaties and pledges, but these were both ambiguous and mutually contradictory. Take the issue of Palestine, for example. According to the French reading of one of the secret treaties, the Sykes-Picot Agreement, Syria was promised to France, and Palestine was part of Syria. According to the Russian reading of the same agreement, Palestine was simply the territory surrounding Jerusalem, and Jerusalem was to be placed under international control. According to the Arab nationalist reading of the letters Sharif Husayn exchanged with the British government before the Arab Revolt, Palestine was to be part of an Arab state or states. And then, of course, there was the Balfour Declaration.

Changed circumstances also muddied the waters of the postwar settlement. For example, during the war, Britain had launched attacks on the Ottoman Empire from India and Egypt. At the close of the war, British troops occupied Iraq and parts of the Levant. This gave Britain leverage in postwar negotiations with other victorious powers. At the same time, the Russian Revolution brought to power a government that, in theory at least, opposed the imperialist designs of the tsarist government. The new Bolshevik government of Russia not only renounced the claims made by its predecessor but embarrassed the other entente powers by publishing the texts of the secret agreements signed by Russia. Furthermore, the Bolsheviks had little use for religion and thus had no desire to make an issue of Orthodox access to Christian holy sites. This left the other entente powers with little incentive to "internationalize" Jerusalem. Nor, with Russia preoccupied with its own internal problems, was it likely to cause trouble in the Middle East. Britain thus had no need for a French buffer between British holdings in the region – centered around the Suez Canal – and the menace to the north.

One last obstacle to implementing the secret agreements came from the United States. When the United States entered the war on the side

10. The official arrival of British troops in Jerusalem, December 1917. (Source: From the collection of the author)

of the entente, President Wilson announced his intention to make his "Fourteen Points" the basis of a postwar peace. These points were an ambitious, if not always practicable, list of proposals for reconstructing the postwar international order. Although they included such seemingly benign items as freedom of navigation on the seas and free trade ("as far as possible"), they also included two items that made European diplomats wince: the right of peoples to self-determination and an end to secret agreements. Nationalist leaders around the world seized on these two promises and demanded that the entente powers make good on them. Increasingly frustrated British and French diplomats humored Wilson as best they could while they seethed in private. Georges Clemenceau, French president and foreign minister, reportedly scoffed at the Fourteen Points, remarking, "Even the good Lord contented himself with only ten commandments, and we should not try to improve on them." Nevertheless, Wilson had let the genie out of the bottle, and delegates to the peace conference ending the war were beset by representatives of a host of nationalist movements, including Zionists and Arabs, all demanding their right to self-determination.

Historians have commonly ascribed Wilson's call for self-determination to his stern, moralistic upbringing or his naiveté when it came to international affairs. In fact, Wilson's call might be seen as an epochal shift in the management of the international order brought about by the emergence of the United States as a Great Power. At the close of World War I, the United States was the leading industrial power in the world. Then, as now, American politicians and diplomats never tired of expounding the virtues of open markets and free trade as means to establish a peaceful and prosperous world order. As President Calvin Coolidge put it only a few years later, "The chief business of the American people is business." But open markets and free trade were incompatible with the colonial system championed by Britain and France. There was no point to annexing territories if colonizing powers could not shut out unwanted competitors from their possessions. Clearly, some compromise had to be reached between these incompatible views. That compromise was to be found in the mandates system.

Meeting in Paris, entente peace negotiators set about unraveling the conflicting claims and contradictory aspirations of their governments. In line with Wilson's fourteenth point, the negotiators agreed to establish a League of Nations that they hoped would ensure the peace and stability of the postwar world. This league would be the institutional expression of an international order that rested on the shared ideals of "civilized" states rather than on discredited balance-of-power politics. Even imperialism was to be justified on the basis of these ideals. Article 22 of the league's charter explained exactly how this would be done:

To those colonies and territories which as a consequence of the last war have ceased to be under the sovereignty of the states which formerly governed them and which are inhabited by peoples not yet able to stand by themselves under the strenuous conditions of the modern world, there should be applied the principle that the well-being and development of such peoples form a sacred trust of civilization and that securities for the performance of that trust should be embodied in the covenant. The best method of giving practical effect to this principle should be entrusted to advanced nations who by reason of their resources, their experience, or their geographical position can best undertake this responsibility.

As for the former Asiatic Arab provinces of the Ottoman Empire,

Certain communities formerly belonging to the Turkish empire have reached a stage of development where their existence as independent states can be provisionally recognized subject to the rendering of assistance by a mandatory [power] until such time as they are able to stand alone, the wishes of the communities must be a principle consideration in the selection of the mandatory.

Accordingly, after World War I, France got the mandate for the territory that now includes Syria and Lebanon, while Britain got the mandate for the territory that now includes Israel, the occupied territories, Jordan, and Iraq.

Although the charter stipulated that the populations themselves would play a role in determining which mandatory power would have supervision over them, the British and French, of course, never seriously considered the desires of the peoples of the Middle East when establishing the mandates system. For example, the elected parliament of Syria that met after the war, the Syrian General Congress, declared that it wanted Syria to be independent and unified. By unity, the representatives meant that Syria should include territories of present-day Syria, Lebanon, Israel/Palestine, and Jordan. If Syria had to have a mandatory power overseeing it, a majority of the representatives declared, it should be the United States. Their second choice was Great Britain. For the representatives, France was unacceptable as a mandatory power. Nevertheless, the territory they defined as Syria was divided, its sovereignty postponed, and a truncated Syria went to France as a mandate.

When it came to the territory that would shortly become Palestine, the British had no illusions about the sentiments of a majority of the politically active Arab population there either. Three months after the armistice, the head of the Arab Bureau – Britain's intelligence unit in the Arab Middle East – sent the following telegram to his superiors in the War Office:

It is convenient in certain circles to attribute local anti-Zionist feeling to influence of [notables] who are spoken of as corrupt and tyrannical landowners, whom it is necessary to consider. This is not a fair statement, as not only are they worthy representatives of their class, but fear and dislike of Zionism has become general throughout all classes. This may be attributed almost entirely to rapid advancement in Zionist demands during last few months. . . . The outcome has been lack of confidence in Great Britain to whom the majority have looked hitherto as the dominant power under whose guidance the future prosperity of Palestine and Syria would best be assured. . . . They argue 1) That Syria must be one and undivided and must include Palestine. 2) That Great Britain and France are bound by agreements that can only lead to a division of the country, to rival control and to a clashing of British-French interests which would be a menace to the peace of Syria and of the civilised world. 3) That France is in any case unsuitable as a mandatory power for Syria, whose economic and commercial interests must be bound up with Egypt and Mesopotamia, both of which are under British control. 4) That Great Britain is debarred by her agreements with France and Zionists from comprehending the only policy which they consider can alone produce a stable and prosperous Syria. 5) That America is only power left. America is tied by no former pledges or agreements in regard to Syria and has no interests which clash with those of Great Britain, by whose influence Syria must always be surrounded, and to whom Syria must always look for much of her economic progress.

Needless to say, the wishes of the territory's indigenous population went unheeded.

The mandates system allowed the mandatory powers complete economic and administrative control over the territory they were allotted. The mandatory powers could also sever and join territories at will. Thus, at the Cairo Conference of 1921, the British detached the territory east of the Jordan River from the Palestine mandate and established a separate administrative unit called, not surprisingly, "Trans-Jordan" (the present-day Hashemite Kingdom of Jordan). Winston Churchill, who presided over the conference as the British colonial secretary, later bragged that at the conference he had "created Jordan with a stroke of the pen one Sunday afternoon." The British established another son of Sharif Husayn, 'Abdullah, as *amir* (prince) of Trans-Jordan (he became king in 1946 when the British granted Jordan independence). Descendants of 'Abdullah have ruled the country ever since. Much to the outrage of Jabotinsky and his followers, the British restricted Jewish immigration to the territory west of the Jordan River. This territory retained the name "Palestine."

In July 1922, in accordance with League of Nations requirements, the British government submitted a "draft instrument" that outlined the procedures it proposed to follow in administering its Palestine mandate. The instrument included the text of the Balfour Declaration in its preamble, thus transforming a wartime pledge into a legally binding statute. Article 2 of the draft instrument stipulated that "the Mandatory shall be responsible for placing the country under such political, administrative, and economic conditions as will secure the establishment of the Jewish national home." Article 4 stated,

An appropriate Jewish Agency shall be recognized as a public body for the purpose of advising and co-operating with the Administration of Palestine in such economic, social and other matters as may affect the establishment of the Jewish National Home and the interests of the Jewish population in Palestine.

Article 6 stated,

The Administration of Palestine, while ensuring that the rights and position of other sections of the population are not prejudiced, shall facilitate Jewish immigration under suitable conditions and shall encourage, in co-operation with the Jewish Agency referred to in Article 4, close settlement by Jews on the land, including State lands and waste lands.

"Other sections of the population" referred, of course, to the indigenous inhabitants of Palestine; the word "Arab" was not used in the instrument.

The "appropriate Jewish agency" mentioned in Article 4 was initially the World Zionist Organization, which was headquartered in London and represented in Palestine by the Palestine Zionist Executive. David Ben-Gurion, a Polish-born Jew who had emigrated to Palestine in the second aliyah and would go on to become the first prime minister of Israel, headed the executive. To garner the support of all Jews, non-Zionist as well as Zionist, the World Zionist Organization abdicated its position as the "appropriate Jewish Agency" in 1929 and established an auxiliary organization called the "Jewish Agency." By including an equal number of non-Zionists and Zionists on its committees, the Jewish Agency hoped to win acceptance in those quarters where Jews supported a cultural or educational presence in Palestine but not a nationalist one. However, because the category of "non-Zionist" included anyone not nominated by the World Zionist Organization in London for their posts – including Zionists in the Yishuv – Zionists could and did maintain their control over the agency. And not just any Zionists either: By 1931, Labor Zionists like Ben-Gurion were firmly in control of the administrative apparatus of the Jewish community in Palestine. As a result, neither the Revisionists (who went so far as to break with the World Zionist Organization and found their own "New Zionist Organization") nor anti-Zionist Orthodox Jews recognized the authority of the Jewish Agency.

Overall, the Jewish Agency had three functions. First, it acted as the foreign office of the Yishuv. In this capacity, it negotiated with the British government on all matters concerning the mandatory power's policy toward the Jewish community in Palestine. In addition, the Jewish Agency controlled colonization and settlement activities. The Jewish Agency governed the two most important Jewish colonization funds: the Jewish National Fund (which, as we have seen, bought land in Palestine) and the Palestine Foundation Fund (which underwrote immigration and settlement activities). Jewish Agency officials estimated the demand for labor – the so-called "absorptive capacity" of Palestine – and proposed immigration schedules to the British. And through its offices in Europe, the Jewish Agency trained and selected immigrants. Since the allocation of visas was in its hands, priority for settlement in Palestine went to Zionists who had been trained in agriculture and manual occupations and had been educated, through a string of academies, in Hebrew. As a result of this selection process, the average age of the Jewish population in Palestine in 1936 was twenty-seven. Finally, the Jewish Agency founded schools, hospitals, and agricultural and medical research centers in Palestine.

Although overall power remained in the hands of a high commissioner appointed from London, the British encouraged each community to organize its own political affairs within the framework of the mandate. The Jewish community in Palestine did so, electing an assembly and general council. The British recognized these bodies in 1927, thus clearing the way for the Yishuv to levy taxes on the members of the community. (While this established an important legal precedent, the tax revenues raised were negligible, and the Yishuv remained dependent on outside sources of funding for its survival.)

Try as they might, however, the British had only limited success in getting the remaining 89 percent of the population of Palestine into the spirit of the mandate. The reasons are not hard to discern. "The [Balfour] Declaration...is not susceptible to change," Winston Churchill wrote in the White Paper of 1922, a futile attempt to clarify British aims in Palestine. "It is essential that [the Jewish community] should know that it is in Palestine as of right and not on sufferance." In case anyone in the indigenous community still missed the point, he added for good measure, "It is necessary that the Jewish community in Palestine should be able to increase its numbers by immigration."

Most leaders of the indigenous community did not believe that their community should participate in a political order imposed on them without their consent – and certainly not one that appeared intent on establishing an alien presence in their midst. Just how that community dealt with the mandate and Zionist immigration is the subject of the next chapter.

SUGGESTIONS FOR FURTHER READING

Fromkin, David. *A Peace to End All Peace: The Fall of the Ottoman Empire and the Creation of the Modern Middle East.* New York: Henry Holt, 1989. Popular diplomatic history of the origins of the state system in the Middle East.

Gelvin, James L. "The League of Nations and the Question of National Identity in the Fertile Crescent." *World Affairs* (Summer 1995): 35–43. Concise overview of nationalism and state building in the region in the aftermath of World War I.

Heikal, Yousef. "Jaffa...as It Was." *Journal of Palestine Studies* 52 (Summer 1984): 3–21. First-person account of World War I told by a Palestinian.

Hurewitz, J. C. "The Entente's Secret Agreements in World War I: Loyalty to an Obsolescing Ethos." In *Palestine in the Late Ottoman Period*, ed. David Kushner, 341–8. Jerusalem: Yad Izhak Ben-Zvi, 1986. Situates the agreements made by the entente powers during World War I within the context of the previous century's diplomatic history.

Keith-Roach, Edward. *Pasha of Jerusalem: Memoirs of a District Commissioner under the British Mandate.* Edited by Paul Eedle. London: Radcliffe Press, 1994. Eyewitness account of the life of a British official in Palestine during the interwar period.

Lockman, Zachary. *Comrades and Enemies: Arab and Jewish Workers in Palestine.* Berkeley: University of California Press, 1996. Rare look at the history of working-class Palestinians and Jews outside the nationalist framework.

Shapiro, Yonathan. *The Formative Years of the Israeli Labour Party: The Organization of Power, 1919–1930.* Sage Studies in Twentieth Century History no. 4. Beverly Hills, CA: Sage, 1976. Institutional and ideological history of party that dominated Israeli politics until 1977.

5

FROM NATIONALISM IN PALESTINE TO PALESTINIAN NATIONALISM

Of all the public utterances made about the Israeli–Palestinian conflict, none sums up each side's sense of victimization at the hands of the other better than two that straddle the 1967 war. On the eve of the war, Ahmad Shuqairy, then chairman of the Palestine Liberation Organization, boasted that the Arab armies would drive the Jews into the sea. Not to be outdone in imprudent remarks, Golda Meir, Israeli prime minister from 1969 to 1974, gave an interview in the *Sunday Times* (London) on the second anniversary of the war. In that interview, she purportedly stated that there were no Palestinians.

Although Meir's attitude toward Palestinians is well known, were she alive today she might cite in her defense Yogi Berra's famous remark, "I didn't really say everything I said." The full text of the question and her answer is as follows:

Q: Do you think the emergence of the Palestinian fighting forces, the Fedayeen, is an important new factor in the Middle East?
A: Important, no. A new factor, yes. There was no such thing as Palestinians. When was there an independent Palestinian people with a Palestinian state? It was either southern Syria before the first world war and then it was a Palestine including Jordan. It was not as though there was a Palestinian people in Palestine considering itself as a Palestinian people and we came and threw them out and took their country away from them. They did not exist.[1]

What is going on here? Meir is not denying that there were indigenous inhabitants in Palestine who were displaced by Zionist settlement (at least not here). Nor does she appear to be denying the existence of a Palestinian nation. To the contrary, her whole point seems to be that the

---

[1] *Sunday Times*, 15 June 1969.

fedayeen represent a new factor because they have goaded that nation into existence. And although her assertion that a Palestinian nation did not exist until after the 1967 war is absurd, the sketch she provides of the historical development of the nationalism that engendered that nation – and her implicit understanding of the unpredictable and conditional evolution of nationalisms in general – is, in the main, accurate.

Palestinian nationalism emerged during the interwar period in response to Zionist immigration and settlement. The fact that Palestinian nationalism developed later than Zionism and indeed in response to it does not in any way diminish the legitimacy of Palestinian nationalism or make it less valid than Zionism. All nationalisms arise in opposition to some "other." Why else would there be the need to specify who you are? And all nationalisms are defined by what they oppose. As we have seen, Zionism itself arose in reaction to anti-Semitic and exclusionary nationalist movements in Europe. It would be perverse to judge Zionism as somehow less valid than European anti-Semitism or those nationalisms. Furthermore, Zionism itself was also defined by its opposition to the indigenous Palestinian inhabitants of the region. Both the "conquest of land" and the "conquest of labor" slogans that became central to the dominant strain of Zionism in the Yishuv originated as a result of the Zionist confrontation with the Palestinian "other."

Indigenous inhabitants of Palestine resisted Zionist settlement almost from the beginning. This resistance took a variety of forms. In the countryside, where a majority of those inhabitants lived, they engaged in forms of resistance associated with peasants everywhere: forced reoccupation and repossession of lands, assaults against settlers, sabotage of crops and property, and the like. In the cities, there were incidents of mob violence. In August 1929, for example, rioting broke out in Jerusalem. Rumors that each community was attempting to restrict the other community's access to its holy sites inflamed tensions, and a demonstration organized by Betar demanding Jewish control over the Western Wall – a site that abutted the Temple Mount/*Haram al-Sharif* – seemed to prove the worst to Muslims. The ensuing riots spread to Hebron, Jaffa, and Safad. Overall, 133 Jews and 116 Arabs died in the violence.

(The parallels to events in 2000 are too close to ignore. In September 2000, Ariel Sharon, who hoped to become the Likud candidate for prime minister, visited the site of the Temple Mount/*Haram al-Sharif* to demonstrate, he claimed, that it belonged to all. This was the immediate spark that set off what has been called "the second intifada." Then, as before, the underlying grievances that contributed to the uprising were ignored by many of those who watched events unfold. Israelis placed the blame for the outbreak of the second intifada on the head of the Palestinian Authority, Yasir Arafat – much as the Yishuv and the British placed the blame for the 1929 riots on the highest-ranking Muslim official in Palestine, the Hajj Amin al-Husayni. No innocents, Yasir Arafat and the Hajj Amin certainly contributed to the rising tensions and sought to exploit the violence for their own ends. Nevertheless, neither was directly responsible for the outbreaks.)

Not all forms of resistance are nationalist, of course. It would be wrong to project prevailing nationalist beliefs further back in history than evidence warrants. The acts of resistance by the indigenous inhabitants of Palestine were what historian Eric Hobsbawm has called "primitive rebellion." There are two characteristics of primitive rebellions. First, primitive rebellions are motivated by a desire on the part of the rebels to redress specific grievances. Rebels act defensively. They do not intend to accomplish anything more by their actions than to reestablish what they consider to be the status quo. In addition, primitive rebellions tend to be spontaneous, localized, and short-lived. Neither of these two characteristics hold for nationalist struggles. Nationalist struggles do not merely attempt to redress grievances; rather, their purpose is to establish a new political order. Nor are nationalist struggles spontaneous, localized, and short-lived. Since they are organized around specific ideologies and require strategies for political reconstruction as well as resistance, nationalist struggles take planning. Although such planning may not occur at the beginning of a nationalist struggle, it must occur at some point for the struggle to succeed. Furthermore, the struggle must mobilize or at least win over a large portion of the population to its side. Such a process takes time.

A separate Palestinian nationalism that reflected a separate Palestinian national identity began to emerge after World War I. Before World War I, most of the Arab inhabitants of Palestine who gave any thought at all to the matter viewed themselves as Ottoman subjects, then, starting about the fifth decade of the nineteenth century, as Ottoman citizens. Three processes served to corroborate their Ottoman identity: their participation in common activities with other inhabitants of the empire, the further intrusion of the state into the lives of its subjects, and the dissemination of an ideology of "Ottomanness" (*osmanlilik*) which inspired loyalty (and served as a model for future nationalist movements).

With the destruction of the Ottoman Empire in World War I, an Ottoman identity was no longer a viable option for the Arab inhabitants of Palestine. Some, particularly among the thin stratum of educated elites, adopted Arab nationalism, the idea that all Arabs comprised a single nation because they spoke the same language, were of the same ethnicity, shared the same history and culture, or any combination of the three. This sentiment, more powerful in retrospect than at the time, was, nevertheless, sustained by roving bands of displaced bureaucrats and exiles, romantic belletrists, and even the Hashemite family (the family to which Sharif Husayn, Amir Faysal, and Amir 'Abdullah belonged) that sought to rule the Arab nation. Many of the aforementioned continued to nourish Arabist sentiments well into the 1950s and beyond.

Other Arab inhabitants of Palestine viewed themselves as Syrians. By the late Ottoman period, Greater Syria had become an economically and socially integrated unit. Not only did infrastructure like railways and carriage roads link together the inhabitants of the region, Greater Syria developed as a consolidated marketplace with its own division of labor. Peasants and bedouin from the territory that is now Palestine regularly migrated back and forth to the rich farmland of the Hawran district, which now belongs to Syria. Urban elites in Damascus and Beirut invested in large landed estates in areas such as the Galilee and arranged marriage alliances with families in Jerusalem and Jaffa (but rarely with families in Cairo or Baghdad). Over the course of the nineteenth century, the economic and social evolution of Greater Syria so diverged from that of its neighbors that neither Syrian nationalists nor the entente representatives meeting in Paris contemplated anything more than a loose affiliation between Greater Syria and the territory that would become Iraq. So great was the identification of the Arab inhabitants of Palestine with Greater Syria that up through the 1930s one of the most important newspapers published in Jerusalem was called *Suriya janubiyya* – Southern Syria.

Over the course of the mandate period, however, both the Arab nationalist and the Syrian nationalist options no longer proved practicable. The mandates system not only divided the Arab world into a variety of proto-states, it severed Palestine from Syria. Because Palestinians could not reasonably expect to unite with Syrians, a Syrian identity eventually lost its hold on Palestinians. Furthermore, the fact that the subsequent history and development of Palestine diverged from the subsequent history and development of Syria and the rest of the Arab world strengthened a Palestinian identity. Syrian elites, for example, would further their education by studying in France, and French became their second language. Since Britain held the mandate for Palestine, Palestinians would study in Britain and learn to speak English.

Further encouraging the emergence of a separate Palestinian identity was the confrontation with Zionism. Zionist settlement not only sparked resistance, it presented the Palestinians with a problem that no other population in the Middle East faced. Zionist colonization was very different from anything the inhabitants of Iraq, Trans-Jordan, Syria, and Lebanon experienced under the British and French mandates. As in Palestine, the British and French ruled their mandated territories indirectly through local collaborators, and as in Palestine their actions disrupted existing social and economic relations in their allotted territories. Nevertheless, neither the British nor the French appropriated land, established a rival and competing economy, or established rival and competing political structures. Furthermore, mandatory rule was, theoretically, temporary – a far cry from the permanent settlement program of the Zionists. Because they faced a different type of enemy, the response of Palestinians came to be different from the response of their neighbors. Had this not been the case, Palestinian nationalism would most likely have evolved along the same lines as Syrian or Iraqi nationalism – if, indeed, it had evolved at all.

Although the first nationalist organizations founded in Palestine during and after World War I did not call for a separate Palestinian state, they paved the way for those that would. There were two types of nationalist organization founded during this period: those that represented the convictions and aspirations of the elites and would-be elites of Palestinian society and those that had a more populist orientation. Each left a legacy for nationalist movements in Palestine that would last through the 1930s.

The first type of nationalist organization included mainly urban notables, former Ottoman bureaucrats, and an emergent stratum of professionals who no longer feared Ottoman repression and were eager to play a role in any future political order. Although a few from these groups had participated in conspiratorial organizations before the war, it was in fact the British who provided the wherewithal for the first openly nationalist organizations in Palestine. As the British army moved north from Egypt to Damascus, political officers assigned to the army organized nationalist clubs to enlist the support of local leaders for the Arab Revolt and, more broadly, the entente campaign against the Ottomans. In the immediate aftermath of the war, these clubs acted as local branches of the Damascus-based Arab Club and even provided the club's Damascus headquarters with two of its chairmen.

The Arab Clubs did not have the political field to themselves for long. Syrian exiles who had spent the war in Cairo followed in the wake of the British army, establishing branches of their nationalist society – the Syrian Union – in Palestine as they journeyed back to Damascus. At the same time, notables, professionals, and former bureaucrats who had stayed in Palestine during the war founded nationalist groups called Muslim–Christian Associations in their hometowns. A host of other clubs, salons, and parties also joined the nationalist fray.

Although there was some differentiation among these groups, most held to a common agenda. Most opposed the mandate, the Balfour Declaration, and the division of Palestine from Syria (although the Muslim–Christian Associations, reflecting the sentiments of indigenous elites, made Palestinian autonomy within a federated Syrian state a central plank of their platform.) All recruited their members from the same layers of the population. Indeed, it appears that the proliferation of these sorts of nationalist groups often had more to do with individuals and families jockeying for position than with disputes over the political future of Palestine.

Populist organizations – branches of the Damascus-based Higher National Committee and committees of national defense – spread to the territory of Palestine from Syria in early 1919. These organizations also opposed the mandate, the division of Palestine from Syria, and the Balfour Declaration. But these organizations differed from other organizations in two ways: Their leadership included a large number of lower-middle-class religious dignitaries and shopkeepers, textile and grain merchants, local toughs, and tribal leaders, and the organizations appealed directly to peasants and nonelite townsmen. Not only did they recruit these peasants and townsmen into militias to resist the French occupation of Syria and Zionist settlement (one of their dispatches called on the indigenous inhabitants of Palestine to "ignite the country"), they framed their nationalism in an idiom that reflected militancy, antielitism, and egalitarianism. Calling on the Arab inhabitants of Palestine to "protect the patrimony of our prophets and our ancestors" and promising "death to those who would betray Palestine," these organizations found an avid following among a population that had become acclimated to the culture of nationalism during the Ottoman period.

In February 1920, representatives of both types of organization met in Damascus to establish a common front. They established the first Palestine General Congress. Soon thereafter the following leaflet appeared on the streets of Damascus:

Palestine is our Country!
The Decision of the Palestinian General Congress
On Friday, 27 February 1920, at 3:00 in the afternoon, a meeting was held at the Arab Club, which included delegates from the Higher National Committee, the Syrian General Congress, and representatives from the Arab Independence Party, the Syrian National Party, the Syrian Union, the Syrian Pact, the Iraqi Pact, the Democratic Party, the Moral Revival Association, the Arab Club, leaders from the Hawrani, Dandashli, Karak, Fadl, Sakhur, and Circassian tribes and communities; finally, a large number of religious leaders, lawyers, journalists, merchants, secondary school students, and the heads of the guilds of Damascus.

Having considered the Palestinian situation, they agreed on the following five points:

1. We confirm what we have always said, that Palestine is an integral part of Syria. We demand that it remain so, and shall use all measures to the last drop of our blood and the last breath of our children to achieve this end.

2. Because we come from all parts of Syria, we consider the Zionist danger to be directed against us and against our political and economic existence in the future. We shall therefore throw back the Zionists with all our force. If the allies continue to let them pursue their activities we shall oppose them by all means possible....

O Arab sons of Palestine:
The Syrian nation and the Palestinian associations are incensed that the [allies] would seek to detach Palestine from its motherland, Syria, under the guise of establishing a national government. How can we accept the life of slaves to the Jews and foreigners and not defend our political and natural rights? Raise your voice, protest this treachery, and never fear threats or intimidation.... If there exists a man among you who, bribed by gold or

honors, rallies to the occupation government, stay away from him, boycott him, and show him your scorn, for he is a traitor to his country and his nation. Likewise, boycott the Jews, sell them nothing and buy nothing from them. Boycott those who sustain them and serve them as underlings. . . .

Life, life, O Brothers!

True to form, the entente powers ignored the resolutions of the Palestine General Congress. In June 1920, the French sent an army into inland Syria to establish their control there. Although it was not until three years later that the boundary separating French-mandated Syria from British-mandated Palestine (the Paulet-Newcombe line) was set, the separation of the two territories was never in doubt. To curtail resistance to their occupation and the division of Syria, the French dismantled the Damascus-based nationalist organizations, including the Arab Club, the Higher National Committee, and the Syrian Union, condemned a number of nationalist leaders to death, and drove others into exile. The various Palestine-based Muslim–Christian Associations fared better for a while, and even came together at the end of 1920 to establish an Arab Executive to coordinate their activities. Acting in the name of "the Arabic-speaking people who were living in Palestine at the outbreak of the Great War," the Arab Executive demanded the termination of the mandate, the withdrawal of the Balfour Declaration, and the end of Jewish immigration and land purchases. It also called for the election of a "national" government in Palestine. In the end, however, most of the Muslim–Christian Associations withered away, and factionalism weakened those that remained. By the mid-1920s, the momentum behind the Arab Palestinian nationalist movements had slowed to a crawl. At the same time, the Zionist movement had already put in place rudimentary institutions of statehood.

Why was it so difficult for the Arab inhabitants of Palestine to organize themselves into a unified nationalist movement? Historians cite a number of reasons. First, as should now be obvious, in the aftermath of World War I most of the indigenous inhabitants of Palestine hitched their nationalist wagon to the wrong mule: Syrian nationalism. Even after the French and the British assumed control over their mandates, some nationalists in Palestine held on to their dream of joining a Greater Syrian state. More pragmatic nationalists agitated for a separate Palestinian nation, but they waged an uphill battle: Not only did they have to formulate a new set of doctrines, they had to disseminate those doctrines while fighting a rearguard action against their Greater Syrian nationalist rivals.

The victory of the former group might have been more assured had the Palestinian national movement been able to use state or statelike institutions to communicate their ideas and make them tangible to the population. But here again indigenous Arab nationalists faced a number of hurdles unknown to their Zionist counterparts. Because Zionists established their colonies in a remote land under conditions that were often adverse, they had to embody their movement in institutions from the start. The nationalist movement in Palestine emerged in a territory that had been part of a functioning empire. Institutions already existed. Not only was there no imperative to create national institutions to govern day-to-day life, those that nationalists attempted to create had to compete with preexisting ones. Further abetting the institutionalization of the Zionist movement and obstructing the institutionalization of nationalism among the indigenous inhabitants of Palestine was the reaction of the leaders of each community to the British-imposed political order. Although groups of Zionists opposed specific policies of the British, they were, in the main, more than willing to work within the framework provided by the mandates system. Most nationalists within the indigenous community refused to sanction either the mandates system or the Balfour Declaration. They thus refused to cooperate with the British and declined to participate in the governing structures the British imposed.

Aspects of the Ottoman legacy also directly impeded the development of national institutions in Palestine. The population of Palestine included a number of non-Muslim religious groups, including Christians, who made up about 10 percent of the population at the time of the first real census in 1922. Under the Ottomans, each religious community of Palestine had regulated many of its own affairs, from social welfare to marriage and divorce. And during the nineteenth century, European powers that had taken a special interest in the religious minorities of the empire intervened in Ottoman affairs, ensuring that the previously informal and loose boundaries separating the various communities would become hard and fast – and sanctified by law. Seeking to enlist reliable local collaborators and redeem what they took to be their "benighted" and "oppressed" coreligionists, European powers extended protection to select minority communities, granted members of those communities honorary citizenship and special commercial privileges, and made sure the Ottomans would apportion them representation at all levels of government according to their number.

When the British received the mandate for Palestine, they carried over many Ottoman-era policies, including those dealing with communal autonomy and minority representation. Thus, for example, when the first British high commissioner for Palestine, Herbert Samuel, attempted to set up an advisory council, he did not create three categories of seats for British, Zionist, and Arab representatives. Instead, he created four categories: British (ten seats), Muslim Palestinian (four seats), Christian Palestinian (three seats), and Jewish (three seats). In addition to granting the 11 percent of the population that was Jewish 30 percent of the seats that did not go to Britons, Samuel's formulation granted legal sanction to the division of the Arab population based on religion.

Many historians point to another way in which the social organization of the Arab community of Palestine frustrated the creation of a unified nationalist movement. As we saw in Chapter 2, a new class of urban notables rose to prominence in Palestine during the nineteenth century. These urban notables derived their wealth from landownership (made possible by the 1858 land code) and their political influence from their membership in newly established municipal, district, and provincial councils. Urban notables forged ties of patronage with urban nonelites and peasants in the villages they owned. The notables intervened with the Ottoman government and performed other services on behalf of their clients. They also lent their urban and rural clients money and supplied peasants with seed and other supplies. In return they gained economic benefit, prestige, or both from their clients. And it did not hurt that notables could use their ties to the urban crowd when they needed to employ a little muscle. But the very links that connected notables to their clients put them in competition with each other: There were just so many clients to go around. This competition naturally made it difficult for notables to act in concert.

Inter-elite rivalries did not abate after the demise of the Ottoman Empire and the imposition of the mandates system. No notable was willing to join a nationalist club or party that enhanced the power and prestige of a rival and his allies. If the Husaynis of Jerusalem founded a branch of the Arab Club, the Nashashibis of Jerusalem would just have to found a branch of another nationalist organization, the Literary

Society. And if, in the years to follow, the Nashashibis were able to acquire position and prestige by cooperating with the British, you could bet that the Husaynis would assume the most uncompromising nationalist stance possible and dismiss their rivals as collaborators.

All too often, however, historians have overestimated the effects of inter-elite rivalries on the evolution of nationalism in Palestine. The competition among rival groups of notables might have created insurmountable hurdles for a nationalist movement to overcome if ties of patronage represented the totality of social relations in Palestinian society. They did not. And over time, the importance and prestige of the notables in society declined. There are two reasons for this. First, the very logic of nationalism runs counter to the logic of a social system built on patronage networks. Nationalisms accentuate the horizontal bonds that unite citizens with each other. Not only were the ties uniting Palestinian notables with their clients arranged vertically, they dissociated the clients of different notables from one another. This ran counter to the ideals of a population increasingly acclimated to the culture of nationalism.

Economic and social changes further undermined the authority held by notables in Palestinian society. What, after all, could urban-based landowners be expected to do for a population that lived in a society defined by market relations, labor migration, Zionist immigration, and foreign control – a society in which notables might sell land to Zionist settlers while large numbers of peasants were losing theirs and being forced into faceless cities to sell their labor? No wonder Palestinian peasants and townsmen increasingly looked to new forms of political organization that addressed their concerns, that enlisted members by appeals to ideology, not ties of patronage, and that engaged them in direct action rather than treating them as bit players in the nationalist drama. The notables and the organizations they sponsored did not disappear from the political scene, but, as we shall see in the next section, they increasingly had to share the stage with mobilized nonelites and mass-based, populist organizations.

THE GREAT REVOLT

At the end of 1935, British officials in Jaffa uncovered a large shipment of arms and ammunition destined for the Zionist community. For many

Palestinians, this could only mean one thing: The Zionist community was arming itself and preparing for war. At around the same time, a popular preacher, ʿIzz al-Din al-Qassam, took to the hills with a band of followers to launch a guerrilla war against the British and the Zionists. The British caught up with the band and killed al-Qassam in a firefight. In the wake of both incidents, Palestine exploded into rebellion. The Great Revolt lasted for three years. It marks a turning point in the history of the struggle between the indigenous inhabitants of Palestine and the Zionists.

While every conflagration like the Great Revolt might be traced to one or more precipitating incidents like the ones just recounted, ascribing the Great Revolt to the discovery of an arms shipment and the killing of a popular preacher would be akin to ascribing the outbreak of World War I to the assassination of the heir to the throne of a fading power. In both instances, the roots of the conflict go much deeper. In the case of the Great Revolt, those roots might be found in the economic peripheralization and growing impoverishment of the indigenous population and the increasing size and intrusiveness of the Zionist community.

While most of the world was reeling from the effects of the Great Depression during the 1930s, the economy of Palestine was actually expanding. According to historian Roger Owen, economic activity in Palestine more than quadrupled during the period between 1922 and 1935. A number of factors contributed to this growth. The fourth and fifth aliyot (1924–8, 1929–39) brought close to 280,000 new immigrants to the Jewish community. Many of these immigrants were highly skilled refugees fleeing the anti-Semitic persecution that would culminate in the Holocaust. As the population of the Yishuv grew to nearly 30 percent of the population of Palestine as a whole, the economy of the Yishuv reached the requisite size and differentiation for what economists like to call an economic "takeoff." British investment in infrastructure provided the foundation for further growth. For example, after the British dredged a deep-water harbor in Haifa and the Iraq Petroleum Company made the city the terminus for an oil pipeline stretching from the oilfields of Mosul to the Mediterranean, Haifa attracted other industrial installations – an Iraq Petroleum Company refinery, the central facilities of the Palestine Railroad – and gained prominence as *the* industrial center of Palestine. During the first ten years of the British mandate, the population of the city doubled. Even the agricultural

11. Jewish immigrants being processed at the Port of Jaffa, ca. 1930s. (Source: From the collection of the author)

12. Tel Aviv, 1937. By the 1930s, Tel Aviv was a showcase for modernist trends in architecture and urban planning, reflecting the Zionist quest to build an "outpost of civilization" in Palestine. (Source: From the collection of the author)

economy of Palestine seemed to prosper during the 1930s, as more land came under cultivation and landowners turned to citrus production to offset declining prices for staples.

But the overall statistics for the Palestine economy are deceptive. Economic growth was not evenly distributed across the two communities. Most of the indigenous inhabitants of Palestine were cultivators, and the Great Depression hit them hard. As with farmers everywhere, collapsing prices for most agricultural commodities increased their indebtedness. But unlike farmers in other places, there was little their government could do to alleviate the crisis: The terms of the mandate prohibited Britain from imposing tariffs that would protect them. As a result, Palestine became a dumping ground for the agricultural products of others. Large numbers of farmers, who carried enormous debts anyway (the going interest rate in rural Palestine at the time was 30 to 200 percent), lost their land as a result of foreclosure. By the outbreak of the Great Revolt, about half of all rural male Palestinians had to engage in labor outside their villages to make ends meet. Some found work in seasonal agricultural labor or on infrastructural projects such as road construction. Others emigrated to cities, where they were often relegated to the lowest rungs of the economic ladder and dwelt in shantytowns.

The upsurge in Zionist immigration aggravated the problem of land-lessness. As more and more Jews entered Palestine, Zionist agents bought more and more land. The price of rural real estate skyrock-eted, and more than a few urban-based landowners decided to make a killing by selling their holdings to the Jewish National Fund. As large estates available for purchase became scarcer, Zionist land agents began buying up smaller plots, both directly and by buying markers from usurers. In the process, they came in contact with ever greater numbers of Palestinians living on the margins of subsistence. By 1931, Zionist land purchases had led to the expulsion of approximately twenty thou-sand peasant families from their lands. Over the course of the next sev-eral years, approximately 30 percent of Palestinian farmers had become totally landless. Another 75 to 80 percent did not have enough land to support themselves. Zionism, which had been an abstract concept for many of the indigenous inhabitants of Palestine, now had become a tangible presence.

These, then, were the circumstances under which someone like 'Izz al-Din al-Qassam could emerge as a champion of the marginalized and dispossessed and as a symbol of resistance. 'Izz al-Din al-Qassam was born in Latakia, on the coast of present-day Syria, in about 1880. His father and grandfather had been ulama (Muslim religious scholars) and belonged to the Qadariyya sufi order. Although it is common to asso-ciate sufism with mysticism, many sufi orders had moved away from mysticism during the nineteenth century. They did this under pressure from their own followers, who sought to use the orders to help them deal with nineteenth-century conditions, and under pressure from the Ottoman government, which used the orders to spread a standardized Islamic orthodoxy. The most prominent Qadari leader in nineteenth-century Syria had been 'Abd al-Qadir al-Jaza'iri. 'Abd al-Qadir had led the resistance against the French occupation of Algeria before he was exiled to Damascus. While in Damascus, he preached the lessons he had learned during that resistance: Muslims not only had to use Islamic law to guide them in their daily lives but had to apply the principles of reason to make that law compatible with modern conditions. Further-more, Muslims had to assimilate Western scientific and technological practices. The ideas 'Abd al-Qadir preached were commonplace in the Middle East during al-Qassam's youth. Al-Qassam's association with like-minded members of other sufi orders in Syria and "modernist" ulama at the Islamic university of al-Azhar in Cairo further reinforced these ideas.

As soon as he returned to Syria from Cairo, al-Qassam began applying the lessons he had learned. In 1911, he collected weapons and supplies for the inhabitants of Tripolitania (in present-day Libya), who were fighting an Italian invasion and occupation, and he even tried to join their resistance with a band of his devotees. After World War I, he joined one of the guerrilla groups associated with the committees of national defense fighting against the French in Syria. When the French seized Damascus, al-Qassam fled to Haifa, where he shared lodgings and pursued scholarly endeavors with the former head of the Higher National Committee. In Haifa, al-Qassam became a popular preacher and registrar of marriages in the surrounding countryside. He used both positions as a pulpit to preach against the British and Zionists. By the time of his ill-fated campaign, he may have had upwards of a thousand followers recruited from among Haifa's casual workers, artisans, peddlers, stevedores, and rail and postal workers.

Al-Qassam's death galvanized anti-British, anti-Zionist resistance among townsmen and peasants. His funeral was the largest in Palestinian history, and he was eulogized in poetry and songs, such as the following:

> Who would imitate Qassam as Islam's ideal soldier
> Follows, if he wishes release from his inherited humiliation,
>   the best master;
> For he forsook words and the weakling's idle chatter.
> Our leaders have stuffed our ears to bursting with talk!
> We believed true what they wrote, but it was only a delusion.[2]

There are two aspects of this eulogy that are worth examining. First, "Qassam as Islam's ideal soldier." Islam has played a role in popular Palestinian nationalism since the inception of popular Palestinian nationalism. Although that role has varied over time (and we shall discuss contemporary Islamic political movements, which use their interpretation of Islam as both a roadmap for the reconstruction of society and the grounds for nationalist struggle, in Chapter 9), what concerns

---

[2] Nels Johnson, *Islam and the Politics of Meaning in Palestinian Nationalism* (London: Kegan Paul International, 1982), 45.

us here is the way in which Islam has provided imagery and vocabulary for the nationalist cause. Sometimes nationalists gleaned words from the vocabulary of religion simply because nationalism was a recent import to the Arab world and a vocabulary of nationalism did not exist in Arabic. Rather than adopting Western terms, they chose the closest approximation. Hence, the use of the word *umma*, which originally referred to the Islamic community of believers, to mean nation. Words that are particularly evocative are the ones that last: Palestinians who die in battle are still referred to as *shuhada'* (martyrs), and Palestinians still sometimes refer to their struggle or those who fight in that struggle with some variant of the word *jihad*. All these terms, of course, predate the nationalist era.

The use of religious imagery and vocabulary in nationalist rhetoric is hardly restricted to the Palestinian case: Nationalisms have commonly taken terms that originated in other settings and transformed their meaning through recontextualization. Think about how the word "martyr" has been applied to Abraham Lincoln or John F. Kennedy, or about how American presidents from Woodrow Wilson to Dwight Eisenhower to George W. Bush have transformed the word "crusade" in their rhetoric from its original meaning – a religiously inspired reconquest of the Holy Land – to signify America's "crusadelike" mission in the world. Americans like to think of the war on terrorism as a "righteous" cause. So, apparently, did a Palestinian rebel leader who made use of a similar rhetorical flourish in the "Proclamation from the General Leadership of the Arab Revolt in Southern Syria-Palestine," issued in 1936:

Palestine summons us to fight in the Path of God so that the world might bear witness to the unity of the nation.... We are called to battle for freedom, independence, and hope, and see the rebellion against oppression as a religious duty.[3]

But why does religious imagery and vocabulary so readily lend itself to adoption by nationalism? The answer lies in the fact that in many places where nationalism and nation-states found a home, religion took on a new meaning and social function. Take the case of Islam in the

---

[3] Nels Johnson, *Islam and the Politics of Meaning in Palestinian Nationalism* (London: Kegan Paul International, 1982), 55.

Ottoman Empire. During the nineteenth century, many in the empire had come to view Islam in the same way that Italians or Frenchmen had come to view the Italian or French language. Just as Italian or French was held up as the characteristic that differentiated Italians or Frenchmen from their neighbors, Islam was held up as the characteristic that differentiated Ottomans from their adversaries in the West. This should not be surprising: As we saw above, as the population of the Middle East came to live their lives in a world of nations and nationalism, they came to live their Islam in the same world. The semiofficial newspaper of the Ottoman Empire once put it this way: "Islam is not only a religion, it is a nationality."

For those living in Palestine during the interwar period, it was not a stretch to do the same. After all, the characteristic that Zionists used to differentiate themselves from the people among whom they settled was their Jewishness. And once Islam had become more than a code of conduct and system of belief and had become a cultural attribute, even non-Muslims could cede to Islam an important role in defining the culture and history of their nation. Thus, the use of Islam in Palestinian nationalism came to parallel the use of Judaism in Zionism.

The second aspect of the eulogy that bears scrutiny are the phrases, "Our leaders have stuffed our ears to bursting with talk! We believed true what they wrote, but it was only a delusion." These lines underscore the social cleavages that affected the course and outcome of the rebellion – and indeed the course of subsequent Palestinian nationalism as well. The Great Revolt broke out in April 1936 in the wake of the murder of two Jews in Nablus. The murders provoked retaliation, and retaliation provoked counterretaliation. The escalating violence prompted two responses in the Palestinian community, one by notables and their allies among the various nationalist parties they dominated, another by nonelites.

Leading notables and their allies decided they had to bury the hatchet and unite their political forces. They formed the Arab Higher Committee, with the Hajj Amin al-Husayni as its leader. The Hajj Amin was born in Jerusalem in 1893, the scion of one the most influential notable families of Jerusalem. Nationalist hagiographers have credited the Hajj Amin with being an implacable foe of Zionism and the British. Actually, this is only partly correct. Although it is true that the Husayni family still enjoys a reputation among Palestinians as one of the few notable families that never sold land to the Zionists, the Husayni family actually enjoyed the favor of the British during the immediate post–World War I period. The Hajj Amin even served as president of the Supreme Muslim Council, a body established to administer Islamic law courts and religious endowments, and as grand mufti (an official who interprets Islamic law) of Jerusalem. Both the council and the position of grand mufti of Jerusalem were British inventions.

The British refused to extend their patronage exclusively to the Husayni family, however. After a bloody anti-Zionist riot in Jerusalem in 1920, the British dismissed the mayor, Musa Kazim al-Husayni, from his post and replaced him with (God forbid!) a member of the rival Nashashibi clan. The British action was certainly an affront to the Husayni family, but it was the position of the family in Palestinian society and the logic of interfamilial competition that virtually compelled its members to take a militant stance toward the mandatory power: The British refused to endorse Husayni claims to preeminence, and since the prestige accorded notable families was directly related to their ability to attract a following, one can imagine the Husaynis thinking, in the words of the anonymous French politician, "I must see where my people are going so I can lead them," no matter what their feelings about the British and Zionists. It was perhaps inevitable, therefore, that a firebrand member of the most influential family of Jerusalem would become head of the Arab Higher Committee.

Although the Arab Higher Committee attempted to provide overall direction during the initial stages of the rebellion, true command belonged to local committees, known confusingly as "national committees," that emerged simultaneously in Jerusalem, Nablus, Jaffa, Tulkarm, and elsewhere. These popularly based committees coordinated a general strike and enforced the boycott of Jewish businesses – two tactics endorsed by the Arab Higher Committee. To minimize the damage their tactics inflicted on Palestinians, the national committees established "nourishment and supply committees" in urban quarters. Financed through a combination of voluntary and involuntary donations, assessments on the salaries of those who continued to work, and contributions from sympathizers throughout the Arab world, these committees furnished the urban quarters with necessities and provided stipends to the families of striking workers. Years later, an elderly Palestinian woman recalled the popular mobilization in these words:

When I was [young], I was with the young students in demonstrations. We would say, "Down with immigration. Down with Balfour." But I didn't know what Balfour was, or what was meant by immigration. I knew that Jews were coming and that we wanted to stop them and that we didn't want them to take our land....

During the strike, my father was one of the committee that collected dry food, wheat, and gave it to the poor whose work stopped during the strike. Once, I remember, British soldiers pushed their way into the house and made a long line to take bags of flour and throw them in the well. My father started to shout, because we used the water.... They went on with what they were doing and my father, a huge man, fell to the floor. I and my sister started to shout and the neighbors came and they carried him to his bed and we called the doctor. It won't go from my eyes. Until now, I can't forget.[4]

British counterinsurgency, while provocative, was effective in quelling the rebellion in the cities. So were the tactics of general strike and boycott chosen by resistance leaders. Mandatory authorities and Jewish employers were more than willing to replace Arab employees who honored the strike with Jewish workers, and the boycott only served to further the economic division between the two communities – a goal the Yishuv leadership advocated anyway. The strike and boycott drained the urban Palestinian population, while the extortion of money and jewelry from richer Palestinians divided the movement along class lines. By July 1936, the revolt in the cities had effectively ended (although the general strike lingered on for another three months). Within a year, the Hajj Amin al-Husayni was on the lam, and the Arab Higher Committee had ceased to function as a body.

With the cities pacified, the site of the rebellion moved to the countryside. Our informant describes it thus:

I used to see the English people helping the Jews in the war. Our men, the Palestinians in the mountains, had to fight against both the British army and the Jews. These men in the mountains had to get their guns from the people. Every family had to collect money and buy a gun for them.

[4] Staughton Lynd, Sam Bahour, and Alice Lynd, *Homeland: Oral Histories of Palestine and Palestinians* (New York: Olive Branch Press, 1994), 27–8.

13. During the Great Revolt, British counterinsurgency took a heavy toll on rebels and Palestinian society alike. Rebel prisoners from Jenin area. (Source: Hulton-Deutsch Collection/Corbis)

These mujahadin, the fighters, would come to a village for a week. The whole village would give them food, cook for them, and clean their weapons for them. When the fighters were in the mountains, someone from the village would go up to the mountains carrying a white flag. This flag would be pointed to the right or to the left and would tell the fedayin whether to stay or to leave. Sometimes while they were eating, the flag would tell them to leave. They would leave the food and flee. This was the life that my people used to live.

By the autumn of 1937, 9,000 to 10,000 Palestinian and non-Palestinian Arab fighters – or mujahidin, as our informant calls them – roamed the countryside, attacking British forces and Zionist settlements and generally wreaking havoc. Whether they were motivated more by nationalist zeal or the promise of loot is anyone's guess. Although our informant would have us believe the former, her words – "Every family *had* to collect money and buy a gun for them" – seem to tell a different story. Whatever their motivation, the rebels hardly swam like fish in the sea. Their appropriation of peasant surplus and whatever valuables they could find filled their ranks with peasants who now, too, had to depend on brigandage to survive. Thus was created an economy of plunder that, in the end, did as much damage to the Palestinian countryside as the attacks launched by the rebels did to the British and Zionists. To pacify the countryside, the British imported an army of 20,000, which worked in tandem with Zionist "special night squads" and "peace bands" organized by the ever-willing Nashashibi family. Employing all the usual tactics of counterinsurgency, including those all too familiar to Palestinians today – the collective punishment of villages, targeted assassinations, mass arrests, deportations, dynamiting homes of suspected guerrillas and sympathizers – the British and their allies eventually snuffed out the rebellion.

With the exception of the nakba of 1948, the Great Revolt marks the most significant turning point in modern Palestinian history. On the positive side of the balance sheet for Palestinians, the Great Revolt marks the point at which we can begin to discuss the phenomenon of a separate, mass-based Palestinian nationalism with confidence. The revolt engaged a broad sector of the indigenous population of Palestine in a programmatic and coordinated movement. The symbols around which the population rallied (such as the example of al-Qassam) were uniquely Palestinian, as was the enemy against which the Palestinians fought, the tactics the rebels employed, and the demands that the rebels made.

Long after its suppression, the Great Revolt continued to provide symbolic sustenance to the Palestinian national movement. It is, of course, true that the Arab Higher Committee, the self-proclaimed leadership of the revolt, all too quickly fell victim to repression and squabbling, that those who led the rebel gangs in the countryside resembled, more often than not, Afghan warlords rather than Robin Hoods, and that the revolt failed to come close to achieving its goal of dislodging the Yishuv. But while all this is true, none of it matters. Nationalist memory is selective. During the first intifada – the uprising against the Israeli occupation of the West Bank and Gaza Strip that broke out in 1987 – the United National Leadership of the Uprising, which coordinated the rebellion, called for a general strike on the anniversary of al-Qassam's death and issued communiqués such as the following:

O masses of our great Palestinian people. O masses of the people of stones and Molotov cocktails. O soldiers of justice who are participating in our people's valiant uprising. . . . A greeting of reverence and admiration to these great people who recorded the most splendid epics of struggle; a greeting to those people who fulfilled the call of duty and shook the earth under the Zionists' feet last week . . . a greeting to you, O grandsons of al-Qassam.[5]

And during the second intifada, the Qassam Brigades of the Islamist organization Hamas have strapped Qassam-19 explosives on to the bodies of suicide bombers and have launched Qassam-2 missiles at Israeli settlements.

(The Great Revolt has also found its way into Israeli collective memory. Take the following editorial from the *Jerusalem Post*, called "Learning from the British." The editorial was written in December 2001, fifteen months after the outbreak of the second intifada. Written by Shlomo Gazit, former head of Israeli military intelligence, it argues that Israelis should draw a very different sort of lesson from the revolt:

Britain proved terrorism can be overcome by force: It established the northern battalion which prevented incursions, infiltrations, and the smuggling of weapons and people from Syria and Lebanon to Palestine. It created a network of police stations, which allowed control of the ground and roads. And mainly it applied massive force, which retook all the areas that had been taken by Arab gangs. Nobody stopped Britain from exercising full military force – not public opinion at home, nor the media, nor the Arab states which had yet to gain political significance, nor the international community.)[6]

Whatever the role the Great Revolt has played in the construction of a Palestinian identity and national narrative, any ledger recording its effects must also include entries on the debit side of the balance sheet. These entries are substantial. The revolt resulted in upwards of 3,000 rebel casualties and the exile or imprisonment of much of the nationalist leadership. Large swathes of the Palestinian countryside lay in ruins, from both rebel actions and British retaliation. Many of the best and brightest of Palestinian society, including a disproportionate number of the educated and wealthy, fled Palestine, some to escape the fighting, others to escape the exactions of the rebels. In all, the Great Revolt might be considered the first nakba of modern Palestinian history. Certainly, it paved the way for the one that followed, and it may even

---

[5] Zachary Lockman and Joel Beinin, eds., *Intifada: The Palestinian Uprising against Israeli Occupation* (Boston: South End Press, 1989), 331.

[6] Shlomo Gazit, "Learning from the British," *Jerusalem Post*, 11 December 2001.

have been the primary reason why 1948 turned out to be the disaster for the Palestinian community that it was.

SUGGESTIONS FOR FURTHER READING

Budeiri, Musa. "The Palestinians: Tensions between Nationalist and Religious Identities." In *Rethinking Nationalism in the Arab Middle East*, ed. James Jankowski and Israel Gershoni, 191–206. New York: Columbia University Press, 1997. Acute analysis of the role of religion in Palestinian nationalism.

Johnson, Nels. *Islam and the Politics of Meaning in Palestinian Nationalism.* London: Kegan Paul International, 1982. An anthropologist looks at the relationship between religion and nationalism in Palestine.

Lesch, Ann Mosely. *Arab Politics in Palestine,1917–1939.* Ithaca, NY: Cornell University Press, 1979. Overview of early period of Palestinian nationalism.

Mandel, Neville J. *The Arabs and Zionism before World War I.* Berkeley: University of California Press, 1976. Examination of early encounters between Zionists and Arabs and their political and cultural effects.

Mattar, Philip. *The Mufti of Jerusalem: Al-Hajj Amin al-Husayni and the Palestinian National Movement.* New York: Columbia University Press, 1988. Biography of figure central to Palestinian politics from the interwar period to the end of World War II.

Miller, Ylana. *Government and Society in Rural Palestine,1920–1948.* Austin: University of Texas Press, 1985. The impact of the mandate on the Palestinian countryside, where a majority of Palestinians lived.

Porath, Yehoshua. *The Emergence of the Palestinian-Arab National Movement,* *1918–1929.* London: Cass, 1974. Standard work on the early history of Palestinian nationalism, based mainly on Israeli sources.

———. *The Palestinian Arab National Movement, 1929–1939: From Riots to Rebellion.* London: Cass, 1977. The second volume of Porath's history of Palestinian nationalism.

Swedenburg, Ted. *Memories of Revolt: The 1936–1939 Rebellion and the Palestinian National Past.* Minneapolis: University of Minnesota Press, 1995, esp. 76–137. Analysis of the role of the Great Palestine Revolt in shaping Palestinian identity.

———. "The Role of the Palestinian Peasantry in the Great Revolt (1936–1939)." In *The Modern Middle East*, ed. Albert Hourani, Philip S. Khoury, and Mary C. Wilson, 467–501. Berkeley: University of California Press, 1993. Overview of the Great Palestine Revolt, with a good dose of social history.

6

FROM THE GREAT REVOLT
THROUGH THE 1948 WAR

The Palestinians and the Zionists were not the only ones to draw lessons from the Great Revolt. The British did as well. The Great Revolt was the first in a series of events that eventually led to the British withdrawal from Palestine. While the British had taken the mandate for Palestine for a number of reasons, high on the list was their belief that control over the area would enhance imperial defense. Ongoing turmoil in Palestine disabused them of this view. Thus, the British ultimately reached the conclusion that, when it came to Palestine, the game was not worth the candle.

In addition to the military response described in the previous chapter, the British attempted to find a political solution to their Palestine problem. Two such attempts are particularly significant. In 1937, during a lull in the fighting, the British government appointed a Royal Commission under the direction of Earl Peel, the secretary of state for India. The report of the commission was a shock to everyone involved, including the British government. According to the Royal Commission, the mandate had been premised on the idea that the Palestinian population would acquiesce to the Balfour Declaration once it came to realize the material benefits of Zionist immigration. Instead of welcoming the "civilizing mission" of the Zionists, however, the indigenous population of Palestine resisted Zionist settlement, and the rift between the two communities grew:

The estranging force of conditions inside Palestine is growing year by year. The educational systems, Arab and Jewish, are schools of nationalism, and they have only existed for a short time. Their full effect on the rising generation has yet to be felt. And patriotic "youth-movements," so familiar a feature of present-day politics in other countries of Europe or Asia, are afoot in Palestine. As each community grows, moreover, the rivalry between them deepens. The more numerous and prosperous and better-educated the Arabs become, the more insistent will be their demand for national independence and the more bitter their hatred of the obstacle that bars the way to it. As the Jewish National Home grows older and more firmly rooted, so will grow its self-confidence and political ambition.

The commission thus concluded that the mandate was unworkable and proposed that Palestine be divided into three parts. Twenty percent of Palestinian territory would go to a Jewish state. Most of the rest would go to an Arab Palestine that would be united with Trans-Jordan. Finally, the commission recommended that the British retain a mandatory zone in Jerusalem, Nazareth, and perhaps other places that would be linked by a corridor to the sea.

Although the leadership of the Yishuv accepted partition in principle (Jabotinsky's Revisionists naturally demurred), it rejected the particular allocation of territory proposed by the commission. The Arab Higher Committee, on the other hand, rejected partition out of hand. Members of the committee pointed out that in the area of the proposed Jewish state Arabs held four times as much land as Jews. Why, they asked, should they be asked to give that up? Furthermore, they asserted, once the Jewish state filled up with immigrants, it would expand into the Arab zone. Thus, the Arab Higher Committee stuck to its original demands: a termination of the mandate, the withdrawal of the Balfour Declaration, complete independence for Arab Palestine, and an end to Jewish immigration and land sales.

Even the British government found the Peel Commission's report difficult to swallow and rejected it. It was then that the Great Revolt entered its second, more devastating phase. As we have seen, the British responded to the new eruption of violence with overwhelming force. Nevertheless, they still looked for a political way out. As a first step, they called a conference in London – the St. James Conference – inviting representatives of the Zionist community, members of the Arab Higher Committee (excepting the Hajj Amin al-Husayni), and representatives from Egypt, Iraq, Saudi Arabia, Trans-Jordan, and Yemen. Although the conferees soon reached an impasse, the conference is important because it internationalized a conflict many in the British government believed should be handled as an internal British affair.

With the conference deadlocked and the international situation going from bad to worse for the British (Nazi Germany had just absorbed Czechoslovakia and signed a pact with the Italians), the British government decided it had to act unilaterally. In May 1939, it issued a White Paper (a government document that was, as the name implies, bound in white). The White Paper would guide British policy for the next eight years.

The White Paper of 1939 included four recommendations. Reversing the Peel Commission report, the White Paper backed away from partition and promised independence for a united Palestine conditioned on good relations between Jews and Arabs (and, it might have been added, pigs learning to fly). It also limited Jewish immigration to 75,000 over the ensuing five years, a figure based on the estimated "absorptive capacity" of the country. Thereafter, Jewish immigration would be allowed only with the consent of the Palestinian population. Finally, the White Paper put the regulation of land sales in the hands of the high commissioner for Palestine, with the stipulation that his principle consideration would be preventing the emergence of a "considerable landless Arab population."

Neither the Arab Higher Committee nor the Zionists accepted the White Paper. According to the Arab Higher Committee,

The last word does not rest with White or Black papers; it is the will of the nation itself that decides its future. The Arab people have expressed their will and said their word in a loud and decisive manner. And they are certain that with God's assistance they will reach the desired goal – Palestine shall be independent within an Arab federation and shall forever remain Arab.[1]

The Jewish Agency also rejected the White Paper. With an eye to events in Europe, the agency declared,

It is in the darkest hour of Jewish history that the British Government proposes to deprive the Jews of their last hope and to close the road back to their Homeland. It is a cruel blow. . . . This blow will not subdue the Jewish people. The historic bond between the people and the land of Israel cannot be broken. The Jews will never accept the closing to them of the gates of Palestine nor let their national home be converted into a ghetto. The Jewish pioneers who,

---

[1] J. C. Hurewitz, *The Struggle for Palestine, 1936–1948* (New York: Schocken Books, 1976), 103.

during the past three generations, have shown their strength in the upbuilding of a derelict country, will from now on display the same strength in defending Jewish immigration, the Jewish home and Jewish freedom.[2]

Although neither of the principals accepted the White Paper, Palestine was relatively quiet during World War II. There are a number of reasons why this was the case. First, neither the leadership of the Zionist community nor that of the Palestinian community was in a position to confront the British over the White Paper, although for different reasons. While the fringe Irgun and the Stern Gang continued their attacks on British targets during the war, the Jewish Agency did not wish to disrupt the Allied war effort against Hitler. It thus declared a truce. In the words of David Ben-Gurion, "We shall fight the war against Hitler as if there were no White Paper, and we shall fight the White Paper as if there were no war." The leadership of the Yishuv even deployed the Haganah alongside British forces to suppress the Stern Gang and Irgun. For its part, the Palestinian community was exhausted and leaderless: British counterinsurgency had taken a heavy toll, as did the economy of plunder and the forced exile of the Palestinian nationalist leadership. The Hajj Amin, for example, escaped Palestine and worked his way, via Lebanon and Iraq, to Nazi Germany, where he spent the war years.

The Hajj Amin's opportunistic wartime residence and propaganda activities in Nazi Germany certainly was not the proudest moment in the history of Palestinian nationalism. And, certainly, opponents of Palestinian nationalism have made good use of those activities to associate the Palestinian national movement with European-style anti-Semitism and the genocidal program of the Nazis. But it should be remembered that the Hajj Amin was not the only non-European nationalist leader to find refuge and succor in Berlin at this time. While in Berlin, the Hajj Amin might have rubbed shoulders with Subhas Chandra Bose, a leader of the nationalist Congress Party of India, who believed that Germany might prove to be an effective ally in the struggle against British imperialism. Bose once remarked, "Britain's difficulty was India's opportunity." Or the Hajj Amin might have bumped into Pierre Gemayel, the leader of a Lebanese Christian group called the Phalange, who believed that

---

[2] Walter Laqueur and Barry Rubin, eds., *The Israel–Arab Reader: A Documentary History of the Middle East Conflict* (New York: Penguin, 1995), 77.

Nazi Germany represented the wave of the future. Gemayel not only took the name "Phalange" from the Spanish fascists allied with Hitler, he was the führer's personal guest in Berlin in 1936. A massacre committed by Phalangists in 1975 sparked the Lebanese civil war (more would follow), and the Israelis invaded Lebanon in 1982 in part to install Bashir Gemayel, Pierre's son and the Phalange's leader, as president. Members of the Stern Gang also sought a tactical partnership with Nazi Germany and even opened negotiations with Hitler's government. According to one Stern Gang document, "There could exist common interests between the foundation of a new order in Europe according to the German concept and the genuine aspirations of the Jewish people as they are incarnated by the Lehi [Stern Gang]."[3] The Stern Gang sought to persuade Hitler's government that sending Jews to Palestine would accomplish the führer's goal of rendering Europe *Judenrein* (free of Jews).

Palestine was also relatively quiet during the war years because of a drop-off in Jewish immigration and the continued expansion of the Palestinian economy. Although the fifth aliyah had brought close to 200,000 new immigrants to Palestine – more than all the other aliyot combined – wartime conditions permitted only 82,000 Jews to emigrate to Palestine during World War II, about 14,000 each year. This was less than the number stipulated by the White Paper and well within British estimates of the absorptive capacity of the country. Indeed, while immigration was declining, the estimated absorptive capacity of Palestine was increasing. According to Roger Owen, from 1939 to 1942, industrial output from Jewish-owned factories increased 200 percent, and the industrial output from Palestinian-owned factories increased by 77 percent. During the same period, overall agricultural output increased by more than 30 percent. With an expansion of both industrial and agricultural production, unemployment reached all-time lows, and it has been estimated that by war's end there was full employment in Palestine. Palestinians would later refer to the wartime period as "the Prosperity."

Two factors contributed to boom times. The first was, ironically, unrestricted submarine warfare in the Mediterranean. The threat that

---

[3] David Yisraeli, *Le probleme palestinian dans la politique allemande de 1889–1945* (Ramat Gan, Israel: Bar Ilan University, 1974), 315–17.

submarine warfare posed to shipping worked like a protective tariff, sheltering Palestinian infant industries from foreign competition. And to cope with the Axis threat, the Allies created the Middle East Supply Center, which brought "national" economic planning to the region. Although the Allies initially designed the Middle East Supply Center to collect data on consumer needs throughout the Middle East so that they might allocate cargo space on freighters more efficiently, over time the center increasingly took on such tasks as regulating imports, guiding and supporting industrial investment, distributing essential commodities, and supervising production on a state-by-state basis. In other words, its rationale was much like that of the New Deal programs implemented a decade earlier in the United States: to streamline production, paper over class antagonisms in the name of efficiency, and improve productivity.

At the same time, Palestine became Britain's second major base in the region (the first being Egypt). The billeting of Allied troops in Palestine created a seemingly unquenchable demand for locally produced goods. Along with this demand came inflation, but even inflation acted to calm the restive population. As prices for agricultural products rose, many farmers were finally able to crawl out from under the burden of debt that had forced so many into poverty and landlessness. For a brief moment, the old adage that "the Palestinian farmer is born into debt, lives in debt, and dies in debt" proved untrue.

But although Palestine remained relatively calm during the war years, the calm was not to last. The war fundamentally changed the terms of the Palestine equation in three ways. First, the British were war-weary and £13 billion in debt. During the war, the British government had borrowed heavily from the United States, from the Dominions, and even from sterling reserves in India and Egypt. The British realized they could no longer maintain the prewar empire in the same form. They also realized that they would have to convince the United States to play a more active role in resolving the problem of Palestine.

The second important change brought about by the war concerned the demands of the international Zionist community. In 1942 an Extraordinary Zionist Conference convened in New York at the Biltmore Hotel. The demands made by the delegates became known as the "Biltmore Program." The program cited the catastrophe facing the Jewish community of Europe and called for the immediate establishment of a Jewish commonwealth in all of Palestine. Its conclusion reads as follows:

The Conference declares that the new world order that will follow victory cannot be established on foundations of peace, justice and equality, unless the problem of Jewish homelessness is finally solved.

The Conference urges that the gates of Palestine be opened; that the Jewish Agency be vested with control of immigration into Palestine and with the necessary authority for upbuilding the country, including the development of its unoccupied and uncultivated lands; and that Palestine be established as a Jewish Commonwealth integrated in the structure of the new democratic world.

Then and only then will the age-old wrong to the Jewish people be righted.

Many historians view the Biltmore Program as evidence of a virtual coup d'etat within the Zionist movement: The Young Turks, represented by David Ben-Gurion of the Yishuv-based Jewish Agency Executive, replaced their more moderate elders, represented by the London-based Chaim Weizmann, at the head of the World Zionist Organization. Weizmann had advocated gradualism, the partition of Palestine between Jews and Palestinians, and negotiation with Britain. Ben-Gurion championed immediate statehood, the establishment of a Jewish state in all of Palestine, and armed resistance, if necessary, to achieve Zionist goals. Ben-Gurion's position owed its popularity among Zionists not only to the crisis of European Jewry but to an increasingly conspiratorial reading of British motives. Many within the Zionist movement read British intentions within the context of Neville Chamberlain's appeasement policy. Just as the British had been willing to sell out Czechoslovakia to Hitler to achieve "peace in our time," Zionists believed the British were willing to backtrack on their promises to the Zionists to placate the "Arabs." What better way to ensure that the Zionist community in Palestine would wither on the vine than by restricting Jewish immigration and land purchases? Hence the immediate need for a Jewish state that could control its own immigration and thereby control its destiny. And hence the image of the "Jewish freedom-fighter," once restricted to the Revisionists, entered the Zionist mainstream.

The final change brought about by the war was the Holocaust and the ensuing refugee problem. When they occupied Poland and Germany, Allied armies came in contact with the concentration camps for the first time and with the tens of thousands of refugees who had been left homeless. Many of these refugees were understandably reluctant to return to their homes in Poland and Germany, if, indeed, they had homes to go back to. The United States representative to the Intergovernmental Committee on Refugees, Earl Harrison, reported to President Truman that the obvious solution to the Jewish refugee problem was to allow 100,000 immigrants into Palestine immediately. Harrison became the first American acting in an official capacity to link the Holocaust, the refugee problem, and Palestine.

After Harrison filed his report, Truman wrote to British Prime Minister Clement Attlee about implementing the committee's findings. Attlee suggested the establishment of an Anglo-American Commission of Inquiry to study the problem. This was, of course, a ploy by the British: They gave in on the issue of linking the refugee problem and Palestine, which they had been reluctant to do previously. In return, they got to suck the Americans into their quagmire. The Americans stood by the commission's recommendation to allow 100,000 refugees into Palestine – a recommendation the British opposed. The British responded that if that was to be the American position, the United States should defray the costs of their resettlement in Palestine and protect them with American troops – a proposition the Americans opposed. In the end, the proposals of the Anglo-American Commission came to naught.

In the meantime, the situation in Palestine was deteriorating. Factional fighting broke out once again among the Palestinians, and each group pushed for maximalist demands. Because the five-year period envisioned in the White Paper for limited Jewish immigration to Palestine had come and gone, Palestinians demanded an end to all further immigration. And because the ten-year waiting period for independence was on the horizon, the Palestinians demanded the implementation of the White Paper provisions calling for independence.

For their part, the Irgun and Stern Gang expanded their terrorist attacks on the British. The most spectacular attack took place in response to the report of the Anglo-American Commission of Inquiry: In July 1946, the Irgun blew up the British headquarters in Palestine at the King David Hotel. Future prime minister of Israel Menachem Begin executed the attack. The British responded with increased repression. At a time when India was about to achieve independence and the Cold War was in its initial stages, the British had to station 100,000 troops in Palestine to keep the peace. Clearly, something had to give.

In February 1947 the British threw up their hands and dumped the Palestine question on the newly founded United Nations – the successor organization to the League of Nations that had granted them the Palestine mandate in the first place. The United Nations General Assembly commissioned the United Nations Special Committee on Palestine (UNSCOP), made up of representatives from Sweden, the Netherlands, Czechoslovakia, Yugoslavia, Australia, Canada, India, Iran, Guatemala, Uruguay, and Peru, to investigate the Palestine problem and make recommendations. In August 1947 the committee issued both a majority and a minority report. The majority report called for the termination of the mandate and the partition of Palestine between Arab and Jewish communities, with the stipulation that the two communities be united in an economic union. The report also called for the internationalization of Jerusalem. (For the record, the minority report recommended the establishment of a single federal state.) Even before the matter came to a vote, the British government announced it was withdrawing its troops from Palestine by mid-May 1948. Thus, when the United Nations General Assembly voted to accept the majority report, both the Zionists and the Palestinians knew there would be no one around to enforce it. It was then that the war for Palestine began in earnest.

Why various countries in the United Nations voted in favor of partition has been a subject of contention for almost six decades. Some historians have noted that most Catholic countries voted for partition, citing as a reason the majority report's endorsement of the internationalization of Jerusalem. This seems a bit of a stretch, and it is far more likely that those countries just followed in the footsteps of the leader of the Western alliance, the United States, on an issue that was not of vital concern to them. Most non-Western countries followed suit. This was, after all, before the period of decolonization, and most non-Western countries that had achieved their independence were still dominated by pro-Western elites. In the cases of Nationalist China, Greece, Haiti, Liberia, and the Philippines, American Zionists in and out of the government, along with representatives of the Jewish Agency, used both carrots and sticks to gain support for partition. The era in which smaller nations sought to assert themselves through the doctrines of nonalignment and Third Worldism lay in the future.

Both the United States and the Soviet Union supported partition, although Soviet support appears to have been surer than that offered by the United States. As a matter of fact, at one point the United States tried to back away from partition and even suggested placing Palestine under temporary United Nations trusteeship. American hesitancy is not hard to fathom: The United States government was hardly united on Palestine policy. Some branches of government – the State Department, the Department of Defense, and the intelligence community – recommended that the United States oppose partition. They argued that American support for partition would injure relations with the Arab states. Although the United States had not yet succumbed to its addiction to Middle Eastern oil, cheap Arab oil was essential for the success of the Marshall Plan in Europe and for Japanese recovery. Many in the government were not willing to jeopardize the central plank of American postwar strategy to pull Britain's chestnuts out of the fire.

Furthermore, American military planners feared that if partition took place, a bloodbath would ensue and the United States would be forced to intervene. The Joint Chiefs of Staff estimated that it would take 100,000 American troops to separate the two sides. Those same planners also feared that the Soviets might use trouble in Palestine as a diversion (they had the same fear when North Korea invaded South Korea). Once the United States committed troops to Palestine, the Soviets would make their move in Europe. This was not just paranoia: While the debate over Palestine was occurring, the Soviet Union had blockaded Berlin, polls predicted a victory for the Communist Party of Italy, communist-led strikes had virtually shut down France, and a coup in Czechoslovakia had brought a communist government to power.

On the other hand, Truman's domestic advisors argued that the United States had a moral commitment to Jews, who had just experienced the Holocaust, and that with American support Israel would become a Western outpost in a potentially hostile region. They also warned the president that the loss of the Jewish vote in Illinois and New York (where most American Jews lived) could cost him the next election. For whatever reasons, Truman came down on the side of partition. He also won reelection (although he lost New York).

Our understanding of the motivations of the Soviet Union is even less sure than our understanding of American motives. The Soviet government under Stalin was not a fount of information about interagency squabbling and turf wars, if indeed such squabbling and turf wars took place. Historians have listed a number of possible reasons why the Soviets backed partition. Least likely is Stalin's belief in a "theory of stages" whereby a social democratic state like Israel was closer to achieving communist revolution than its Arab neighbors, which, Stalin believed, lived under feudalism. It is more likely that the Soviets saw the Middle East as a British playground and supported partition simply to make mischief. Regardless of the reason, the Soviet Union was the first state to grant Israel *de jure* recognition (recognition by legal right). Although the United States was the first nation to grant Israel *de facto* recognition (recognition regardless of legal niceties), it held off granting *de jure* recognition until Israel held its first postindependence elections.

THE 1948 WAR

The 1948 war for Palestine, called by Israelis the "War of Independence" and by Palestinians the nakba, actually consisted of two wars: a civil war fought between the Yishuv and the Palestinian community (which lasted from December 1947 to May 1948) and a war fought between the newly proclaimed State of Israel and its neighbors (which began in May 1948 and ended in various armistice agreements negotiated in the first six months of 1949). The war had two immediate effects. First, the war resulted in the establishment of the State of Israel within its commonly recognized borders. Under normal circumstances, we might say that with the proclamation of Israeli independence the Zionist project had achieved what it had set out to achieve and that now the Yishuv could focus on performing the mundane tasks of an ordinary state, from stamping passports to issuing postage stamps. This was not to be, however. The surrounding Arab states, which had invaded Palestine ostensibly in defense of the Palestinian people, refused to recognize Israeli sovereignty and refused to validate the consequences of the war by signing peace treaties with their enemy. Israel remained in a state of war with Egypt until 1979 and with Jordan until 1994. It still remains in a state of war with Syria and Iraq.

Israeli independence came at a high price for Palestinians. During the war, close to three-quarters of a million Palestinians who had lived within the territory over which Israel claimed sovereignty became refugees, prohibited from returning to their homes in the Jewish state. It was, in the words of former Israeli prime minister Ehud Barak, the "shattering and exile of a whole society, accompanied by thousands of deaths and the wholesale destruction of hundreds of villages."[4] Other settler states, such as the United States, had been built on the ruins of indigenous societies, of course. But it was Israel's misfortune that it did so under the harsh lights of the mid-twentieth century, a period when the West's imperial reach – along with the self-proclaimed civilizing mission that provided the rationale for its imperial reach – was no longer taken for granted and, in fact, was beginning to be challenged worldwide. Despite the self-conception of the post-Biltmore Zionists of the Yishuv that they were freedom fighters, few others in the throes of decolonization viewed them as such. It was also Israel's misfortune that it attempted to build a state on the ruins of a society that had nationalist aspirations of its own.

The military victory of the Yishuv over the surrounding Arab states and the displacement of the Palestinians living within Israel's borders transformed the nature of the conflict in a fundamental way. Before 1948, two communities of equal stature (although of unequal endowment) engaged in a face-to-face struggle for control of Palestine. By May 1948, one of those communities had declared itself a sovereign state whereas the other had experienced a cataclysm. The Palestinian community was dispersed and had no territory to call its own. The Yishuv had incorporated close to 80 percent of Palestine into their new state, and Egypt and Jordan held the remainder. In the meantime, the international community turned its attention to what it considered to be the issue at hand: ending the state of war between Israel and its neighbors. The best the Palestinian community could hope for was that its claims would be broached in international councils by proxy and resolved in the context of an "overall settlement" or a "comprehensive peace." The conflict between Zionists and Palestinians thus became the "Arab-Israeli dispute." It remained as such for over forty years, until, in 1993, Israelis and Palestinians once again met face to face – but this time in an effort to find common ground to resolve a conflict that was, after all, all about them.

Because the 1948 war might be considered *the* seminal event in the history of the Zionist-Palestinian conflict, it has generated more mythologizing and demythologizing than perhaps any other event in

---

[4] Benny Morris and Ehud Barak, "Camp David and After – Continued," *New York Review of Books*, 27 June 2002.

modern Middle Eastern history. Each side has done more than its share of mythologizing. Pro-Zionist accounts portray the 1948 war in terms of David versus Goliath. Take, for example, the portrayal of the war in Leon Uris's novel *Exodus*, a best-seller published in 1958. The book sold more than two million copies in the United States and reached an even broader audience as a movie (starring, improbably enough, Paul Newman as a Jewish freedom fighter and Eva Marie Saint as the girl who comes to love him):

After the November 1947 partition vote the Yishuv of Palestine begged the Palestine Arabs to remain calm, friendly, and to respect the unassailably legal rights of the Jewish people.

Despite wanton aggression, the State of Israel, in its Declaration of Independence, held out its hand in friendship to its Arab neighbors, even at the moment her borders were being violated.

The avowed intention of murdering the Jewish people and completely destroying the State of Israel was the Arab answer to law and friendship.

Israel today stands as the greatest single instrument for bringing the Arab people out of the Dark Ages.[5]

Uris's account is not important because of its novelty. To the contrary, it is important because it contains all the elements common to Zionist accounts of 1948: The Zionists accepted the United Nations partition plan and were willing to live in peace with their neighbors; the Arab states rejected the partition plan and launched a war against the Jewish state; the Arab states acted as a monolithic bloc; the outnumbered, outgunned Zionist forces fought heroically against overwhelming odds; in spite of Zionist assurances of protection, Palestinians left at the urging of Arab governments to make way for the advancing Arab armies.

Not to be outdone when it comes to misrepresentation, the standard accounts from the Arab side are just as spurious and self-serving. These accounts commonly tell the story of battlefield victories and behind-the-scenes betrayals. They begin with the heroic exploits of the Arab armies, which, acting in concert to rescue their Palestinian brethren, defeated the gangs of Zionist terrorists wherever they met in combat. Unfortunately, the Arab armies were unable to take advantage of their success (and here is where the accounts diverge). According to some accounts, the Americans and British conspired to ensure a Zionist victory by providing

---

[5] Leon Uris, *Exodus* (New York: Bantam Books, 1958), 552.

logistical and even combat support to the Zionist gangs. According to other accounts, the Arab armies were unable to press on to victory because they were stabbed in the back by the reactionary and corrupt regimes that ruled them. These regimes were more than willing to act as imperialist lackeys – which is why they had to be replaced in the aftermath of the war by the very military regimes that sponsored the rewriting of national histories. (One popular account, related to me by an individual who should know better, has King 'Abdullah of Jordan providing his troops with rifles that fired backwards. Every time a Jordanian soldier discharged his weapon in the battle to liberate Palestine, he shot himself in the head.)

Although neither the pro-Zionist nor the conventional Arab account of the 1948 war can be taken seriously, it was not until the 1980s that historians were able to shed new light on the war and its devastating impact on Palestinian society. Those most responsible for revising our knowledge of the 1948 war are a group of Israeli historians known as the "New Historians." Taking advantage of the "thirty year rule" and consulting government documents that the Israeli government had kept under wraps for three decades, these historians have challenged what have become known as "the founding myths of Israel." By combining their findings with those of historians working in British and American archives, it has become possible to challenge the most egregious myths concerning the 1948 war. Unfortunately, it is still not possible to pull together a definitive narrative of events. Not only does the discipline of history work through constant visions and revisions, no New Historian group has emerged in the Arab world to complement the work of Western and Israeli scholars. There is no thirty year rule for the declassification of documents in the Arab world, and given the lack of openness there, there is not likely to be one.

The picture of the 1948 war that emerges from recent research certainly does not support the image of David versus Goliath. In spite of the fact that the Palestinian population outnumbered the population of the Yishuv Zionist community 1.4 million to 600,000, Palestinian society, as we have seen, had never recovered from the effects of the 1936–9 Great Revolt. Not only had the population been literally decimated during the revolt (upwards of 10 percent of the male population had been killed, wounded, imprisoned, or exiled), at the time the British announced their withdrawal from Palestine little in the way of leadership or even institutions remained. With the end of World War II, the Hajj Amin found his way to Egypt from Germany, while the newly formed Arab League founded a new Arab Higher Committee that operated under its auspices. Neither the Hajj Amin nor the new Arab Higher Committee were able to exert effective control over Palestinian affairs.

The intervention of Arab forces during the second phase of the war did little to improve Palestinian fortunes. The Arab states did an abysmal job of preparing for and waging war. The armies they fielded never matched those of the Yishuv in size, and whatever advantages they might have initially had in terms of equipment had eroded by war's end. This was in part because no Arab state had the capability or desire to undertake full war mobilization, in part because of the Arab states' colonial or mandatory heritage. Not only had the mandatory authorities designed armies to preserve domestic stability and not to wage war abroad, the liberation of Palestine was just not a wise avenue to take for governments that had just secured their independence (Lebanon, Syria, Jordan) or still had to contend with an continued imperialist presence (Egypt). In case after case, it was fear of the mob and those who would exploit the mob that drove fragile governments to intervene in Palestine against their better judgment.

The Arab states might have been able to overcome these difficulties had they truly been joined in a common cause. They were not. The Arab League, which theoretically supervised the efforts to liberate Palestine, was never more than the sum of its parts. Originally proposed by the British as a means to maintain their influence in the postwar Arab world, the Arab League was established among states jealous of their prerogatives. Just as the Cold War had weakened the ability of the United Nations to act with unanimity and effectiveness, interstate rivalry undermined the effectiveness of the Arab League. In 1948 the Arab states were divided into two rival camps: Jordan and Iraq, on the one hand, and, by default, Egypt, Syria, and Saudi Arabia, on the other. Because Jordan and Iraq were ruled by two branches of the same Hashemite family that enjoyed a close relationship with the British, leaders of Egypt, Syria, and Saudi Arabia feared a British-backed "Hashemite conspiracy" intent on dominating the Arab world. Making matters even more complex, the leaders of Jordan, Egypt, and Iraq each had ambitions to lead the Arab world. As a result, there was no agreement on strategy or war aims in 1948. No wonder no state was willing to put its military under the command of a potential rival or offer more than a veneer of cooperation with others.

Jordanian war aims were driven by the desire of King 'Abdullah to create a Greater Syrian state led by Jordan and encompassing Syria, Lebanon, and Palestine as well. As a result, the Jordanians displayed closer coordination with the Zionists than with other Arab states. As a matter of fact, King 'Abdullah of Jordan had been meeting with leaders of the Yishuv since Trans-Jordan had been created in 1921. Because Jordanian and Zionist leaders had already negotiated the boundaries of their respective states, the Jordanians arrayed their forces as peace-keepers and occupiers, not as liberators. As a matter of fact, virtually no fighting took place between Jordanians and Zionists outside of Jerusalem.

Needless to say, none of the other Arab participants in the war had illusions about Jordanian ambitions or war aims. The government of Syria never fully trusted the officers of the Syrian army, fearing that they supported 'Abdullah's Greater Syria scheme – which, indeed, many did. Nor did the Syrian government trust local elites, who were often willing to offer up Syria to one or another Greater Syria or Pan-Arab scheme to further their personal ambitions. The Egyptians feared a Jordanian land grab that would carve a corridor from Jordan through southern Palestine to the Mediterranean Sea, thus cutting Egypt off from the eastern Arab world. Even the Palestinian leadership viewed Jordanian ambitions as a threat. There was no love lost between the Hajj Amin al-Husayni and 'Abdullah. Both wanted to rule Palestine. The mufti, fearing for Palestinian independence and his own political future, even argued against intervention by Arab armies.

Overall, then, when the Arab states intervened in the conflict, their military capabilities were inadequate for the job, their efforts were never particularly well coordinated, and they were not joined in a common cause. A little more than half a century after the 1948 war, historian Avi Shlaim concluded, "The Arab coalition was one of the most divided, disorganized, and ramshackle coalitions in the entire history of warfare."[6] The results were what one might expect: In a military campaign

---

[6] Avi Shlaim, "Israel and the Arab Coalition in 1948," in *The War for Palestine: Rewriting the History of 1948*, ed. Eugene L. Rogan and Avi Shlaim (Cambridge: Cambridge University Press, 2001), 82.

interrupted only by a thirty-five–day truce, the forces of the Yishuv, resupplied and reinforced, delivered a final knockout blow to their enemies.

Now, it seemed, all that remained for the international community was to arrange some sort of settlement, preferably peace treaties, between the newly proclaimed State of Israel and its opponents. This was not to be. Although the United Nations sponsored peace talks on the island of Rhodes, the talks stalled on two issues: the fate of Jerusalem and the fate of the Palestinians who had fled their homes during the fighting. The Arab states argued for repatriation. Thus was born the "right of return." The Israelis, on the other hand, argued for resettlement. The Israeli stand against repatriation was justified on the basis of the refusal of the mainstream Zionist movement to acknowledge Palestinian nationness. Zionist polemics presented Palestinians simply as Arabs, and as Arabs they could just as easily find a home in any number of Arab states, from Mauritania to Iraq. Here is how the American Zionist Louis Brandeis presented the argument:

People have a right to live the way they want. That is inalienable. They have a right to live in squalor, in dirt, in disease or any form they choose. The question, however, is on *how much land*. The Arabs have millions of acres uncultivated and unexploited. There is Iraq, Syria, Saudi Arabia, the Hedjaz, etc., etc. In some way, it should be shown how much land the Arabs occupy in the East, and how all their aspirations may be fulfilled without interference of Jewish development in Palestine.

And here's how Abba Eban, Israel's representative to the United Nations in the 1960s, used this argument to absolve Israel from the responsibility of repatriating Palestinian refugees: "It is impossible to escape the conclusion that the integration of Arab refugees into the life of the Arab world is an objectively feasible process which has been resisted for political reasons."

Eventually, the United Nations mediator, Ralph Bunche, broke the impasse at Rhodes by adopting the formula used to suspend the hostilities at the end of World War I: Rather than negotiating peace treaties between Israel and its neighbors, the United Nations mediated armistice agreements. Those agreements informally confirmed the boundaries of the State of Israel. The Gaza Strip, the area taken by the Egyptian army during the war, remained under Egyptian control, while the Jordanians

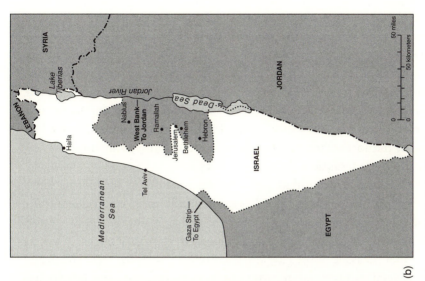

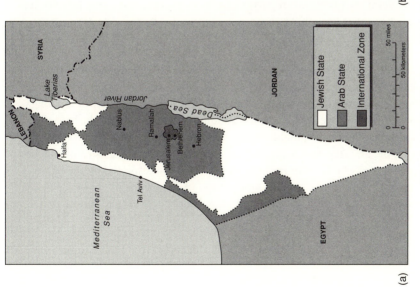

Map 6. (a) United Nations partition plan, 1947. (b) Armistice lines, 1949.

went so far as to annex the West Bank, claiming that annexation would not prejudice the "final settlement" of the Palestine question. (Palestinian nationalists would continue to fight a rearguard action against Jordanian claims to act on their behalf and Jordanian attempts to integrate the West Bank into Jordan for the next four decades.) Whereas residents of the West Bank came to hold Jordanian passports, use Jordanian currency, and submit to Jordanian law, Palestinian residents of the Gaza Strip were truly stateless in the most fundamental sense of the term. No formal solution to the Jerusalem issue was reached, but a working relationship between Israel and Jordan divided the city into an Israeli-controlled "new city" and a Jordanian-controlled "old city." In 1960, the Jordanians decided to replace ambiguity with confusion by proclaiming Jerusalem their "second capital."

Thus, the problem that captured the attention of the international community came to be defined as turning the armistice agreements into full-fledged peace agreements, and the principals in the conflict came to be defined as those who could speak to that issue. This is not to say that the issue of the Palestinians dropped out altogether. The Arabs continued to press for repatriation or compensation, the Israelis for resettlement. Nevertheless, a revolution had taken place. According to historian Albert Hourani,

By refusing to consider the refugee problem except in the framework of a peace settlement with the surrounding Arab States, they linked together two matters which had no moral connection: for the return of the refugees was an obligation which they owed not to the surrounding Arab States but to the Palestinian Arabs themselves, as inhabitants of the land they had conquered.... After 1948, the first step to peace was that Israel should recognise its responsibility to the Arabs who lived in its territory but had been displaced by the fighting. Only this could have set in motion a train of events leading towards peace; and only Israel could have taken the step. Israel never did so, and its attitude was accepted by the Western Powers.[7]

"SHATTERING AND EXILE"

The United Nations defined Palestinian refugees as those Palestinians who fled their homes and were subsequently trapped behind the

[7] Walter Laqueur and Barry Rubin, eds., *The Israel-Arab Reader: A Documentary History of the Middle East Conflict* (New York: Penguin, 1995), 273.

14. Palestinian refugees, carrying whatever possessions they can, make their way to safety during the 1948 war. (Source: Bettman/Corbis)

armistice lines. Of an estimated total population of 1.4 million Palestinians, a little over half – about 720,000 – became refugees. Anywhere from 65 percent to more than 85 percent of Palestinians living within the boundaries of Israel were forced into permanent exile, while upwards of another 25 percent of those who remained were uprooted and became internal refugees in Israel. Those Palestinians who remained in Israel were subject to martial law until 1966.

Why Palestinians fled their homes has been a topic of controversy and mythmaking ever since. Leon Uris relates one set of myths as follows:

The Arabs created the Palestine refugee problem themselves. . . . The first reason for this was that the Palestine Arabs were filled with fear. For decades racist leaders had implanted the idea of mass murder in their minds. . . . Was this fear founded upon fact? No! At one place, Neve Sadiq, there was an unforgivable massacre of innocent people. Otherwise, the Arabs who remained in Palestine were completely unmolested. No Arab village which remained at peace was harmed in any way by the Israelis. . . . The second major cause of the refugee situation comes from the absolutely documented fact that the

Arab leaders wanted the civilian population to leave Palestine as a political issue and a military weapon. The Arab generals planned an annihilation of the Jewish people. They did not want a large Arab civilian population present to clutter their operational freedom. . . . If the Arabs of Palestine loved their land, they could not have been forced from it, much less run from it without real cause. The Arabs had little to live for, much less to fight for.[8]

Not all of Uris's account is wildly inaccurate. For example, historians do agree that most Palestinians fled from fear, although they would disagree with Uris on the cause of that fear. Theirs was not the sort of fear that came from years of brainwashing at the hands of unscrupulous leaders; it was the very reasonable fear of being trapped inside a war zone. Uris is also correct when he asserts that Arab governments have shamelessly exploited the plight of the Palestinian refugees when it has suited their interests. During periods when crocodile tears were no longer required, those governments remained indifferent to the circumstances of the refugees, or even treated the presence of Palestinian refugees in their countries with hostility.

Nevertheless, much of the narrative Uris reproduces is baseless. Take the old canard about Arab leaders urging the Palestinians to get out of the way of incoming tanks. The New Historian Benny Morris does cite evidence that the Arab Higher Committee issued orders in certain villages for the evacuation of women, children, and the elderly. Still, no records in the Israeli, British, or American archives indicate that leaders of Arab nations directed Palestinians to leave. As a matter of fact, some Arab governments did the exact opposite, appealing to the Palestinians to stay where they were. Thus, although politicians like Abba Eban might claim that "as early as the first months of 1948 the Arab League issued orders exhorting the people to seek a temporary refuge in neighboring countries, later to return to their abodes in the wake of the victorious Arab armies and obtain their share of abandoned Jewish property," it is hardly an "absolutely documented fact."[9] (Neither, of course, is Uris's assertion, "If the Arabs of Palestine loved their land, they could not have been forced from it." If that were the case, why would second- and third-generation refugees still hold onto the keys

[8] Leon Uris, *Exodus* (New York: Bantam Books, 1958), 552.
[9] Walter Laqueur and Barry Rubin, eds., *The Israel-Arab Reader: A Documentary History of the Middle East Conflict* (New York: Penguin, 1995), 158, 160.

to their abandoned homes and pass them down as keepsakes to their descendants?)

Perhaps the most erroneous assertion Uris makes concerns what has become known in the last few decades as "ethnic cleansing." Because this term is so charged with meaning, historians of Zionism have opted for the more inoffensive term "transfer thinking" when describing the rationale for the removal of the indigenous inhabitants of Palestine. Transfer thinking dates back to the beginnings of the Zionist movement. For example, Theodor Herzl wrote in his diary,

We must expropriate gently . . . We shall try to spirit the penniless population across the border by procuring employment for it in the transit countries, while denying it any employment in our country. . . . Both the process of expropriation and the removal of the poor must be carried out discreetly and circumspectly.[10]

Forty years later, Ben-Gurion reiterated this view:

The transfer of population has already taken place in the Jezreel Valley, in the Sharon Plain, and in other places. You are aware of the work of the Jewish National Fund in this respect. Now a transfer of wholly different dimensions will have to be carried out.[11]

During the 1948 war, Ben-Gurion put his recommendations into practice. In a campaign known as "Operation Hiram," a wholesale transfer of population took place in the Galilee region. During this campaign, Morris writes, Zionist forces engaged in "an unusually high concentration of executions of people against a wall or next to a well in an orderly fashion."[12] In his work, the indefatigable Morris cites twenty-four incidents of terror or massacre, the worst taking place at Saliha (seventy to eighty killed), Lod (250), Dawayima (hundreds) and, of course, the previously cited Dayr Yassin. Some of these massacres were probably carried out for tactical reasons: In Dawayima (near Hebron), for example, "a column entered the village with all guns blazing and

---

[10] Benny Morris, "Revisiting the Palestinian Exodus of 1948," in *The War for Palestine: Rewriting the History of 1948*, ed. Eugene L. Rogan and Avi Shlaim (Cambridge: Cambridge University Press, 2001), 41.

[11] Benny Morris, "Revisiting the Palestinian Exodus of 1948," in *The War for Palestine: Rewriting the History of 1948*, ed. Eugene L. Rogan and Avi Shlaim (Cambridge: Cambridge University Press, 2001), 43.

[12] Ari Shavit, "Survival of the Fittest," *Haaretz*, 8 January 2004.

killed anything that moved." Others had the strategic purpose of panick-
ing the population so that it would flee. These acts of massacre were
hardly hidden from the Palestinian population. After all, as Lenin once
put it, the purpose of terrorism is to terrorize. (Morris, by the way, now
justifies Zionist actions using the logic of Lenin's well-known aphorism:
"To make an omelette, you have to break a few eggs.") According to
one eyewitness in Dayr Yassin,

Deir Yassin was a village that was attacked by the Israelis, or by the Zionists,
on the ninth of April 1948.... You would meet people who would tell you,
"This is what happened at Deir Yassin," because they were there. I met a
woman who said that they brought her son and they asked her to put him on
her lap and they killed him. They used knives, bayonets. It was really slaugh-
tering, not fighting. There was nobody to fight. They were mostly women and
children. Many, many people were massacred at that village. This massacre
scared the *whole* of Palestine. Everyone talked about the massacre in Deir
Yassin.[13]

In all, more than five hundred Palestinian villages disappeared forever.

Most of the Palestinians who fled ended up in the West Bank, the
Gaza Strip, and neighboring Arab countries. Those with an education,
skills, or money tried to rebuild their lives as best they could on their
own, sometimes in places as far away as the Persian Gulf, Europe,
and the Americas. Those who were not so lucky ended up in refugee
camps supported initially by an agency called United Nations Relief for
Palestine (UNRP). Arab states initially believed that the construction of
the camps would create an international problem that begged solution.
Either the international community would be so moved by the plight of
the refugees – or so tired of paying for their support – that it would have
no choice but to pressure Israel to repatriate them. The international
community had other ideas, however. UNRP, which distributed direct
aid for the refugees, gave way to the United Nations Relief and Works
Agency (UNRWA). In the spirit of the day, when diplomats actually
believed that peace could be achieved through economic development
and that economic development could be achieved by large-scale, New
Deal–style public works projects, UNRWA promised to bring prosperity to the Middle East by employing Palestinians on such projects in

---

[13] Staughton Lynd, Sam Bahour, and Alice Lynd, *Homeland: Oral Histories of Palestine
and Palestinians* (New York: Olive Branch Press, 1994), 47–9.

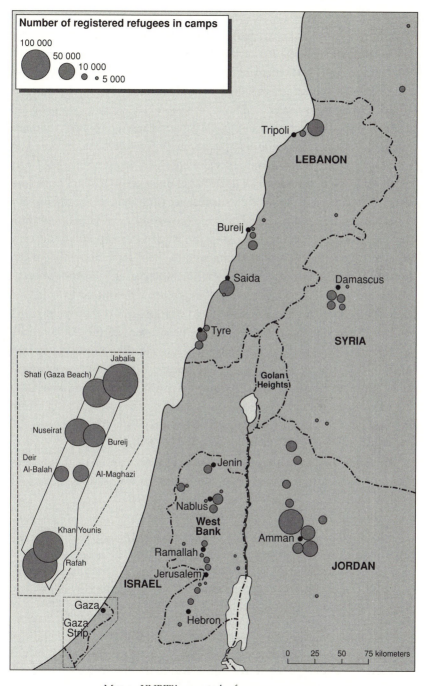

Number of registered refugees in camps

100 000

50 000

10 000

● 5 000

Tripoli

LEBANON

Bureij

Saida

Damascus

Tyre

SYRIA

Jabalia

Shati (Gaza Beach)

Golan
Heights

Nuseirat

Bureij

Deir
Al-Balah

Al-Maghazi

Jenin

Nablus

Khan Younis

**West
Bank**

Amman

Rafah

Ramallah

JORDAN

Jerusalem

ISRAEL

Gaza

Gaza
Strip

Hebron

0   25   50   75 kilometers

Map 7. UNRWA-operated refugee camps, 2005.

the states where they had taken shelter. The Arab governments would have none of it. Not only would the proposal shift much of the financial burden for the upkeep of the Palestinians to them, it would mark the triumph of resettlement over repatriation. Without their cooperation, UNRWA continued to support the refugees in the same manner as UNRP, only with a larger budget.

As of this writing, fifty-nine UNRWA camps shelter about 1.3 million refugees and their descendants (this number includes those uprooted by the 1967 war and their descendants as well). The largest number of camp dwellers reside in the occupied territories, followed by Jordan, Lebanon, and Syria. The rights enjoyed by the refugees and their descendants vary from country to country. Jordan is the only country in which Palestinians are entitled to full rights of citizenship. This explains why only about 307,000 of 1.7 million refugees and their descendants in Jordan live in camps. In Syria, Palestinian refugees and their descendants cannot become citizens. Nevertheless, they are legally entitled to work – a right severely restricted in neighboring Lebanon. It is not only the camp dwellers who have experienced an uncertain fate in the Arab world, however. Kuwait went so far as to expel its Palestinian guest workers after the 1991 Gulf War because the Palestine Liberation Organization had supported Saddam Hussein's invasion of the sheikhdom. When the Kuwaitis discovered they needed the skills possessed by the Palestinians, they recanted. The Libyans also expelled their Palestinian guest workers, ostensibly in protest against the 1993 Oslo Accord.

Adjusting to camp life has not been easy. One refugee in southern Lebanon recounts the miserable conditions in an UNRWA camp as follows:

At the camp people started living in tents and later began to build concrete walls. People from the same village in Palestine lived in the same section of the camp. So you could say, "This is the Hattin area." Up to the present time, it is easy to find any person in the camp without having his address. All you have to do is ask which village he is from in Palestine. You say, "He's from Hattin." "OK, this is the Hattin neighborhood. . . .

Families got bigger and bigger. People could not afford to go and buy houses in the city unless they were working and making good money, which very few were doing. Most of the people had to use the area on which they already lived to accommodate additional children. So they changed the corrugated ceilings into concrete roofs and built another story. Now some houses have three stories. You can see parents living on the first floor of a house, and their children and grandchildren on the other floors.....

The infrastructure was all planned by the United Nations. But it's not great. In the winter the sewage pipes are flooded all the time. The streets are filled with water. Most of the time you are walking in mud. In the summer, water is scarce. Drinking water comes just to the lower level of homes.[14]

No wonder many Palestinians still hold onto the keys to their former homes in what is now Israel.

The segregation of Palestinian refugees in camps has had a dual effect on the Palestinian national movement. On the one hand, it has worked to keep a separate Palestinian national identity alive. Not only did the camps become hotbeds of nationalist activism, the structure of life in the camps reaffirmed Palestinian identity. As our informant relates, refugees from the same villages lived together in camp neighborhoods and named them after the villages they had left behind. Memories of village life were frozen in time, embellished, and passed down from generation to generation. Traditions that had been flexible and adaptive became fossilized, while others were invented. Each village became identified with one or another style of embroidery, for example, which is still sold in the boutiques of Europe and America as authentic folk art.

On the other hand, the segregation of Palestinians who had fled their homes in 1948 opened up cleavages in the Palestinian movement that had not existed before. Before 1948 the leadership of the Palestinian national movement had rejected partition unequivocally. In the early 1970s a faction of the movement's leadership once again put the issue on the table, and over the course of the next decade and a half the idea of establishing a Palestinian "mini-state" in the West Bank and Gaza Strip gained momentum. When the Palestinian leadership accepted the Oslo Accord of 1993, it officially recognized partition, although it never took the right of return off the table. Those who fled and their descendants have been more reluctant to abandon the right of return than those who had roots in the West Bank and Gaza Strip. Thus, in the aftermath of Oslo, when a reporter from the *New York Times* asked an elderly camp dweller his opinion about the possibility of a Palestinian

[14] Staughton Lynd, Sam Bahour, and Alice Lynd, *Homeland: Oral Histories of Palestine and Palestinians* (New York: Olive Branch Press, 1994), 36.

15. Nationalisms transform what people once wore into traditional "national costumes." Palestinian Authority stamps, 1995.

state in the occupied territories, the old man shrugged, held up an old key, and replied with indifference, "My house is not within those borders."[15]

SUGGESTIONS FOR FURTHER READING

Bell, J. Bowyer. *Terror out of Zion: Irgun Zvai Leumi, LEHI, and the Palestinian Underground, 1929–1949.* New York: St. Martin's Press, 1977. Account of the extreme Zionist right in Palestine before independence.

Hurewitz, J. C. *The Struggle for Palestine, 1936–1948.* New York: Schocken Books, 1976. The diplomatic and political history of Palestine during the period leading up to Israeli independence.

[15] James Bennett, "Mideast Turmoil: Palestine: In Camps, Arabs Cling to Dream of Long Ago," *New York Times*, 10 March 2002.

Khalaf, Issa. "The Effect of Socioeconomic Change on Arab Societal Collapse in Mandate Palestine." *International Journal of Middle East Studies* 29 (1997): 93–112. Highlights social and economic factors that led to the Palestinian nakba of 1948.

———. *Politics in Palestine: Arab Factionalism and Social Disintegration, 1939–1948.* Albany: State University of New York, 1991. The name says it all.

Rogan, Eugene L., and Avi Shlaim. *The War for Palestine: Rewriting the History of 1948.* Cambridge: Cambridge University Press, 2001. Essays on the war by some of the leading revisionist scholars.

Shlaim, Avi. *Collusion across the Jordan: King Abdullah, the Zionist Movement, and the Partition of Palestine.* New York: Columbia University Press, 1988. Account of the relationship between the king of Jordan and the Zionists in the period leading up to the 1948 war.

7

ZIONISM AND PALESTINIAN NATIONALISM: A CLOSER LOOK

We are about to enter the world of the Arab-Israeli dispute, the world of "Black September," Henry Kissinger, the "Year of Decision," the "Decade of Decision," the "Rejectionist Front," three Arab-Israeli wars (1956, 1967, 1973), the Israeli invasion of Lebanon, massacres at Sabra and Shatila, the Johnston Plan, the Rogers Plan, the Rogers Initiative, the First Geneva Conference, the Second Geneva Conference, the 1978 Framework for Peace in the Middle East, the Schultz Plan, the Reagan Plan, and the Madrid Conference. We might therefore be forgiven if we pause before we dive into this rather depressing phase of the conflict and take one more look at the nationalisms that lie at the conflict's core.

When I say "nationalisms that lie at the conflict's core," I mean, of course, Zionism and Palestinian nationalism. Defining the conflict in these terms, however, is a bit of an oversimplification. As we have seen, neither nationalism is monolithic. In the case of Zionism, I have described Labor Zionism, Revisionism, and Religious Zionism. In the case of Palestinian nationalism, I have described it as it was conceived by society's elites and as it was conceived by its nonelites. Even these breakdowns are oversimplifications, since not all Revisionists are the same, nor do all nonelite Palestinians hold to the same agenda. Although every nationalism attempts to present itself to the world as a monolithic bloc, beneath its indivisible exterior lurk class, gender, geographic, generational, and ideological cleavages. This fact alone is enough to raise a number of questions. How do nationalisms draw their doctrinal boundaries? How does one strain of a nationalism achieve dominance over others? What happens to those other strains when this occurs? How do the symbols chosen by nationalist movements to represent themselves restrict the meaning of the nationalisms they advocate? How do those symbols enable nationalist movements to incorporate those who hold diverse views into their fold? This chapter explores these questions by examining two episodes in the history Zionism and Palestinian nationalism – the construction of the "Jewish Palestine" pavilion at the 1939–40 New York World's Fair and the 2000 effort by Israeli educational reformers to include a poem written by a Palestinian in Israeli textbooks.

"JEWISH PALESTINE" GOES TO THE FAIR

World's fair pavilions constructed during the golden age of international expositions had two purposes. Their first purpose was to associate the sponsoring nation with the forward march of universal progress. Every world's fair had a theme – "Century of Progress" (1933), "Building the World of Tomorrow" (1939), "Peace through Understanding" (1964) – and just by participating in the fair a nation associated itself with that theme. The second purpose of world's fair pavilions was to display to the world the characteristics of the sponsoring nation that distinguished it from other nations, justified its sovereign existence, and made its contribution to the international community unique. To achieve these goals, nations spoke through their pavilions with a single voice, using the dominant, state-supported version of the national narrative to marginalize, incorporate, or eliminate alternatives to the official nationalist ideology.

For sixty years, the "Jewish Palestine Pavilion" constructed at the 1939–40 New York World's Fair has been portrayed as fitting the model of a typical world's fair pavilion. As a result of post-Holocaust nostalgia and such popular works as E. L. Doctorow's *World's Fair* and David Gelernter's *1939: The Lost World of the Fair*, the pavilion has become a symbol of Jewish solidarity on the eve of disaster. At the same time, a singular Zionist vision associated with the pavilion has been projected backward, while the memory of struggles among anti-Zionist, non-Zionist, and alternative Zionist voices within the Jewish community has been diminished.

The reality of the pavilion was, in fact, quite different from that held in memory for two reasons. First, unlike other world's fair pavilions, the Jewish Palestine Pavilion did not represent an established nation-state. Rather, it represented a community (the Yishuv) that relied on nonnationalists (mostly Jewish non-Zionists) as well as nationalists (Zionists) for financial and political backing. Second, since Zionism was still in its formative period and needed to expand its base of support, pavilion organizers were forced to acknowledge – and thus validate – the assorted beliefs held by supporters and potential supporters. The result was a pavilion whose representational goals were, to put it charitably, ambiguous. A close examination of the pavilion thus provides the historian with a unique vantage point from which to recover a range of beliefs associated with Jewish settlement in Palestine and view their interaction during a particularly critical period in Zionist history.

In general, the organizers of the pavilion recognized three constituencies that merited representation on its planning board. These constituencies not only provided financial support for the pavilion, they composed the pavilion's primary target audience. The first constituency consisted of non-Zionist Jews who rejected what one prominent leader called "the nationalistic Jewish philosophy." Although, more often than not, this rejection did not conflict with their support for a Jewish presence in Palestine, non-Zionists resented the attempts Zionists made to present Jewish nationalism as the culmination of Jewish history. Many non-Zionists were thus apprehensive of participating in the pavilion project, which they rightly feared would be hijacked by Zionists seeking to glorify Jewish national aspirations.

The second group that participated in planning the pavilion was made up of those who represented what might be called an "indigenous American Zionism." Although supportive of Jewish national aspirations, this group rejected three doctrines associated with the Zionism popular in eastern Europe: First, it refused to equate exilic culture with degeneration, the foundation for the principle of "negation of exile." Second, it rejected the idea that the Jewish people worldwide made up a single subject nationality deserving the same political rights as other subject nationalities – a doctrine known as "diaspora nationalism." American Zionists considered their nationality to be American (or, to be more precise, Jewish-American) rather than simply Jewish. As a result, the American Zionist movement rejected the campaign to bring about a Jewish national revival in the United States (a doctrine known in the business as *Gegenwartsarbeit*). American Zionism confined its activities to supporting European Jewish immigration to Palestine. American

Zionists felt that this support not only would provide the answer to the uniquely European "Jewish question" but would enable the Americans to participate in a project they associated with the march of universal progress. In short, indigenous American Zionism was more a support system for other people's nationalism than a nationalism in its own right. Like the non-Zionists, the American Zionists sought to use the Jewish Palestine Pavilion to show off the good works and the civilizing role taken on by Jews in Palestine.

The third group to participate in planning the pavilion consisted of Yishuv Zionists, whose ideals reflected their roots in the second and third aliyot. This group advocated the very principles rejected by indigenous American Zionism: negation of exile, diaspora nationalism, and Gegenwartsarbeit. Although dependent on financial support from those committed to the American brand of Zionism, the Yishuv Zionists involved in the pavilion project were impatient with what they regarded as the American tendency to reduce Zionism to a mere philanthropic enterprise. Instead, they regarded Palestine as the site of a regenerative social revolution. In their correspondence, they expressed three ambitions for the pavilion: to attract non-Zionists to Zionism, to disseminate an officially sanctioned (Labor) Zionist ideology within the diverse Zionist community, and to attract support for Zionist ambitions in Palestine among non-Jewish fairgoers.

Although Zionists, non-Zionists, and American Zionists had lived in relative harmony before the 1930s, during the 1930s their relationship began to unravel. There were several reasons for this. The resistance of the indigenous inhabitants of Palestine to the Yishuv not only made a mockery of the popular assumption that those inhabitants would welcome the "civilizing mission" of the Zionists, it raised doubts about the future of Jewish settlement in Palestine. So did Italian military successes in the region. Finally, the Peel Commission report put the divisive issue of a Jewish state front and center. In the words of the prominent non-Zionist Maurice J. Karpf,

If you ask [non-Zionists] why they entered the Jewish Agency, they answer that when they entered the Agency they did not expect that within their lifetime the Jewish State would be a problem for consideration.... Now that a Jewish State is actually proposed, and may almost be had for the taking, they suddenly found themselves forced to face a problem they did not envisage, and they are frank to say they will not accept a Jewish State.[1]

The Yishuv leadership feared the fragmentation of the fragile Yishuv Zionist, American Zionist, non-Zionist coalition, but it also feared the dilution of Zionist ambitions during a period of crisis. It thus assumed primary responsibility for organizing the pavilion. Working through a handpicked design and administrative team, it worked to ensure that the pavilion design and the exhibits housed within would reflect Zionist accomplishments in Palestine and the Zionist narrative of Jewish history. They loaded up the pavilion with symbols of Zionism. Atop the pavilion, for instance, designers placed a stylized version of the seven-branched menorah (candelabrum). Derived from an image sculpted on the Arch of Titus in Rome, the same menorah motif was later incorporated into the Israeli national emblem. Its significance as a Zionist symbol has been perceptively described by anthropologists Don Handelman and Lea Shamgar-Handelman:

The biography of this menorah paralleled that of the Jewish nation. It was understood as a mirror image of the Second Temple menorah, of the singular centricity of the land of Israel. It too went into exile, paraded and degraded in the Roman triumph, enchained on a monument that commemorated the oppression of the Jewish nation. In secular Zionist views, the menorah was frozen on the arch – time stopped for the menorah, as, in a sense, significant time had stopped for the Jewish people, until their revival. Now the menorah returned, free, redeemed, reunited, as were the Zionists, with that place that offered the fruitful realization of nation and self. This menorah, then, denied the permanence of exile, as did messianic beliefs, and bore witness to the generations of absence by bringing them to a close.[2]

In case the message of the menorah and like symbols was too subtle, the pavilion included more direct displays of the Zionist narrative of history. Stonemasons carved the most important dates in the Zionist narrative of Jewish history on the entranceway of the pavilion. The dates began with 2000 BC ("Abraham goes up to the land of the Jordan"), continued through the return of the Jews to Palestine from exile in Egypt,

---

[1] Samuel Halperin, *The Political World of American Zionism* (Silver Spring, MD: Information Dynamics, Inc., 1985), 118.

[2] Don Handelman and Lea Shamgar-Handelman, "Shaping Time: The Choice of the National Emblem of Israel," in *Culture through Time: Anthropological Approaches*, ed. Emiko Ohnuki-Tierney (Stanford, CA: Stanford University Press, 1990), 223.

Babylon, and Assyria, and ended with the Zionist reconstruction of the Jewish nation in the modern period ("1896: 'The Jewish State' published by Theodor Herzl," "1922: U.S. endorses national home"). Once inside the pavilion, visitors had to ascend a "staircase of rising immigration," which was inscribed with the names and dates of Jewish settlements. Visitors then entered the exhibition halls themselves, including one that provided the focal point of the pavilion: animated dioramas depicting "the transformation of a backward and neglected land into a thriving modern country by the devoted labors of heroic Chalutzim [pioneers]." As visitors watched, Haifa, Tel Aviv, and Esdraelon were transformed from a "tiny village," a "stretch of sandy beach," and a "marshy waste" into "a modern seaport," "the great metropolis it is today," and "a fertile cultivated valley." "For centuries this ancient land lay barren and neglected, ravaged by wars fought over its holy sites," guides recited, following their prescribed text.

In these dioramas you will see how the countryside had grown arid because of the drying up of wells and springs, how sand dunes covered fields once fruitful, hills stood bare of timber, valleys were marshy with the unguided waters of streams which once had nourished grain and fruit-trees. A primitive population lived a semi-nomadic life in this land, which could barely provide them with a meager sustenance.... Into this land came Jewish settlers, inspired with the hope of establishing there a new home for the oppressed.

To ensure visitors understood exhibits such as these as their designers intended them to be understood, organizers distributed booklets and posted labels.

It would seem that the message of the pavilion would have been clear to all who visited it. But since Yishuv leaders felt the need to placate diverse groups with divergent goals and took them into their councils, much of the meaning of the pavilion was muddled. Take, for example, the issue of how to portray the relationship of Jewish settlers and the indigenous inhabitants of Palestine – an issue that caused problems for the pavilion organizers from the start and set representatives of the Yishuv against both non-Zionists and American Zionists. The jurist Louis Brandeis, who was closely identified with American Zionism, weighed in on the issue early. Brandeis and his allies advocated using the pavilion to present Zionism as a Pilgrim-style "mission in the wilderness" and Zionists as representatives of the "civilized" world bringing enlightenment to the far reaches of the globe. Brandeis thus argued that displays should show how life expectancy among Arabs in Palestine had increased following Zionist immigration, or how the Arab economy in Palestine had improved. "We must show something of the effort made by Zionists to cultivate Arab-Jewish goodwill," his representative on the planning board wrote, "we must have statistical as well as visual evidence of how the Zionist work in Palestine has benefitted the Arabs, and we must also indicate our vision as one aiming at Jewish-Arab friendship and cooperation."

The political department of the Jewish Agency treated the utopian visions of Brandeis and his associates with a mixture of bemusement and horror. This was, they argued, to be a *Jewish* Palestine Pavilion, not a Palestine Pavilion. Moshe Shertok of the political department was adamant. Shertok made it clear to Brandeis that Jews had *not* come to Palestine for the purpose of improving the lot of Arabs; rather, they had come to find national self-expression. The Arabs of Palestine, Shertok wrote, were free to find their own national self-expression in Iraq, Arabia, and Trans-Jordan. After all, Palestine had never been and was not now a "national center" of the Arabs.

For all Shertok's bluster, the Yishuv Zionists could not afford to alien-ate American Zionists. Yishuv Zionists needed the Americans' financial support and needed them to persuade the American government to play a more active role in Palestine. Thus, a compromise was reached: The two sides agreed that exhibits should recount the history of Anglo-American support for Jewish political rights in Palestine, compare the Arab condition before Zionist immigration to the Arab condition after, point out that Palestine was never an Arab country "politically or even culturally," and demonstrate that Palestine could comfortably hold all the Jews of the diaspora if they chose to emigrate there. Most impor-tant, both sides agreed that the portrayal of the indigenous inhabitants of Palestine should be subdued.

Ironically, it was the design team itself that placed Arab-Yishuv rela-tions at center stage. Whereas board members associated with American Zionism advocated a pavilion design that would have as its "*leitmo-tif*. . . the universal meaning of the civilization that is being born on the shores of the Mediterranean," the political department of the Jewish Agency had charged the architect it selected to showcase "authentically

16. The Jewish Palestine Pavilion at the 1939–40 New York World's Fair. In the background, the pointed Trylon and spherical Perisphere, the symbols of the fair. (Source: From the collection of the author)

Palestinian" design elements. The architect therefore designed the pavilion in what he considered to be the most authentically Palestinian design scheme he could imagine: a modernist interpretation of a "tower and stockade" settlement. Tower and stockade settlements were a relatively recent innovation in Palestine. Zionist settlers began constructing them during the Great Revolt in those areas of Palestine where the Yishuv sought to expand its presence. Their design was purely utilitarian: Threatened by attack from the indigenous inhabitants, Jewish settlers hastily erected a rampart enclosing prefabricated shelters. Overlooking the garrison stood a central tower housing a searchlight that scanned the countryside, probing for "bedouin" and "terrorists" bent on mischief. By the late 1930s, the tower and stockade had become a key symbol for residents of the Yishuv. As the pioneering spirit popularly associated with the second and third aliyot surrendered to the urban-orientation of the fourth and fifth aliyot, the tower and stockade came to encapsulate two myths central to the Yishuv and its supporters: Jewish Palestine as an outpost of civilization in a savage land, and the Zionist settler, with rifle in one hand and plow in the other, as heroic ideal.

Although it symbolically concentrated the focus on Arab-Yishuv relations, organizers well understood that the myth of the intrepid pioneer confronting a barren land and the savage "other" would strike a familiar chord with the Americans they hoped to reach. The American director of the pavilion described it as follows:

A group of youngsters, boys and girls, enter hurriedly to take in the Palestine Pavilion while "doing" the Fair. They pause before an expressive photomural showing pioneers prepared to defend a new-built colony. One boy, whose face the distorted vocabulary of the present day would call typically Nordic, turns to his friends and whispers: "That's just like American history. Those pioneers defending their stockades against Arab terrorists are no different from our ancestors fighting off the howling Indians."

As if the representation of the indigenous inhabitants of Palestine was not enough of a problem, organizers faced another representational nightmare of equal magnitude: the portrayal of women in the pavilion. Although the Yishuv leadership wanted to display the social revolution that Labor Zionism was bringing to Jewish Palestine, they feared estranging socially conservative non-Jewish visitors to the pavilion as well as American Zionist and non-Zionist Jews who were uncomfortable with the social agenda of the second and third aliyot.

Women had provided crucial support to the Zionist movement in the United States at a time when support for organized Zionism in general was declining: During the 1920s, Hadassah, the American Zionist women's organization committed to raising money for health and welfare projects in Palestine, more than tripled its membership. During the same period, the Zionist Organization of America lost more than half its members. During the 1930s, Hadassah membership expanded another threefold. The organization owed a large share of its success to its single-minded commitment to charitable activities and its unwillingness to participate in doctrinal disputes that divided much of organized Zionism. By engaging in "gender-appropriate" activities for a cause that was nonetheless "progressive," and by standing above the fray, Hadassah commanded a base that was both broad and ideologically diffuse. The influence and reputation of Hadassah and likeminded women's organizations in the Jewish community and the financial support they provided the pavilion alerted designers to the danger of privileging the "new Jewish Palestinian woman" by portraying her as the sole model for emulation and a symbol of the Yishuv as social laboratory.

The attitude toward women and the "women's question" expressed through the pavilion project was thus equivocal. On the one hand, the designers integrated into the pavilion images of women as selfless helpmates in the colonization of Palestine, picturing them as nurturers, domestic handworkers, educators, and the transmitters of culture. The designers represented Hadassah with a statue of a nurse holding a child, the Women's League for Palestine with a girl at work on a handloom, and the Pioneer Women's Organization with a display of handicrafts tooled in trade schools built by the organization for poor immigrant girls. This effort to portray women in "conventional" roles was augmented by the designers' attempt to appeal to female visitors as consumers. "The Palestine Pavilion's exhibit includes many items that fascinate feminine visitors," a publicity release announced. "A beautiful exhibit of handmade jewelry has proved very attractive, and the display of Palestinian-made cooking utensils, canned goods, leather goods, and clothing is usually surrounded by admiring women."

On the other hand, photomurals and guidebooks prepared under the supervision of the political department of the Jewish Agency depicted women in a very different manner, rendering them as exemplars of the social transformation taking place in Palestine. Promotional releases likewise approved by the Jewish Agency portrayed women as pioneers who "fought a double fight, for not only have they had to fight the vicissitudes of pioneer life, but they have had to fight for the right to share those hardships with men." The releases went on to cite those who "blazed the trails for women" by planting fields, laying bricks, building roads, painting walls, manning ships, bearing rifles, and spilling their blood.

The manner in which pavilion organizers punted on the issue of depicting women's roles in "Jewish Palestine" for an American audience is perhaps best illustrated by the attempt to find a suitable "chief of guides" from among Yishuv women. According to the plan submitted by the pavilion's publicity director, the ideal candidate not only should have provided invaluable service to her kibbutz or to the defense corps ("if they have girls in it"), but also should be the most attractive young woman in Palestine, chosen in a beauty contest. "But for heaven's sake," the director warned, "don't let them talk you into accepting a middle-aged crone just because she is the wife or relative of some big shot."

The Zionists who acted as the principal designers and managers of the pavilion were not unaware of the mixed messages the pavilion was sending and sought to overcome the problem in two ways. First, they swathed the pavilion in signs of nationhood – the Zionist ("national") flag, an honor guard of chalutzim, and the like – to such an extent that, in the words of the chief architect, "They don't say in New York, 'Let us go to the Palestine Pavilion but let us go to Palestine' because they see in the Pavilion a piece of Palestine soil." Second, they sponsored demonstrations and ceremonies at the pavilion. The largest ceremony was held to mark the opening of the pavilion – an event that coincided with the public announcement of the British White Paper of 1939. Taking advantage of the timing of the British announcement, pavilion organizers transformed the ceremony into a protest rally against British policy and a reaffirmation of American Jewish support for the Yishuv. Albert Einstein, whose scientific achievements, cosmopolitanism, and inchoate, sentimental support for Zionism made him the personification of the movement's commitment to progress and modernity, was a featured speaker.

In the end, it was the very White Paper the demonstrators protested, not a mere pavilion, that did the most to promote Zionist outreach in the Jewish community. As discussed in the previous chapter, the White Paper undercut the position of those who favored a Jewish presence in Palestine but balked at the idea of a Jewish state. As Zionists argued, only the establishment of an independent Jewish commonwealth in Palestine that controlled immigration and institutional development could ensure the viability of Jewish Palestine.

Nevertheless, the very diffuseness of the message offered by the pavilion may have benefitted the Zionist movement more than any directed message could have. At a time when the Zionist Organization of America counted about 28,000 members and the number of those Americans who contributed fifty cents or more was approximately 82,000, the pavilion attracted from 2.5 to four million visitors, making it the fourth most popular at the fair. Significantly, although about a third of those who toured the pavilion in the second season had previously toured it in the first, 87 percent of the first year's visitors had avoided the hall that the Yishuv planners had intended to be the pavilion's centerpiece – the hall that contained the dioramas. According to one designer, the purpose of the hall was to disseminate a "controlled message to produce enthusiasm in directions wanted." This objective was probably not lost on the visitors, who refused to be fooled twice. By the close of the fair, even the political department of the Jewish Agency took notice of the benefits of presenting Zionism as a "big tent." Immediately after the New York World's Fair closed, they ordered the reopening of the exact same pavilion at the Cleveland International Exposition so that it might become a focal point for Zionist organizing in the American Midwest.

THE EXPERIENCE OF EXILE: PALESTINIAN POETRY
AND ISRAELI POLITICS

When the novelist Willa Cather asked poet W. B. Yeats to contribute a poem to an anthology she was putting together in the middle of World War I, he replied with one entitled, appropriately enough, "On Being Asked for a War Poem." In it, Yeats put on record his opinion about the relationship between poetry and politics:

> I think it better that in times like these
> A poet's mouth be silent, for in truth
> We have no gift to set a statesman right;
> He has had enough of meddling who can please
> A young girl in the indolence of her youth,
> Or an old man upon a winter's night.

On Yeats's death a little more than two decades later, W. H. Auden wrote a tribute poem in which he repeated Yeats's sentiment:

> For poetry makes nothing happen: it survives
> In the valley of its saying where executives
> Would never want to tamper, it flows south
> From ranches of isolation and the busy griefs,
> Raw towns that we believe and die in; it survives
> A way of happening, a mouth.

Apparently, Israeli politicians never got the message. In 2000, proposed changes in the Israeli school curriculum created a stir that threatened to topple the country's coalition government. At the center of this controversy was a poem that education reformers sought to include in Israeli textbooks. The poem was written by Mahmoud Darwish, whom many Palestinians consider to be their poet laureate.

Not all poetry written by Palestinians would provoke the same controversy as the one chosen by the reformers. Palestinian poetry is diverse. It addresses the usual range of themes poetry addresses, such as love, loss, nature, and spirituality. Nevertheless, Palestinian poets, like Supreme Court justices, wake up every morning and read the newspaper. Since the nakba was a defining event in Palestinian collective memory, it should come as no surprise that Palestinian poets would represent the usual themes of poetry through the image of exile or depict the experience of exile through those themes. As a result, there has emerged a genre of Palestinian poetry that might be called "poetry of exile." This poetry has not only been shaped by Palestinian collective memory, it has helped shape that memory.

Palestinian poets have reacted to the experience of exile in a number of ways. For some, the experience induces nostalgia. In their work, they commonly represent Palestine as paradise lost. Take the following selection from the poem "I Love You More,"[3] written by Abu Salma (1907–80). Abu Salma came from the town of Tulkarm in the occupied West Bank. He practiced law in Haifa until 1948 and eventually ended up in Damascus.

> The more I fight for you, the more I love you!
> What land except this land of musk and amber?
> What horizon but this one defines my world?
> The branch of my life turns greener when I uphold you
> And my wing, Oh Palestine, spreads wide over the peaks.
>
> Has the lemon tree been nurtured by our tears?
> No more do birds flutter among the high pines,
> or stars gaze vigilantly over Mt. Carmel.
> The little orchards weep for us, gardens grow desolate,
> the vines are forever saddened...
> Oh Palestine! Nothing more beautiful, more precious, more
> pure....

Other poets have approached the experience of exile fatalistically, using it to explore the afflictions of alienation and tragic loss that they present as essential components of the human condition. It was in this

---

[3] Salma Khadra Jayyusi, ed., *Anthology of Modern Palestinian Literature* (New York: Columbia University Press, 1992), 97.

spirit that the Jerusalem poet Yusuf 'Abd al-'Aziz (b. 1956) wrote "The Traveler":[4]

> He visits the station,
> buys a ticket, and goes away.
> He dreams of the unblinking sun,
> of inns by the sea,
> and the woman like a lily.
> He drinks her kiss
> in bed
> near a quiet window.
>
> Always he had gathered his days
> as the sea gathers its waves at twilight.
> He watched them closely, then departed
> for inscrutable destinations.
> – Did you find the right departure date?
> – No, I found the road that has severed the river from
>   its source.

Many Palestinian poets reject such fatalism. Among them are those who were children in 1948 or were born after the nakba. The anger expressed in their poetry is, of course, aimed primarily at the Israelis, but it frequently is aimed in another direction as well: How was it possible, they ask their parents' generation, that you could so readily flee Palestine and surrender our birthright? This anger comes through in a poem by Sameeh al-Qasim entitled "Anti-Aircraft Amulets."[5] Al-Qasim was nine years old at the time of the nakba. Being Druze (that is, a member of a religious sect that branched off from mainstream Islam in the eleventh century) and not, strictly speaking, Palestinian, he found employment as a teacher in Israeli public schools – until he was dismissed because of his politics.

> They taught me that
> The affairs of earth
> Are in the hands of heaven
> They taught me that He gives life
> Or death
> To whomever He chooses

---

[4] Salma Khadra Jayyusi, ed., *Anthology of Modern Palestinian Literature* (New York: Columbia University Press, 1992), 83.

[5] Naseer Aruri and Edmund Ghareeb, *Enemy of the Sun: Poetry of Palestinian Resistance* (Washington, DC: Drum and Spear, 1970), 44.

They taught me to obey the prophets
Without asking
Who are they?
And what have they done for the wretched?
Defeated father – humbled mother
To hell with
My inheritance of tribal teachings,
My savage rites.
I cut the stupid customs
From the roots and spit my hate
My shame
Into the faces of the devout
The holy ones
I kick the garbage of my defeat and
My humility
Into the face of the dervishes –
The barking half men – the office holders.

Finally, there are poets who have taken on the role of witness. Although the phrase "role of witness" originally referred to those Christians who would testify to their faith among the heathen, it is now commonly applied to anyone who puts himself forward as a guardian of memory to prick the conscience of the world. Yusuf 'Abd al-'Aziz takes on this role in his poem "The Shaqeef Moon."[6] The poem derives its title from the site where for a time thirty-three Palestinians held off Israeli forces during the 1982 invasion of Lebanon. All thirty-three died in the engagement.

For an evening laden with prophets
for thirty-three gardens
for the red seed bursting in the rock
for the rock that pierces the clouds
and for the free sun.

I shall tune my strings to the wind and sing.
For those who burned like morning birds
I shall sing.
The blood that springs from their bodies flows from
mine.

[6] Salma Khadra Jayyusi, ed., *Anthology of Modern Palestinian Literature* (New York: Columbia University Press, 1992), 86.

All this brings us back to the controversy stirred by the attempt to include a poem by Mahmoud Darwish in Israeli textbooks. The state school system of Israel, established in 1953 by the State Education Law, was designed to inculcate "the values of Jewish culture," "love of the homeland," and "loyalty to the Jewish state." David Ben-Gurion referred to the State Education Law as one of the country's two "supreme laws" – a law that, along with the Law of Return, embodied the historic mission of the Jewish state. (We shall discuss the Law of Return in the next chapter). For Ben-Gurion, education was essential to the project of *mamlachtiyut* (statism), the centralization of power and authority in the hands of the Israeli state.

Benzion Dinur, one of the founders of the so-called Jerusalem school of history, was the principal designer of the first curriculum. The Jerusalem school of history consisted of a group of historians who constructed a historical narrative of Jewish history based on two assumptions. First, they believed that Jews are a unique and distinct people who remained united during their exile from Palestine by the belief that they would some day be restored to Zion. Second, they believed that the establishment of the State of Israel was the realization of a thousand-year-old dream. Accordingly, the curriculum designed by Dinur began with the Kingdom of David and culminated with Israel's "War of Independence" in 1948.

Although historians revised the curriculum in the 1970s, it was not until 1991 that the government commissioned an entirely new one. The new curriculum reflected changes in the discipline of history, on the one hand, and changes in Israeli politics and society, on the other. By 1991, no historians believed that nationalism existed before the modern period, and those historians who believed that nations existed before the modern period had been put on the defensive. These beliefs ran counter to the assumptions of the Jerusalem school. By 1991, historians had also challenged the tidiness of the historical narrative provided by the Jerusalem school. Not only had the work of the New Historians thrown the founding myths of Israel into question, social scientists were questioning the value of writing national histories in general. National histories, they argued, exalted the voices of the dominant layers of society at the expense of those they dominated (minorities, the poor, women, etc.), ignored the fluidity and "hybridity" of cultures, overemphasized consensus and downplayed conflict, and presented the establishment of whatever nation-state they glorified as the inevitable endpoint of history.

The complaints lodged by social scientists in the 1980s were difficult to ignore for two reasons. First, Israeli citizens not of European descent were increasingly making their voices heard. These included the *mizrahis* (Jews who immigrated to Israel from Arab lands after the establishment of the State of Israel) and the Arab citizens of Israel (those Palestinians who were living inside the borders of Israel in 1948 and refused to leave their homes). Just as these groups could no longer be ignored in Israeli society, they could not be ignored in Israeli textbooks and the Israeli national narrative. Furthermore, many felt that the educational curriculum had to reflect the changing status of Israel as the conflict itself began to shift into a new phase of its history. Although reformers began working on the new curriculum two years before the Oslo Accord, it was becoming increasingly apparent that defining the conflict as a dispute between Arab states and Israel was no longer adequate. In 1987, Palestinians in the occupied territories launched an open revolt known as the (first) intifada, and a year later the Palestine Liberation Organization went on record in support of a two-state solution. For some Israelis, the possibility of a final settlement no longer appeared hopeless. Indeed, some Israeli academics began to discuss the possibility of a "post-Zionist Israel" – an Israel devoid of its claim to represent the special mission and historical embodiment of the Jewish nation, an Israel comfortable with being just another small Mediterranean country living at peace with its neighbors.

Not everyone in the Israeli educational establishment and the Israeli government saw the appeal of curriculum reform, educational "multiculturalism," or the possibility of a post-Zionist Israel. A poet chosen by the reformers for inclusion in the curriculum provided conservatives with an opening that was too good to ignore. The poet had once written a poem entitled, "Those Who Pass between Fleeting Words,"[7] which contains the following lines:

> It is time for you to be gone
> Live wherever you like, but do not live among us.
> It is time for you to be gone

---

[7] Mahmoud Darwish, "Those Who Pass Between Fleeting Words," in *Intifada: The Palestinian Uprising Against Israel: Occupation*, ed. Zachary Lockman and Joel Beinin (Boston: South End Press, 1989), 26–7.

Die wherever you like, but do not die among us
For we have work to do in our land.

... get out of our land
our continent, our sea
our wheat, our salt, our sore
our everything, and get out.

Conservatives argued that the poem expresses an implacable Palestinian hostility to Israel. The author of the poem, Mahmoud Darwish, answered their criticism by asserting that the "our land" from which the Israelis must go is the occupied territories.

Although Darwish's rebuttal might seem a bit disingenuous to an outsider, his political stance is certainly not as simplistic as his critics have made it out to be. Mahmoud Darwish was born in 1942 in the village of al-Barweh, where his father was a farmer. Zionist forces destroyed the village in 1948. His family initially fled across the border to Lebanon, then returned to the Galilee region. Darwish worked as a journalist for the Communist Party newspaper in Haifa. In 1971, he moved to Beirut, where he remained until the Israeli invasion of 1982, at which time he fled to Paris. After he had left Haifa, the Israeli government banned him from the country. It lifted the ban in 1996, but even then he was only allowed to live in the territories under the control of the Palestinian Authority.

Beginning in the 1970s, Darwish had acted as an advisor to the chairman of the Palestine Liberation Organization, Yasir Arafat. From 1978 to 1993, he was a member of the PLO Executive Committee, which acts, at least in theory, as the central committee of the organization. Nevertheless, Darwish could never be considered a "kept poet." Once, when Arafat complained that Palestinians were an ungrateful people, Darwish snapped back at the chairman, "Find yourself another people, then." Darwish resigned from the executive committee after Arafat signed on to the Oslo Accord because, as he put it, "There can be no peace between master and slave." He explained his stand against Oslo in a poem he wrote to Arafat, entitled "Reality Is Two-Faced, Snow Is Black":[8]

Who will strike our flags: us or them? And who
Will proclaim the "peace accord" to us, O King of extinction?

---

[8] Mahmoud Darwish, *Ahda ᶜashara kawkaban* (Beirut: Dar al-Jadid, 1995), 19.

Everything has already been prepared for us. Who will erase
Our names from our identity cards: you or they? And
   who will proclaim among us
The official account of our wandering in the desert:
   "We could not raise the siege
So let us surrender the keys of our Paradise to the
   Minister of Peace, and be saved . . ."

Like Yeats and Auden, Darwish has no illusions about the power of
poetry. In an interview with *Newsweek* in 2000, Darwish stated, "Poems
can't establish a state. But they can establish a metaphorical homeland
in the minds of the people. I think my poems have built some houses in
this landscape."[9]

Many Israelis have found Darwish's politics galling. Others seem to
object to the fact that Darwish not only cloaks the Palestinians with the
mantle of victimization in his poetry, he has no qualms about parading
them in that mantle before the eyes of a people who numerically rank
among the greatest victims of the twentieth century themselves. But if
Israelis were to look beyond the poem "Those Who Pass between Fleeting Words" to a poem entitled "Eleven Planets in the Last Andalusian
Sky,"[10] they would see a poet whose symbolic world closely approxi-
mates their own. The "eleven stars" of the title are the eleven stars seen
by Joseph in a vision related to his grandfather Isaac. The story is related
in the Qur'an. Like Joseph, Darwish invests himself with prophetic powers. "The last Andalusian sky" alludes to the expulsion of the Moors
from Spain (*al-andalus* in Arabic); the Spanish expelled the Jews at
the same time. Here, of course, Darwish uses the expulsion from the
earthly paradise of Spain to represent the expulsion of the Palestinians
from their own earthly paradise. Nevertheless, should committed Zionists read the poem in the context of their own historic memory, they
would have no difficulty understanding its sentiment:

On the last evening
we tear our days down from the trellisses

---

9 "The Politics of Poetry," *Newsweek*, 20 March 2000.
10 Mahmoud Darwish, "Eleven Planets in the Last Andalusian Sky," in *The Adam of Two Edens*, ed. Daniel Moore and Munir Akash (Syracuse, NY: Syracuse University Press, 2000), 147–70.

tally the ribs we carry away with us
and the ribs we leave behind.

On the last evening
we bid farewell to nothing,
we've no time to finish,
everything's left as it is,
places change dreams the way they
change casts of characters.

Suddenly we can no longer be lighthearted,
this place is about to play host to nothing.

On the last evening
we contemplate mountains surrounding the clouds,
invasion and counter-invasion,
the ancient era handing our door keys over
to a new age.
Enter, O invaders, come, enter our houses,
drink the sweet wine of our Andalusian songs!
We are night at midnight,
no horseman galloping toward us
from the safety of that last call to prayer
to deliver the dawn
Our tea is hot and green – so drink!
Our pistachios are ripe and fresh – so eat!
The beds are green with new cedarwood
    – give in to your drowsiness!
After such a long siege, sleep on the soft down of our dreams!
Fresh sheets, scents at the door, and many mirrors.
Enter our mirrors so we can vacate the premises completely!

Later we'll look up what was recorded in our history
    about yours in faraway lands.

Then we'll ask ourselves,
"Was Andalusia
here or there? On earth
or only in poems?"

SUGGESTIONS FOR FURTHER READING

Aburish, Said K. *Children of Bethany: The Story of a Palestinian Family*. London:
    I. B. Tauris, 1988. Memoir of Palestinian life spanning several generations.

Barghouti, Mourid. *I Saw Ramallah*. Translated by Ahdaf Soueif. New York: American University in Cairo Press, 2000. Memoir of exiled Palestinian poet.

Berkowitz, Michael. *Western Jewry and the Zionist Project, 1914–1931*. Cambridge: Cambridge University Press, 1997. The story of the evolution of Zionism outside eastern Europe continues.

Darwish, Mahmoud. *The Adam of Two Edens: Poems*. Edited by Munir Akash and Daniel Moore. Syracuse, NY: Syracuse University Press, 2000. Good introduction to the poetry of Palestine's poet laureate.

Gelvin, James L. "Zionism and the Representation of 'Jewish Palestine' at the New York World's Fair, 1939–1940." *The International History Review* 22 (March 2000). Examination of the relationship between Yishuv and American Zionists and the construction of Zionism through symbols.

Jayyusi, Salma Khadra, ed. *Anthology of Modern Palestinian Literature*. New York: Columbia University Press, 1992. Contains poetry, short stories, excerpts from larger works, etc.

Mendelsohn, Ezra. *On Modern Jewish Politics*. New York: Oxford University Press, 1993. Good overview of the evolution of various strands of Jewish thought in the United States.

8

THE ARAB-ISRAELI CONFLICT

The 1948 war between Zionists and Palestinians, then between Israel and Arab states, left two unresolved issues. First, although the State of Israel received the recognition of most other states in the world, the surrounding Arab states refused to grant it recognition. Representatives from those states balked at confirming Israeli sovereignty by sitting opposite their Israeli counterparts at state-to-state negotiations held to resolve the dispute. And to further isolate and increase the pressure on Israel, the Arab League imposed a diplomatic and economic boycott on the new state soon after the war. The second unresolved issue – which provided Arab states with the justification for their refusal to accord Israel recognition – was the problem of the Palestinian refugees.

Israel attained its independence during the great wave of decolonization that began after World War II. When the United Nations was founded in 1945, it included 51 states as members. By 1965, there were 118 members. But Israel differed from other states that achieved independence during this period in three ways. First, most other newly independent states had to adapt institutions imposed by a colonial power or create those institutions from scratch. Israel, on the other hand, entered its period of independence with a strong heritage of institutions built from the bottom up during the previous half century. Furthermore, whereas other newly independent states had to subjugate recalcitrant groups living within their borders or win them over to the nationalism of the ruling elites, Israel had reduced its most recalcitrant internal adversaries – the Palestinians – to a manageable minority, leaving the Jewish majority to debate the finer points of a commonly held nationalist ideology, Zionism. Although it is true that political debate in Israel has often resembled a bloodsport, the fractiousness that divided other emerging states was kept within limits. Finally, unlike other states that achieved their independence during the era of decolonization, Israel could draw on a worldwide diaspora for political and economic support. Indeed, as we have seen, by the time of independence the Zionist movement had already worked out a division of labor between statebuilders in Palestine and their benefactors in North America and western Europe. Israel thus had an economic security blanket available to few other new states.

Rather than comparing Israel to other states that emerged during the period of decolonization, then, the Israeli-American historian Jehuda Reinharz has suggested that it might be more accurate to compare Israel during its immediate postindependence period to the United States during its period of mass immigration, 1880–1920. Immigrants who flooded into Israel in the mid-twentieth century, like immigrants who had flooded into the United States earlier, found political and economic institutions already in place. Although their arrival in such large numbers certainly modified existing institutions, the immigrants did not have to build those institutions themselves. Furthermore, they found upon their arrival a political system with established "rules of the game."

The first ten years of Israel's existence might be thus considered a period of radical demographic change and more subtle institutional modification. The demographic change was the result of two factors. Most obviously, there was the flight of the Palestinians. After the war, Israel repatriated only a tiny number of the Palestinians who had fled – a gesture it made to win the goodwill of the international community. (Documents recently found reveal that United States president Harry S Truman grew increasingly impatient at Israeli reluctance to repatriate refugees and threatened to withdraw American support for Israel if the new state did not take in at least a token number as a sign of good faith.) The issue of repatriation and restitution is a complex one that has yet to be resolved. Israel is a Jewish state. In 1950, the Israeli parliament, the *Knesset*, passed the Law of Return, which stipulated in its first article, "Every Jew has the right to immigrate to the country." Israel could hardly retain its Jewish character if it extended the right of citizenship to large numbers of non-Jews, such as Palestinians.

Making the problem of repatriation and restitution all the more complex was the fact that the Israeli government took over approximately 94 percent of the property abandoned by the Palestinians who fled and distributed it to Jewish Israelis. Some Palestinians attempted to reclaim

17. A view of mainstreet in the Jewish quarter of Fez, Morocco during the 1930s. As late as the early 1950s, approximately thirteen thousand Jews lived in Fez. Twenty years later, only a thousand remained. (Source: From the collection of the author)

their property by crossing the armistice lines to harvest crops or carry away moveable property to their new homes. Others crossed the lines to commit acts of sabotage. The Israeli government did not differentiate between the two groups. To deal with the problem of "infiltration," it launched reprisal raids against the states from which the infiltration occurred. In part, the Israeli government adopted this policy to encourage the emergence of the "new Zionist man." In the words of the first prime minister of Israel, David Ben-Gurion, "We must straighten [the Israelis'] backs and demonstrate that those who attack them will not get away unpunished, that they are residents of a sovereign state which is responsible for their safety." The second reason reprisal was adopted as a policy was that the Israeli government felt that this strategy would induce the Arab states to police their borders more diligently. Obviously, the policy of reprisals did little to endear Israel to its neighbors. In 1953, an Israeli raid into Jordan resulted in sixty-six civilian casualties. In 1955, an Israeli raid on an Egyptian military post in Gaza left thirty-eight Egyptian soldiers dead and about forty wounded. Both raids were led by future Israeli prime minister Ariel Sharon.

The other factor that changed the demographic balance of Israel was immigration. During the first four years of Israel's existence, approximately seven hundred thousand new immigrants arrived. This doubled the state's population. Another seven hundred thousand arrived over the next fifteen years. A large number of the new immigrants came from Muslim countries. Some Arab Jews immigrated to Israel at the urging of Israeli Zionists. Others came because they were persecuted at home. For example, beginning in 1947, the Iraqi government passed discriminatory legislation against Iraqi Jews. This legislation restricted Jewish freedom of movement and required Jews to put up bonds if they wanted to leave Iraq. In 1948, discrimination against Jews became systematic in Iraq. There were anti-Jewish riots in Baghdad, probably encouraged by the Iraqi government (although some historians, such as Elie Kedourie, claim that Israeli agents instigated or fanned the flames of the riots); Jews were arrested; and Jews who worked for public concerns (ports, railroads, etc.) were dismissed from their jobs. There was even a show trial and execution of a prominent Jewish Iraqi business-man. Most of the Jewish community of Iraq saw the writing on the wall. Over a hundred and twenty thousand Iraqi Jews emigrated to Israel. Some were Zionists, others not. They were joined by a hundred and sixty-five thousand Jews from Morocco, thirty-one thousand from Libya, forty thousand from Yemen (flown to Israel in "Operation Magic Carpet"), eighty thousand from Egypt, ten thousand from Syria, and so on. Jewish communities that had existed sometimes for centuries, sometimes for millennia, disappeared seemingly overnight. By the year 2000, only about five thousand Jews remained in the entire Arab world.

It appeared at first that Israel had absorbed Jews from the Arab world without a hitch. During the 1960s, however, Israeli Jews of Arab descent began to complain about institutional discrimination, and like other ethnic groups around the world, they organized themselves against it. Their complaints were numerous. Immediately after their immigration to Israel, for example, many were housed in tent cities whereas Jewish immigrants from Europe received housing allotments. They also complained of discrimination in employment and educational opportunities, which resulted in a lower standard of living than that enjoyed by European Jews, and of the patronizing attitudes of the Israeli establishment, which presumed that Arab immigrants were in need of "civilizing." Many expressed their dissatisfaction by joining the right-wing parties of the Likud bloc (a coalition that did not become a unified party until 1988). The bloc seemed to include almost every group in

Israeli society that harbored grievances against the "Labor aristocracy" or felt excluded from the mainstream. Its appeal to Arab Jews stemmed from its more bellicose stand against the very Arab countries from which the immigrants came and its populism and nonsocialist ideology, which was in harmony with the petit-bourgeois sentiments of many of the immigrants.

Nevertheless, Labor Zionists remained in control of the institutions of state. Because the Histadrut continued to distribute benefits to its members and play an important role in the labor market (enterprises associated with the Histadrut employed a quarter of the Israeli workforce), the ranks of Labor Zionism continued to swell. As a result, the institutions of the new state closely resembled the institutions that had governed the Yishuv during the mandate period – institutions created during the second and third aliyot.

Of course, these institutions had to be modified to meet the needs of a sovereign state. Although a network of voluntary organizations had assumed wide-ranging responsibilities during the prestatehood period, now it was up to the state to coordinate their activities or take on their functions. The state did this to ensure that it and it alone would be the focal point of loyalty. This was the rationale behind the doctrine of mamlachtiyut. Thus, while the Israeli government allowed the Histadrut to continue to provide social services (such as the settlement of new immigrants), it insisted that the Histadrut surrender its educational functions to the government. To ensure the state possessed a monopoly on the legitimate use of violence, it amalgamated the party-affiliated militias into an Israeli army, the Israel Defense Forces (IDF). The government's power in this matter was soon put to the test. In June 1948, the S.S. Altalena arrived on the coast of Israel with a supply of weapons and ammunition destined for the Irgun. When Irgun leader Menachem Begin refused to turn over the weapons, Ben-Gurion had the ship shelled. Sixteen Irgun fighters died in the confrontation, but the point was made.

Centralizing authority in the hands of the state may have made good political sense, but it was expensive. Israel was, and continues to be, heavily dependent on a form of income known as "rent." Social scientists define rent as income derived from sources other than internal taxation. Although Israel does tax its population at a level in line with other social democracies, it has also benefitted from contributions and investment from Jews outside the country. To encourage private contributions, the Israeli government severed its official connection to the Jewish Agency and the Jewish National Fund. This enabled American Jews to make tax-deductible contributions to those institutions. In addition, Israel has benefitted from grants and loans from foreign governments. These began early and of course continue to the present. In 1953, the West German government pledged over $700 million in reparations for the Holocaust. Soon thereafter France began to supply military assistance. American assistance began in 1949 with a loan from the Export-Import Bank. For the past quarter century, the United States government has contributed about $3 billion in direct aid annually, along with close to $3 billion in indirect aid (loan write-offs, special grants). Since foreign aid and contributions go directly to the state and to state-affiliated organizations, Israel's dependence on rent has enabled the state to assume a dominant role in the economy and maintain the socialist-style institutions and benefits associated with the second and third aliyot. Only at the end of the 1980s, when the free market doctrines of Reaganomics and Thatcherism became the building blocs of the new "globalized" international economy, did the Israeli state begin a slow retreat from its founding social democratic principles.

Israel was not the only state undergoing transition in the Middle East during the immediate post-1948 period. Beginning in the late 1940s, a series of military coups d'etat overturned governments in Syria, Egypt, Iraq, North Yemen, and Libya and threatened the governments of other states in the region. These coups brought to power a new generation of Arab leaders, who over the course of the 1950s and 1960s increasingly championed the policies of anti-imperialism, nonalignment, and state-guided economic development, which were popular throughout the developing world at that time. The most prominent of these leaders was Gamal 'Abd al-Nasser of Egypt.

Nasser was born in 1918 on the outskirts of Alexandria. The son of a postal clerk, he graduated from the Royal Military Academy of Egypt and rose to the rank of major in the Egyptian army. During the 1948 war, Nasser's unit was surrounded by Zionist forces, and he was seriously wounded. For Nasser, as for many of his cohort, the war marked a turning point. Not only did it result in the establishment of an alien presence in their midst, it once again confirmed their worst fears: The corruption of their governments and the backwardness of their societies rendered their states both unwilling and incapable of standing up to imperialism.

According to biographers, it had been Nasser's experience with imperialism that steered the young military officer to politics in the first place. In 1942, while Nasser was stationed in Cairo, the British ambassador delivered an ultimatum to the Egyptian king demanding that the king appoint a British-approved candidate as prime minister. When the king hesitated, the ambassador ordered British tanks to surround the unfortunate monarch's palace. Soon thereafter, Nasser began organizing the Free Officers movement. The Free Officers took power in 1952, and by 1954 Nasser was the undisputed leader of Egypt.

Neither Israel nor the Palestinians was high on the list of Nasser's priorities when he took power. Instead, Nasser focused on consolidating power and negotiating a final treaty with the British that would end Britain's seventy-year military presence in Egypt forever. Egyptian and Israeli representatives even met in secret to negotiate issues of mutual concern. These contacts came to an end in the wake of two incidents. In the summer of 1954, the Egyptian government uncovered a plot by Israeli agents to blow up American and British installations in Cairo. The conspiracy was hatched by the Israeli defense minister, Pinhas Lavon, who assumed that the Americans and British would lay the blame for the attacks on the Egyptian government. The British would then break off negotiations over the withdrawal of British troops from the Suez Canal Zone, and the Americans would refuse to sell arms to Egypt. The "Lavon Affair," worthy of Inspector Clouseau, infuriated Nasser. Then came the Israeli raid into Gaza.

The Israeli raid triggered a chain of events that led first to the Suez War of 1956, then to the 1967 war. In wake of the raid, Nasser turned in earnest to the West for arms. When the West balked, he decided to take his business elsewhere. Declaring Egypt nonaligned, he signed an arms deal with the Eastern Bloc state of Czechoslovakia and, for good measure, further tweaked America's whiskers by granting mainland China – "Red China" – official recognition. In the eyes of the American government, Nasser had clearly crossed the line. Secretary of State John Foster Dulles later went so far as to call him "nothing but a tin-horn Hitler." To teach him and other Third World leaders a lesson about the high cost of disloyalty, the United States government vetoed Egypt's request for a loan from the World Bank to finance the Aswan High Dam. Nasser had staked his reputation on the dam, which promised to revolutionize Egyptian agriculture by regulating the unpredictable flow of the Nile.

It was then that the cash-strapped Nasser hit upon a scheme to kill two birds with one stone: By nationalizing the Suez Canal (of which the British government was majority shareholder), the Egyptian government could simultaneously acquire a cash cow and end the British presence in Egypt once and for all. This was the spark that set off the Suez War.

In the immediate aftermath of the nationalization, Britain, France, and Israel entered into a conspiracy to invade Egypt. The complexity of the conspiracy was matched only by its folly. All three nations harbored grievances against Nasser: the British because he nationalized the canal, the French because he provided material and political support for the Algerian revolutionaries they were fighting, and the Israelis because . . . , well, Nasser was Nasser and Israelis were Israelis. Rather than toppling Nasser, however, the invasion provoked an international outcry. Coming in the wake of the Soviet invasion of Hungary, it outraged the United States because it drew attention away from what should have been a propaganda bonanza for the West. Perhaps more important, the invasion also marked the last hurrah of the old colonial powers in the region before they finally conceded that the torch had been passed to a new power. In the wake of the Suez War, the United States assumed its role as the unrivalled outside power in the Middle East – a role it has played ever since. Under American pressure, Britain, France, and Israel were forced to withdraw their forces. Not only did Nasser remain in power, the invasion raised his political stock in Egypt and throughout the region.

There is a direct line connecting the events of 1956 with those of 1967. As a result of the Suez War, Nasser came to view the West in conspiratorial terms – a view that, as we have seen, was not far from the truth. Because he believed that no Arab state had the capacity to resist the conspiracy of the Western powers on its own, he began to pursue Arab unity actively. In 1958, Egypt merged with Syria to form the United Arab Republic and soon thereafter entered into negotiations to bring Iraq into the union. The breakdown of those negotiations and the withdrawal of Syria from the union in 1961 merely confirmed for Nasser the strength of the conspiracy he was up against. It also confirmed for Nasser the threat to Arab unity posed by Israel, whose very presence divided Arab territory like "a dagger stuck in the heart of the Arab nation." But if Arab nations could not consolidate themselves into a single state, at least they could coordinate their policies. Thus it was that Nasser fell victim to his own rhetoric: When Syria and Israel clashed over Israel's unilateral diversion of the Jordan River in 1964, when the Soviet Union reported (falsely, as it turned out) that Israel was massing troops on the Syrian border in May 1967, Egypt just had to do something. That something turned out to be disastrous not only for Egypt but for Syria, Jordan, and the Palestinians as well. It also resulted in a fundamental change in the nature of the conflict between Israel and the Arab states.

WAR AND DIPLOMACY

On 14 May 1967, Gamal 'Abd al-Nasser placed Egyptian armed forces on maximum alert and sent the Egyptian army into the Sinai. Egyptian newspapers reported that Nasser's actions were a response to information provided by the Soviet Union that Israel was planning to attack Syria. Soon thereafter, the Egyptian government took two steps that escalated tensions dramatically. First, it demanded that the United Nations remove its observers from Egyptian soil. The observers had been stationed on the Egyptian side of the Egyptian-Israeli border since the withdrawal of Israeli troops from the Sinai in 1956. Then Nasser ordered the closing of the Strait of Tiran to Israeli shipping. The strait connected Israel's southern port of Eilat (via the Gulf of Aqaba) to the Red Sea. Since the strait lay off the coast of the Sinai peninsula, Nasser claimed it as Egyptian territorial waters. The Israelis insisted it was an international passage, as did the United States. As a matter of fact, to expedite Israeli withdrawal from the Sinai in 1956, the United States sent Israel an *aide mémoire* (diplomatic memorandum) backing the Israeli government's position. For Israel, the closing of the strait was an act of war.

World War I broke out when European leaders threw caution to the wind and took it upon themselves to revise an already unstable balance of power. Nine decades after the event, historians are still trying to piece together the wrong-headed gambles, erroneous assumptions, and real and imaginary grievances that brought on the catastrophe. Such is the case with the 1967 war. Just what was going through the principals' minds during this crisis will never be known with certainty. What could the Soviets have been thinking when they sent Nasser a false report of an Israeli military buildup on the Syrian border? What could Nasser have been thinking when he used the report – which he apparently knew to be false – as the basis for escalating an already tense situation? Whatever their reasoning, the Soviet report seems to have had the same effect as the famous "blank check" offer of unconditional support the Germans sent the Austrians after the assassination of Archduke Franz Ferdinand. The Egyptians, like the Austrians before them, read the message they received as the endorsement by their stronger ally to raise the stakes.

Some historians argue that Nasser made a deliberate decision to weather the first Israeli blow. He may have believed that by doing so he could isolate Israel diplomatically and gain international support for the Arab military coalition that he had been building since the end of May. If this was the case, it was a miscalculation. In the first hours of the war, Israeli airstrikes destroyed 90 percent of the Egyptian airforce, about 70 percent of the Syrian airforce, and almost all of the Jordanian airforce. In the wide open spaces of the Middle East, whoever controls the air controls the battlefield. The war was over in six days. Not only did the Israeli army prevail, by war's end Israel found itself in control of territory belonging to Arab states – the Sinai Peninsula (belonging to Egypt), the Golan Heights (belonging to Syria), and a narrow strip of land on the Jordanian frontier – as well as the West Bank, the Gaza Strip, and East Jerusalem.

Ironically, Israel's conquest of territory belonging to its neighbors opened up new prospects for resolving the diplomatic stalemate that had frustrated the international community for almost twenty years. In spite of the turmoil of the 1950s, the Arab-Israeli dispute had reached a political impasse before the 1967 war. The war broke that impasse and provided both sides with a completely different set of goals and options. Before the war, the issue lurking in the background for both Israelis and their Arab neighbors had been the continued existence of Israel. On the eve of the war, for example, Nasser had defined the conflict as a "clash of destinies" between Israelis and Arabs. "The issue is . . . the aggression against Palestine that took place in 1948," he told the Egyptian national assembly. "[People] want to confine it to the Strait of Tiran, the United Nations Emergency Force, and the right of passage. We say: We want the rights of the people of Palestine – complete."

After the war, the issue at stake was no longer the existence of Israel. Instead, the return of the territories occupied during the hostilities became the overriding concern for the Arab states. For their part, the

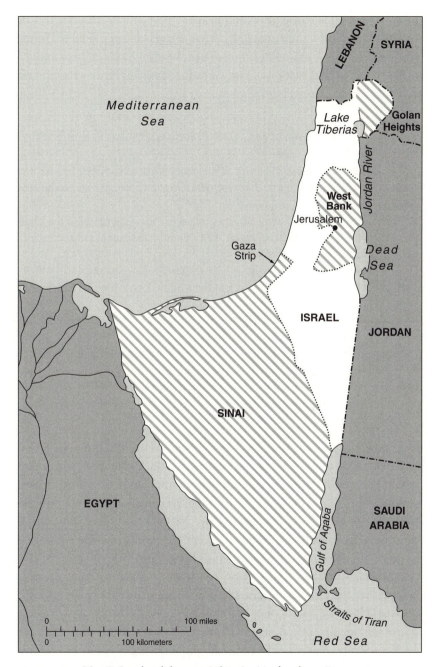

Map 8. Israel and the occupied territories after the 1967 war.

Israelis demanded recognition and peace settlements as the price for the return of land. The exchange of land for peace was embodied in United Nations Security Council Resolution 242, written by the British ambassador to the United Nations, Lord Caradon. United Nations Resolution 242 reads in part as follows:

The Security Council,

Expressing its continued concern with the grave situation in the Middle East,

Emphasizing the inadmissibility of the acquisition of territory by war and the need to work for a just and lasting peace in which every state in the area can live in security,

Emphasizing further that all Member States in their acceptance of the Charter of the United Nations have undertaken a commitment to act in accordance with Article 2 of the Charter,

   1. Affirms that the fulfillment of Charter principles requires the establishment of a just and lasting peace in the Middle East which should include the application of both the following principles:

     (i) Withdrawal of Israel armed forces from territories occupied in the recent conflict;

     (ii) Termination of all claims or states of belligerency and respect for and acknowledgement of the sovereignty, territorial integrity and political independence of every State in the area and their right to live in peace within secure and recognized boundaries free from threats or acts of force.

The Security Council of the United Nations adopted the resolution in November 1967. The Israelis, Egyptians, and Jordanians (who anticipated the return of the West Bank to Jordanian control) affirmed their support for it soon thereafter, as did the Syrians in 1973. Not surprisingly, the Palestinians, represented by the Palestine Liberation Organization (PLO), at first refused to accept the validity of the resolution because it did not refer to Palestinians as one of the principals in the dispute. Instead, the resolution's only reference to the Palestinians was as refugees whose fate was inserted into the resolution as an item on a "to do" list: "The Security Council . . . affirms the necessity . . . for achieving a just settlement of the refugee problem." For the PLO, this was a far cry from the recognition of Palestinian national rights. The PLO did not formally accept Resolution 242 as a basis of negotiations until 1988. Even then, the PLO placed its acceptance within the context of a demand for Palestinian statehood. It was only with Oslo and its affirmation of

Palestinian national rights that the PLO endorsed the resolution without qualification.

The land-for-peace formula provided the foundation for every serious effort at peacemaking from the end of the 1967 war to the Oslo Accord of 1993 and even after. This, in spite of the fact that it took the Palestinians more than two decades to jump on the bandwagon and that Israeli support for the formula has been erratic. (The official position of the Likud has been that Israel should not have to enter into negotiations with its neighbors on the basis of prior conditions, that the "Land of Israel" is an inviolable trust that cannot be negotiated away, and that peace is its own reward. Thus, Likud prime ministers from Yitzhak Shamir to Ariel Sharon have advocated exchanging "peace for peace" rather than land for peace.) Accordingly, from November 1967, when the United Nations sent Swedish mediator Gunner Jarring to the region to work out a settlement, to March 2002, when Saudi Arabia proposed the "Arab Peace Initiative" at an Arab League summit conference, members of the international community – acting alone, in multiples, or in concert – launched more than a dozen major initiatives to resolve the Arab-Israeli dispute on the basis of Resolution 242. As Oscar Wilde asserted about second marriages, such persistence bears all the hallmarks of the "triumph of hope over experience."

Not that these initiatives did not go through some interesting permutations over the course of thirty-five years. Sometimes the sponsors of these initiatives attempted to bring together all interested parties at the same time to negotiate a comprehensive settlement. Thus, the Geneva Conference of 1973 and the Madrid Conference of 1991. At other times their sponsors – or, since it was always the United States that encouraged this alternative approach, their sponsor – adopted the "Rhodes format." The Rhodes format was named after the island on which Ralph Bunche worked out his armistice agreements. Under the Rhodes format, Israel and each of its adversaries would communicate through a mediator. They would never engage in direct negotiations and would only meet face to face at the end of the process to sign an agreement. Henry Kissinger's "shuttle diplomacy" represents the most famous use of the Rhodes format. In the wake of the 1973 war, Kissinger traveled back and forth from Tel Aviv to Damascus and from Cairo to Tel Aviv working out a blueprint to disengage armies that had become entangled during the last days of the war and jump-start individual peace negotiations between Israel and its two neighbors. Although shuttle diplomacy inextricably entwined the United States in peace negotiations and reduced the Soviet Union to a mere observer of events – a main objective of Kissinger's overall Middle East strategy – it, too, failed to bring about a final resolution of the conflict.

Both of the two formats for negotiations – conferencing and the Rhodes format – had advantages and disadvantages. Since the conference format brought in everyone at once and everyone would be forced to make compromises at the same time, no one was left to snipe at the proceedings from the sidelines. Furthermore, some United States policymakers hoped that if the Soviet Union were included in an international conference, it would use the occasion to bring pressure to bear on its allies in the region, particularly Syria. But while some American policymakers believed, in the words of an old Arabian proverb, that it was better to have a camel inside your tent pissing out than a camel outside your tent pissing in, others were horrified at the idea of making America's principal Cold War foe a "partner for peace" in the region. After all, the primary goal of American foreign policy in the post–World War II period was to "contain" the Soviet Union. This meant keeping the Soviet Union out of regions like the Middle East – not inviting it in – and diminishing its influence where it had already made inroads. Policymakers opposed to the conference format also argued that international conferences encouraged grandstanding and intransigence. In an effort to bring everyone on board, they claimed, conference participants would have to give in to the demands of the most radical holdouts or risk sacrificing a comprehensive settlement.

In the end, neither the conference format nor the Rhodes format resulted in peace treaties based on the exchange of land for peace. Instead, in the two cases where such treaties were signed – the treaty between Israel and Egypt in 1979 and the treaty between Israel and Jordan in 1994 – it was the principals themselves who negotiated the deals face to face (although the United States played an essential role in the former case and sweetened the pot with pledges of military assistance and debt relief in the latter). In the first case, it was domestic circumstances that induced President Anwar al-Sadat, who succeeded Nasser as president of Egypt in 1970, to make peace. Anwar al-Sadat never enjoyed the popularity of his predecessor and had to find something he could use to shore up his weak base of support at home. If he could regain the Sinai, which Nasser had lost, if he could sweeten the deal by getting buckets of American aid, if he could divert resources destined for defense to strengthen the civilian economy, he believed he just might be able to win the devotion of his people, which had always eluded him. (Anwar al-Sadat was assassinated in 1981.) The Israeli-Jordanian treaty was worked out in the immediate aftermath of the signing of the Oslo Accord, when the Jordanians no longer laid claim to the West Bank and when ongoing negotiations between the Israelis and Palestinians had transformed the logic of the dispute. After all, if the Palestinians themselves were willing to make peace with Israel, what earthly reason was there for the Jordanians to hold out?

The exchange of land for peace is a simple formula. That it should take more than a decade to reach the first land-for-peace settlement, then another decade and a half to reach the second, seems to defy logic. Historians cite a number of reasons for the inability of Israel and its neighbors to reach agreements based on Resolution 242. First, the resolution itself is ambiguous. This was no accident. After all, not only did the resolution have to accommodate the conflicting concerns of United Nations Security Council members, it could only provide the basis for negotiation if it was acceptable (or at least only mildly irritating) to Israel and the Arab states. Thus, a document whose ambiguous wording rivals that of the Balfour Declaration.

As in the case of the Balfour Declaration, diplomats carefully vetted every word of every phrase of Resolution 242. For example, the resolution calls for the withdrawal of Israeli forces "from territories occupied during the recent conflict." The Israelis like to point out that the resolution nowhere states that they must withdraw from *all* the occupied territories. In fact, the phrase "withdrawal of Israel [*sic*] armed forces from territories occupied in the recent conflict" read, in the first draft, "withdrawal of Israel armed forces from *the* [italics added] territories occupied in the recent conflict"; it was deliberately revised to give the parties more wiggle room. The resolution also calls for the "termination of all claims or states of belligerency and respect for and acknowledgement of the sovereignty, territorial integrity, and political independence of every state in the area and their right to live in peace within secure and recognized boundaries free from threats or acts of force." The Arab states like to point out that the resolution does not call for formal peace treaties with Israel. They have claimed that they could fulfill the terms of the resolution simply by issuing statements of nonbelligerency (whatever those may be). Needless to say, each party to the dispute has challenged the interpretation of the other.

The postwar strategy adopted by the Arab states also complicated the application of Resolution 242, although this was never the intention. Soon after the war, the heads of the Arab states met in Khartoum, Sudan, to negotiate a unified position. At Khartoum, Arab leaders decided on the famous "three no's": no negotiations with Israel, no peace with Israel, no recognition of Israel. At the time, observers interpreted this as representing the height of intransigence. In fact, the three no's marked a subtle tactical shift. The Arab states agreed to unify efforts to "eliminate the effects of aggression" – not eliminate Israel. And they agreed to take political, not military, action. Although the Arab heads of state agreed not to negotiate with Israel, they did not agree not to negotiate. The Arab heads of state instead looked to the superpowers – the United States and the Soviet Union – to resolve the dispute. But since the Soviet Union had broken all diplomatic relations with Israel, it was up to the United States to bring the Israelis around. This is how the United States came to hold "ninety-nine percent of the cards" in the region, to borrow Anwar al-Sadat's telling phrase.

This tactic was dangerous for the Arab states because it assumed that the Americans so wanted a settlement that they would put pressure on Israel to get it. This assumption was overly optimistic. Taking the initiative on the Arab-Israeli dispute was politically risky for American presidents, particularly if taking the initiative involved putting pressure on Israel. As a result, after the 1967 war the United States was all too willing to sit back and wait for the Arab states to come round. If the Arab states wanted their land back, American policymakers argued, all they had to do to get it back was to sign peace treaties with Israel. And if they did not want to negotiate directly with Israel, they could come to the United States first. As a matter of fact, in the zero-sum game that was the Cold War – a game in which a gain for the United States was a loss for the Soviet Union, and vice versa – it would be all the better if they did. To foreclose the war option once and for all, the United States adopted the policy of supplying Israel with enough weaponry to keep it stronger than the sum total of its enemies. This policy began in 1968 with the sale of fifty of America's latest Phantom fighter-bombers to Israel and continues to the present day.

The American policy was logical but certainly not foolproof. As early as 1969, Egypt launched the so-called War of Attrition against Israel to break the stalemate that had settled in after the 1967 war. The war started with artillery duels, then aerial dogfights between Egyptians and Israelis across the Suez Canal. When the Israelis began deep penetration bombing runs over Egypt, Soviet pilots began flying missions for the Egyptians. The Americans certainly did take notice. American policymakers were horrified at the idea that their ally might trigger World War III by shooting down a Soviet-piloted MIG. The Americans therefore launched the Rogers Initiative and the Rogers Plan (both named after Secretary of State William Rogers) to bring about a ceasefire and, once both sides cooled off, a solution. After the failure of the Rogers Plan, the United States once again "bought into a stalemate" (to use a phrase from the Nixon administration). American inattention lasted until October 1973, when Egypt and Syria once again launched a war against Israel.

Unlike 1967, the Egyptians and Syrians did not launch the 1973 war to revise the results of 1948. Rather, they launched their attack to break the stalemate and capture superpower attention once again. Anwar al-Sadat was particularly distressed that not only had the United States bought into a stalemate, it had gotten the Soviet Union to do so as well. At a summit meeting held in April 1972, the United States and the Soviet Union agreed that, when it came to the Middle East, they would "do everything in their power so that conflicts or situations do not arise which would seem to increase international tensions" and that neither would seek "unilateral advantage at the expense of the other." Anwar al-Sadat and his Syrian allies needed to do something to get the process going again.

The 1973 war resulted in eleven to sixteen thousand more Arab and Israeli casualties and was used by Arab members of OPEC as an excuse to hike oil prices, which rose 380 percent in a few months. Even more ominously, after the Soviet Union agreed to an Egyptian request to send troops to the region to force the Israelis to abide by a ceasefire, the United States government placed its military on the highest state of alert, bringing the world to the brink of nuclear war. As had been the case with the War of Attrition, the 1973 war got America's attention. At a time when the United States had bigger fish to fry – the United States was still involved in Vietnam, had just opened up relations with China, and had to figure out the intricacies of détente (cooperation) with the

Soviet Union – Henry Kissinger, who had replaced William Rogers as secretary of state, was spending his time shuttling between Damascus, Cairo, and Tel Aviv working out minutiae of Israeli and Arab troop redeployments.

The period leading up to the 1973 war was not the last time the skills of politicians and diplomats operating in the post–Resolution 242 environment would be put to the test and be found wanting. The years 1983 to 1987 mark another such period of stalemate bookended by crises – the Israeli invasion of Lebanon and the outbreak of the first intifada. Diplomats had embraced Resolution 242 because it promised to provide a framework for resolving the Arab-Israeli dispute. Instead, the world created by the resolution was one in which a crisis followed each period of stalemate, a flurry of diplomatic activity followed the crisis, and a new period of stalemate followed the flurry of diplomatic activity, starting the cycle once again.

THE OCCUPIED TERRITORIES

There was a third reason why the land-for-peace formula was difficult to implement: Israeli attitudes toward the conquered territories. Some of the territories were relatively easy for Israel to part with. Some, more difficult. And the Israelis refused to put one piece of real estate – the portions of Jerusalem they annexed – on the table at all.

In part, Israeli attitudes toward the value of the conquered real estate might be traced to ideology. Take the issue of Jerusalem. As we saw in Chapter 1, Jerusalem had always played a special symbolic role in Zionist ideology. As the capital of David and Solomon's kingdom, it provided a reminder of the golden age of the ancient Israelite kingdom that was central to the Zionist narrative of history. Thus, in January 1950 the Israeli Knesset not only declared Jerusalem the capital of Israel but declared that Jerusalem had been the capital of Israel since the state had proclaimed its independence in 1948. The only problem was that Israel was only in possession of the western part of the city. With the 1967 war, Israel came into possession of the remainder of the city. Two weeks after the war ended, the Knesset declared Jerusalem unified for all time. To confirm the Knesset declaration, the Israeli government severed the political connection between Jerusalem and the West Bank and began encircling what had been East Jerusalem with neighborhoods to be inhabited by Israelis. Since 1967, East Jerusalem has become home to approximately 200,000 Israelis, and its boundaries have been extended far into the West Bank. In 1967, the territory of East Jerusalem included 6.5 square kilometers. As of this writing, it includes 71 square kilometers. The Israeli government does not consider the Israelis who live there to be settlers, nor does it consider the new neighborhoods around East Jerusalem to be settlements. In other words, they are nonnegotiable and have never been on the post-Oslo bargaining table.

While Jerusalem lies on one end of the Zionist ideological spectrum, the Sinai Peninsula lies on the other. The Sinai had never been part of the "Land of Israel," and although it does play a role in Jewish historical memory (after all, Moses did receive the Ten Commandments there), that role is hardly overwhelmingly positive: For most Jews, the Sinai has represented a place to get out of, even if it takes forty years. Thus, the ideological reasons to remain in the peninsula were not compelling. There were other considerations, of course. The Sinai contains some oil and some nice beaches ripe for development, and it does form a geographic buffer zone separating Israel and Egypt. And for true believers – the secular Revisionists and like-minded religious zealots – withdrawal from any territory is unthinkable. For most Israelis, however, none of these considerations made the Sinai worth retaining when weighed against the possibility of a peace treaty with Egypt and increased American financial assistance. Thus, the Israelis agreed to withdraw from the Sinai as part of the peace treaty they signed with the Egyptians in 1979. American monitors have been stationed there since the withdrawal, although only a token force now remains.

Ideology has not been the only factor Israelis have taken account of when considering the value of the various territories Israel occupied in 1967. There is also the question of defense. Although a majority of Israeli military experts came to believe that the military benefits Israel might obtain from keeping the Sinai Peninsula could be finessed, the question of the Golan Heights, taken from Syria, was an entirely different matter. The Golan Heights overlook the Galilee region of Israel and therefore their strategic importance seems apparent. Israeli tour guides still take tourists up to the heights to point out the vulnerability of Israeli communities below. The strategic value of the Golan Heights has not been uncontested, however. The Israeli defense minister in 1967, Moshe Dayan, argued that the risk involved in taking the heights was far greater than any strategic benefit the Israelis would derive from it. In an interview granted after the war, Dayan went so far as to attribute pressure for the Israeli assault on the heights to their agricultural value rather than their defense value. "Along the Syrian border there were no farms and no refugee camps – there was only the Syrian army," he bitterly remembered. "The kibbutzim saw the good agricultural land and they dreamed about it."[1]

Overall, the importance of the occupied territories for Israeli defense is still debated among experts. Some assert that the territories provide Israel with defensible frontiers, deny Israel's enemies sites from which to launch attacks, and act as territorial shock absorbers that not only distance Israel from hostile armies but ensure that future battles will be fought outside Israel's borders. Others contend that the territories undermine Israeli defense. Their logic seems to be based on the famous aphorism of the early nineteenth century Prussian strategist Karl von Clausewitz, who stated that "war is a continuation of politics by other means." Retaining the territories, they assert, escalates the threat to Israel because it increases the hostility of the Palestinian and other Arab populations, frustrates a peaceful settlement with the Syrians, undermines support for Israel in the international community, and unites Israel's Arab foes in a common cause. They also question the value of a territorial buffer zone in an age when geosynchronous satellites and early warning systems can keep track of enemy troop movements, and Scud missiles can fly over miles of intervening territory.

In addition to ideology and defense, two other factors have shaped Israeli attitudes toward the occupied territories, particularly the West Bank and Gaza Strip: economics and settlements. Immediately after the 1967 war, Moshe Dayan, whose ministry of defense managed the occupied territories, instituted what became known as the "open bridges policy." Dayan reasoned that economic instability in the West Bank would frustrate Israeli control, feed Palestinian national aspirations, and swell the ranks of the various guerrilla groups that were challenging Israeli occupation by force of arms. Under the open bridges policy, West Bankers would continue to be able to cross back and forth to Jordan to work, engage in commerce, and visit relatives. This, Dayan hoped,

---

[1] "Dayan Reveals Regrets over Golan, Hebron in Newly Disclosed Interview," Associated Press, 11 May 1997.

would make the occupation appear less irksome. The Israelis soon supplemented the connection to the east with one to the west. They granted West Bank and Gaza Strip Palestinians the right to travel throughout all of historic Palestine and even take jobs in Israel (although Palestinian laborers had to return to their homes in the occupied territories at the end of each workday). Over time, the Israeli government broadened and deepened the economic linkages between Israel and the occupied territories and even made the territories a factor in national economic planning.

Israeli policies transformed the economy of the territories. The Israelis found a captive market in the West Bank and Gaza Strip. They enjoyed exclusive rights to export manufactured goods to the territories and, because Israeli farmers had access to subsidies denied residents of the territories, were able to flood the Palestinian market with cheaper agricultural products. Land-use restrictions, production and marketing quotas, Jordanian import controls, and access to the Israeli labor market all served to change the orientation of the Palestinian workforce away from agriculture toward (usually unskilled) employment in Israel. Within four years of the 1967 war, about half of all workers from the occupied territories regularly commuted to jobs in Israel. In addition, the Israelis integrated the electrical grid in the occupied territories with their own and increased their dependence on water resources from the West Bank. Currently, Israel derives almost 40 percent of its water from aquifers it shares with the West Bank and about 25 percent from aquifers located exclusively in the West Bank.

Overall, after the 1967 war, Israel integrated the economies of the West Bank and Gaza Strip with its own. This has made separation all the more difficult. And because this integration occurred under compulsion, and because the level of Israeli economic development had far outstripped that of the territories, the effect was to create a colonial-style dependent economy in those territories. At first, the creation of this dependent economy seemed to bring benefits to both peoples. Israeli officials noted that Israeli policies had produced a rate of employment in the territories in the range of 98 percent. According to Harvard scholar Nadav Safran,

[The employment of Palestinians in Israel] eliminated unemployment in the territories, caused wages there to rise, triggered a revolution in agriculture, multiplied spending, saving, and investment, stimulated trade, and precipitated many processes of social change. All this did not make the Israeli occupation acceptable, but it did give the majority of the population a vested interest in the avoidance of seemingly pointless trouble.[2]

To paraphrase humorist James Thurber: This may be a naive little idea, but we ought not to be too amused by its presumption. Safran wrote those lines in 1978, before the Israelis began imposing a policy of closure – obstructing the daily flow of labor from the territories to Israel – on a regular basis. He also wrote those lines before 1993, when Israelis began a policy of weaning themselves from Palestinian labor by importing workers from East and South Asia, Eastern Europe, and Africa (as of this writing, these guest workers make up about one-sixth of the population of Tel Aviv). With the outbreak of the second intifada in 2000, the Israeli government, citing security concerns, began restricting the entry of Palestinian labor into Israel on an almost continuous basis. According to International Labor Organization statistics, within two years unemployment rates in the territories jumped to about 50 percent, with about 68 percent of the Gaza population living below the poverty line. The problem with a dependent economy is not just that it skews economic development; it also makes the population living in a state of dependency vulnerable to the policies of an outside power.

Although defense, ideology, and economics all obstructed the simple exchange of land for peace, no factor has been more troublesome than the Israeli settlements built on occupied lands. This is no accident. Indeed, various Israeli governments have described the construction of settlements as "creating facts on the ground." What they have meant by this is that each settlement confirms Israeli control over the territory upon which it is built. Each settlement provides Israel with either a permanent foothold in the territories or at least an expensive bargaining chip to be traded away only if the price is right.

It is difficult to present exact figures for the number of Israeli settlers and settlements in the occupied territories for several reasons. Not only are the numbers constantly changing through immigration and natural increase, the Israeli government considers some settlements "legal" whereas others are classified as "illegal" – that is, neither authorized

[2] Nadav Safran, *Israel, the Embattled Ally* (Cambridge, MA: Belknap Press, 1978), 269.

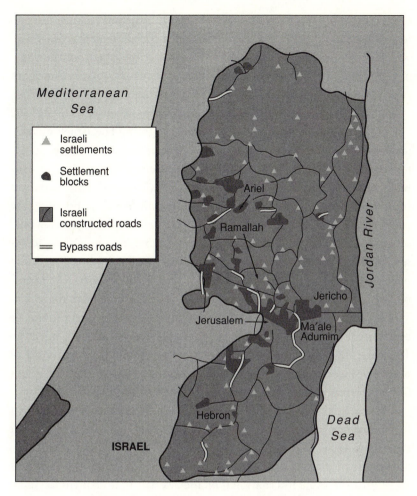

Map 9. Israeli settlements in the West Bank, 2005.

nor counted as settlements by the Israeli government. Furthermore, the government does not include the Israeli inhabitants of East Jerusalem in its census of settlers. Excluding those settlers, there are more than 225,000 settlers living in more than 150 "legal" settlements on the West Bank, more than 7,500 settlers living in more than 20 settlements in Gaza, and more than 18,000 settlers living in more than 30 settlements on the Golan Heights. The size of settlements varies widely, from the "small cities" (as they are classified by the Israeli government) of Ma'ale Adumin and Ariel on the West Bank, which are populated by about 25,000 and 15,000 settlers respectively, to illegal settlements consisting of nothing more than a trailer or two on a hilltop and lacking any permanent inhabitants. The social structure of the settlements also varies widely, from neo-kibbutzim and moshavot to regular bedroom communities that would not be out of place on the outskirts of any American city.

In the main, the considerations cited above – defense, ideology, and economics – drove the Israeli settlement program. The Israeli government authorized the construction of settlements for military purposes immediately after the 1967 war. These settlements were built on the fringes of the territories: in the Jordan River Valley next to the Jordanian frontier, along the Golan Heights on the Syrian frontier, and along the edges of the Sinai Peninsula. It was hoped that the settlements would serve as an Israeli Maginot Line, slowing or halting any attack across one of the frontiers. The ideologues of the ruling Labor Party also believed that building kibbutz- and moshav-style military settlements might revive images of the tower and stockade settlements of the 1930s. This would restore luster to the image of the warrior-pioneer that is so central to Labor Party lore. These hopes were soon dashed, however. The settlements did not attract or retain anywhere near the number of hearty pioneers originally envisioned. Presently, no more than about three hundred settlers live in the largest of these settlements.

During the 1970s, Labor Party ideologues had every reason to despair for the future of Labor Zionism. Much of the electorate held Labor Party politicians responsible for the near disaster of the 1973 war. Economic growth slowed dramatically during the 1972–81 period, partly as a result of the same international financial crisis that brought "stagflation" to the West, partly as a result of the rigidity of Israel's political and economic institutions. Throughout the world, populations held the welfare state accountable for their economic problems, and the Israeli population was no different. Just as serious, in the years following the 1967 war, the Labor Party–dominated governments had been unable to articulate a clear vision for the future. Some Laborites, arguing from the standpoint of demography, asserted that Israel could not retain its Jewish character if it incorporated large amounts of Palestinian-inhabited territory. They opposed establishing facts on the ground that would make Israeli withdrawal from the West Bank more difficult. For them, the Maginot Line settlements were enough. Others envisioned a future in which joint Israeli-Jordanian control over the West Bank would hold a resurgent Palestinian national movement in check. They advocated creating facts on the ground as the first step to achieving that end.

While the ruling coalition dithered, however, others approached the issue of settlements with monomaniacal zeal. Among them were that old standby, the Likud bloc, and a new factor in Israeli politics, the religiously inspired Gush Emunim settler movement.

Like Jabotinsky, the Likud bloc advocated the construction of a "Greater Israel." It thus weighed in early and often on the settlements issue. Before 1977, the Likud and its allies exerted steady pressure on the Labor government to sponsor or at least permit settlement activity. Their efforts proved effective, and under Labor Party–dominated governments eighty-five settlements were constructed throughout the territories. In 1977, Likud bloc candidates for the Knesset ran on a platform that read, in part, as follows:

The right of the Jewish people to the land of Israel is eternal and indisputable and is linked with the right of security and peace; therefore, Judea and Samaria will not be handed to any foreign administration; between the sea and Jordan there will only be Israeli sovereignty. . . .

Settlement, both urban and rural, in all parts of the Land of Israel is the focal point of the Zionist effort to redeem the country, to maintain vital security areas and serves as a reservoir of strength and inspiration for the renewal of the pioneering spirit. The Likud government will call the younger generation in Israel and the dispersions to settle and help every group and individual in the task of inhabiting and cultivating the wasteland, while taking care not to dispossess anyone.[3]

The 1977 elections brought a Likud prime minister, Menachem Begin, to power for the first time. With Ariel Sharon as his agriculture minister and point man on settlement activities, the expansion of settlements began in earnest. But while the government supported the expansion of settlements, its policy could only succeed if there was a steady stream of settlers willing to inhabit them. Begin and Sharon thus worked hand in glove with newly formed settler organizations, of which the most prominent was the Gush Emunim.

Although the Gush Emunim – the "bloc of the faithful" – was founded in 1974, its doctrines can be traced back to the teachings of the chief

---

[3] Walter Laqueur and Barry Rubin, eds., *The Israel-Arab Reader: A Documentary History of the Middle East Conflict* (New York: Penguin, 1995), 591–2.

rabbi of the Yishuv from the 1920s to the 1940s, Rabbi Abraham Isaac Kook, and his son Zvi Yehuda Kook. Like the followers of Jabotinsky, the Kooks' disciples were dissatisfied with the territory allotted them by the mandatory power. Unlike the secular Likudniks, however, members of the Gush Emunim have considered Jewish resettlement of "Eretz Israel" a religious mission. They view the 1967 triumph in messianic terms and Israel and the occupied territories as God's sacred patrimony bestowed on the Jewish people. According to one of the movement's founders,

The entire matter of the Land of Israel is a mysterious issue whose basis is a spiritual attachment to matter and soil. If one goes deeply into the understanding of the relation between the body and the soul or of the relationship between man and woman and penetrates the mystery of the unity of matter and spirit one is able to understand the love and the appreciation for each part of the Land of Israel just as there is value for every limb of the human body. The Land of Israel has an element of life in it, and is tied to spirit so that a surrender of any part of it is like giving up a living organ.[4]

The Gush undertook a twofold strategy in their quest to secure what it perceived to be God's sacred trust to Israel. To ensure that no Israeli government would surrender that sacred trust, Gush members established their own facts on the ground, often with a wink and a nod from the government. Under the Likud, the Gush provided the ideal "cutout": The government could insist to its international benefactors that it was not doing anything to sabotage the possibility of trading land for peace, all the while offering more than tacit support to those who were. But the Gush was willing to exploit the party system of Israel directly as well. By 1977, the Gush had won over a majority of the members of the National Religious Party (NRP) to its position on settlements. Not only was the NRP a member of the ruling coalition dominated by the Likud, the coalition would have collapsed had the NRP withdrawn its support. The Gush thus acquired direct access to the corridors of power and exploited it to the hilt. With Likud support, it established settlements not only near centers of Palestinian habitation but in such centers as well. Today, for example, 400 to 500 settlers, protected by 4,000 soldiers, inhabit Hebron, a city of 120,000 Palestinians.

---

[4] Ehud Sprinzak, *The Ascendance of Israel's Radical Right* (Oxford: Oxford University Press, 1991), 112.

18. West Bank or suburban New Jersey? Many Israelis have found settlements attractive not only because of government incentives, but also because of the lifestyle they promise. Above: The settlement of Ofra in the West Bank. (Source: Sipa Press/Rex Features)

Although the Gush represents a particularly combative strain within the settler movement, however, it still represents only a strain. Not all settlers have been motivated by religious or political ideologies. Many of the settlements built closest to Israel consist of Israelis looking for cheap housing or an affordable "good place to raise kids." (Tel Aviv currently ranks thirty-third on the list of the most expensive cities in the world to live, six slots down from Los Angeles but above Chicago.) These settlements are mixed in with others inhabited by "ultra-Orthodox" Jews who are unmoved by the cultlike messianism of the Gush but who want to live their lives in an affordable environment surrounded by other ultra-Orthodox Jews and ultra-Orthodox institutions. The Israeli government has encouraged the expansion of these settlements by offering settlers a wide array of incentives, including tax breaks, grants, and low-interest loans. The Israeli academic Avishai Margalit explains the system of incentives as follows:

If a settler buys an apartment for $100,000, he will receive from the government a standing loan of $20,000, which in practice comes close to turning into a grant after five years. Moreover, he also gets $12,000 as a flat grant; and he pays such low interest on his mortgage (2.5 percent compared to

5.5 percent in Israel proper) that he saves $40,000 in mortgage payments over twenty years. . . . Nor do government subsidies stop with money for housing. Living in a settlement like Ma'ale Adumin (ten minutes from the Mount Scopus campus of the Hebrew University of Jerusalem) means, among many other benefits, that income taxes are reduced by 10 percent, health taxes by 30 percent, and kindergarten fees by 50 percent.[5]

Besides the fact that the Israeli government acquires the land for settlements through expulsions and selective enforcement of the 1858 Ottoman Land Code (particularly the provision that allows the state to take over land if its owner cannot prove title or leaves it barren for a given length of time), it is this very policy of providing incentives for settlements that supplies their opponents in the international community with ammunition against them. Opponents of the Israeli settlement policy argue that the settlements violate the Fourth Geneva Convention of 1949. According to the convention, "The occupying power shall not deport or transfer parts of its own civilian population into the territory it occupies." By giving tax incentives and other forms of encouragement to settlers, it is argued, the Israeli government is encouraging such a transfer of population. Needless to say, the United Nations has condemned Israeli settlement activity countless times.

Before the Reagan administration, the United States government also called Israel's settlement policy illegal. The Reagan administration began the practice of rhetorically sidestepping the issue of the legality of the settlements by referring to them as "an obstacle to peace." Only recently did the United States definitively reverse its long-standing dissatisfaction with Israel's settlement policy. On 14 April 2004, President Bush wrote Israeli prime minister Ariel Sharon a letter in which he stated,

In light of new realities on the ground, including already existing major Israeli population centers, it is unrealistic to expect that the outcome of final status negotiations will be a full and complete return to the armistice lines of 1949, and all previous efforts to negotiate a two-state solution have reached the same conclusion. It is realistic to expect that any final status agreement will only be achieved on the basis of mutually agreed changes that reflect these realities.

The reversal of America's position on the settlements coheres with the Bush administration's Manichean worldview, which divides states into

<hr>

[5] Avishai Margalit, "Settling Scores," *New York Review of Books*, 20 September 2001.

19. Hilltop settlements in the West Bank act as a constant reminder to Palestinians of Israeli authority and dominance. (Source: David G. Houser/Corbis)

those "with us" and those "against us" in the War on Terrorism, and grants to the former the right to act unilaterally against the latter if they deem it appropriate.

For their part, Israeli governments have ignored the condemnations of most of the international community, going so far as to contest the applicability of the Fourth Geneva Convention. The Geneva Convention covers occupied territories, Israeli government lawyers assert; those territories taken in the 1967 war are not occupied, since no state since the Ottomans has had rightful sovereignty over them. They are merely "disputed." When it comes to the West Bank and the Gaza Strip, successive Israeli governments have advanced the "homeland doctrine," which asserts that these territories are not really occupied at all but rather part of the Jewish homeland.

Whatever the arguments back and forth, Israeli settlements have certainly proved to be an "obstacle to peace." They have been a stumbling block in all negotiations between Israel, its neighbors, and the Palestinians since they were first built. They are a daily reminder to Palestinians and others of Israeli power and territorial claims. The settlements assert these claims both symbolically and tangibly. Those placed on hilltops in the West Bank are not built to blend in with the surrounding environment. To the contrary, they are built to stand out, like Crusader fortresses of old. In the Gaza Strip, where settlers make up .5 percent of the population, settlements take up 40 percent of the land and siphon off scarce water supplies to nourish the lawns and fill the swimming pools of settlers. Adding insult to injury, settlements are connected to each other and Israel through a network of "access" and "bypass roads" – 160 kilometers' worth in the West Bank – that cut through the Palestinian countryside and make the dream of a unified Palestinian state all the more elusive.

Finally, the settlements have proved to be anything but a reliable or even useful bargaining chip in negotiations. Settlers have been reluctant to withdraw from any territory they claim as theirs. On those rare occasions when the Israeli government has floated the idea of limited withdrawal from the settlements, settlers have been able to mobilize political support – both inside and outside the Knesset – far in excess of their numbers. In part, their power in the Knesset is a result of the internal dynamics of that body: Ruling coalitions in the Knesset need to draw their support from a number of political parties, many of which represent a single issue – such as those that represent the settler movement. The power of the settler movement outside the Knesset also unnerves Israeli governments. Government officials cringe at the memory of 1982, when the Israeli army had to be sent in to roust settlers and squatters from settlements in the Sinai – a territory that by no stretch of the imagination could be claimed as part of "Eretz Israel." When prime minister Ariel Sharon – perhaps the most influential proponent of Israel's settlement policy – announced his plan for unilateral Israeli withdrawal from the Gaza Strip in early 2004, leaders of the settler movement went so far as to threaten civil war. The settlements may thus prove not only to be the undoing of a negotiated agreement with the Palestinians, but an imposed one as well.

SUGGESTIONS FOR FURTHER READING

Kuniholm, Bruce. *The Origins of the Cold War in the Near East*. Princeton, NJ: Princeton University Press, 1980. Standard work on U.S.-Soviet rivalry in the region during the first decade after World War II.

Liebman, Charles S., and Eliezer Don-Yehiya. *Civil Religion in Israel: Traditional Judaism and Political Culture in the Jewish State*. Berkeley: University of California Press, 1983. Examination of the interplay between ideology and the public sphere in Israel.

Lustick, Ian. *Arabs in the Jewish State: Israel's Control of a National Minority.* Austin: University of Texas Press, 1980. A look at Israel's Arab citizens in Israeli society and politics.

Margalit, Avishai. "Settling Scores." *New York Review of Books,* 20 September 2001, 20–4. Concise overview of the settlements issue.

Morris, Benny. *The Birth of the Palestine Refugee Problem, 1947–1949.* Cambridge: Cambridge University Press, 1987. Revisionist account by one of Israel's leading New Historians.

———. *1948 and After: Israel and the Palestinians.* Oxford: Oxford University Press, 1994. Scholarly account of the relationship between the two peoples after the 1948 war.

Neff, Donald. *Warriors at Suez: Eisenhower Takes America into the Middle East.* New York: Linden Press, 1981. Popular account of 1956 war, told from the vantage point of those who were involved.

Parker, Richard B., ed. *The Six-Day War: A Retrospective.* Gainesville: University of Florida Press, 1996. Excellent collection of essays on the war and its aftermath.

Quandt, William B. *Decade of Decisions: American Policy toward the Arab-Israeli Conflict, 1967–1976.* Berkeley: University of California Press, 1977. American diplomacy in the region from the Johnson through the Ford administrations, told by an insider.

Roy, Sara. *The Gaza Strip: The Political Economy of De-development.* Washington, DC, 1995. Analysis of the Gazan economy and society since the Israeli occupation.

Safran, Nadav. *Israel, the Embattled Ally.* Cambridge: Belknap Press, 1978. History of Israel told by sympathetic scholar.

Silberstein, Laurence J., ed. *New Perspectives on Israeli History: The Early Years of the State.* New York: New York University Press, 1991. Wide-ranging collection covering everything from institutional history to the construction of national symbols.

Segev, Tom. *The Seventh Million: Israelis and the Holocaust.* Translated by Haim Watzman. New York: Hill and Wang, 1993. Provocative account of Israeli attitudes toward the Holocaust told by a leading Israeli journalist/New Historian.

Smith, Pamela Ann. "The Palestinian Diaspora, 1948–1985." *Journal of Palestine Studies* 59 (Spring 1986): 90–108. Good overview of the effects of exile on Palestinian society.

Sprinzak, Ehud. *The Ascendance of Israel's Radical Right.* Oxford: Oxford University Press, 1991. Traces the rise of the Likud Party, the settlers movement, and their allies and the challenge they offer to Labor Zionism.

Troen, S. Ilan, and Noah Lucas, eds. *Israel: The First Decade of Independence.* Albany: State University of New York Press, 1995. Large collection of essays on a variety of topics dealing with the consolidation and early history of Israel.

Weisbrod, Lily. "Gush Emunim Ideology: From Religious Doctrine to Political Action." *Middle East Studies* 18 (1982): 264–75. Good introduction to religious nationalism in Israel.

9

THE PALESTINIAN
NATIONAL MOVEMENT
COMES OF AGE

In the late summer of 2001, Mary Robinson, the United Nations high commissioner for human rights, convened the World Conference against Racism, Racial Discrimination, Xenophobia and Related Intolerance in Durban, South Africa. Attendees included the member states of the United Nations General Assembly and assorted observer missions and nongovernmental organizations. At the end of the conference, participants agreed on a final report that included a list of 122 "General Issues" and a 219-point "Programme of Action." Not surprisingly, the report condemned racism, racial discrimination, xenophobia, and related intolerance. The report also urged the world community to be more sensitive to these evils and undertake efforts to eradicate them. All this was set down in a style of rhetoric once caricatured by former American vice president Nelson Rockefeller as BOMFOG – Brotherhood of Man (under the) Fatherhood of God. It's a small world after all.

The blandness of the final report masks one of several controversies that had threatened to tear apart the conference before it had even convened: An early draft of the report had condemned the "practises of racial discrimination against the Palestinians as well as other inhabitants of the Arab occupied territories," going so far as to single out Zionism as a particularly virulent form of racism. "The World Conference recognises with deep concern the increase of racist practises of Zionism and anti-Semitism in various parts of the world," the draft read, "as well as the emergence of racial and violent movements based on racism and discriminatory ideas, in particular the Zionist movement, which is based on racial superiority." In the end, the final report deleted the offending passages, but not before the American and Israeli delegations staged a walkout.

Although the equation of Zionism and racism never made it to the final draft, the report did not entirely ignore the Israeli–Palestinian conflict. Article 63 on the list of General Issues, for example, stated,

We are concerned about the plight of the Palestinian people under foreign occupation. We recognize the inalienable right of the Palestinian people to self-determination and to the establishment of an independent state.

Although not as controversial as the red meat of the Zionism equals racism equation, the inclusion of Article 63 was still anomalous. While the report expressed broad sympathy with the causes of indigenous peoples throughout the world, descendants of enslaved Africans and colonized Asians, trafficked women and children, and persecuted Roma (Gypsies), the Palestinians were the only *national* group whose rights the attendees championed.

This and similar expressions of international solidarity with Palestinian national aspirations have become commonplace in both official and unofficial gatherings during the past thirty years. Nevertheless, these expressions, and even the continued existence of the Palestine question, were never foregone conclusions. The 1936–9 Great Revolt and the 1948 war were catastrophes of such magnitude that it would not have been surprising had the Palestinian national movement and a distinct Palestinian national identity vanished forever. Indeed, as we have seen, in the aftermath of the establishment of Israel and the nakba, members of the international community dismissed or ignored Palestinian national aspirations or cynically manipulated them for self-serving ends. With little international support, a powerful adversary committed to destroying it, no base of operations, and few resources upon which it could draw, the Palestinian national movement – the repository of Palestinian national identity – seemed fated for destruction.

Yet, this was not to be. In previous chapters, we discussed some of the factors that militated against the destruction of Palestinian national identity. Included among them was the history of the Palestinian struggle against Zionism, the memory of national tragedy ("Where national memories are concerned, griefs are of more value than triumphs, for they impose duties, and require a common effort"), the physical and legal segregation of Palestinian refugees and their descendants from the populations among whom they lived, and the invention and reinvention of peculiarly Palestinian national traditions. There is another factor that must be added to this list, however: the existence and efforts of the Palestine Liberation Organization (PLO). Indeed, as tarnished as the reputations of the PLO and its former chairman, Yasir Arafat, have become among both Palestinians and non-Palestinians in the past decade, it would not be a stretch to claim that they bear primary responsibility for keeping Palestinian national aspirations alive. As we shall see, this has been both a blessing and a curse for the Palestinian national movement.

Ironically, the individual most responsible for the founding of the PLO was not a Palestinian at all. Rather, it was Gamal 'Abd al-Nasser, who engineered the formation of the organization in 1964. The raids launched by Palestinian guerrillas (fedayeen) into Israel and rising tensions between Israel and Syria over the allocation of Jordan River water threatened to bring on a crisis that Nasser had hoped to defer. He thus convened a summit meeting in Cairo at which thirteen Arab leaders put their stamp of approval on the founding of an organization that was ostensibly committed to representing Palestinian national interests but was, in fact, designed to mollify and rein in those interests. Nasser hand-picked the first leader of the PLO, Ahmad Shuqairy, an unimaginative and uncharismatic Palestinian diplomat introduced at the beginning of Chapter 5. Besides his famous comment about pushing the Jews into the sea, Shuqairy's sole contribution to the Palestinian cause was to oversee the drafting of the Palestine National Charter, which has continued to define the Palestinian nation and national movement to this very day. The charter begins as follows:

1. Palestine is the homeland of the Palestinian Arab people and an integral part of the great Arab homeland, and the people of Palestine is part of the Arab nation.
2. Palestine with its boundaries that existed at the time of the British mandate is an integral regional unit.
3. The Palestinian Arab people possesses the legal right to its homeland, and when the liberation of its homeland is completed it will exercise self-determination solely according to its own will and choice.
4. The Palestinian personality is an innate, persistent characteristic that does not disappear, and it is transferred from fathers to sons. The Zionist occupation, and the dispersal of the Palestinian Arab people as a result of the disasters which came over it, do not deprive it of its Palestinian personality and affiliation and do not nullify them.

The charter was adopted in 1964. Modified in 1968 and after Oslo, it remains the constitution of the PLO.

By making the PLO a wholly owned subsidiary of the Arab League, Nasser hoped to ensure that the liberation of Palestine would remain an *Arab* problem. It would not remain so for long. The disastrous showing of the Arab states in the 1967 war demonstrated to many Palestinians that, whatever their rhetoric, those states were incapable of defeating Israel. In the wake of the war, many Palestinians came to believe that the liberation of Palestine could only take place if Palestinians took matters into their own hands. This belief received its first validation in March 1968, when the Israelis launched a raid into the Jordanian town of Karameh to root out Palestinian guerrilla groups based there. The outnumbered fedayeen, backed by Jordanian artillery, inflicted more than a hundred casualties on the invaders and forced the Israelis to withdraw. The Battle of Karameh achieved mythic status in Palestinian lore. Three hundred Palestinian irregulars repulsed an invading force three times their number, accomplishing what entire Arab armies had been unable to achieve. And as far as mythmaking was concerned, it did not hurt that *karameh* means "honor" in Arabic.

The Battle of Karameh changed the balance of power in Palestinian politics. Before the battle, Fatah – the largest of the guerrilla groups and the one led by Yasir Arafat – included between two hundred and three hundred fighters. Within weeks after the battle, Fatah leaders boasted they could field fifteen thousand. Before the battle, the guerrilla groups had kept their distance from the PLO. After the battle, they assumed a dominant role in the organization, and in 1969 the members of the organization elected Yasir Arafat chairman – a position he held until his death.

Yasir Arafat was born in Jerusalem (his own story) or Cairo in 1929. His father was a well-to-do Palestinian merchant, perhaps a descendant of the Hajj Amin al-Husayni. Whether he was in fact related to al-Husayni remains a matter of dispute, but even as myth it is telling: Arafat lacked the social position and political credentials of the Hajj Amin and, as an upstart, was not averse to drawing from the reputation of a more established personality to enhance his own. Arafat studied engineering at King Fuad University in Egypt, from which he was graduated in 1951. He thus reached political maturity during the period of decolonization and might even be considered part of a younger group within the original cohort of Third World leaders that included Marshal Tito of Yugoslavia (born 1892), Chou En-lai of China (born 1898), Achmed Sukarno of Indonesia (born 1901), Kwame Nkrumah of Ghana (born 1909), Gamal 'Abd al-Nasser (born 1918), Ahmed Sékou Touré of Guinea (born 1922), Patrice Lumumba of the Congo (born 1925), and Fidel Castro of Cuba (born 1926). The 1950s were the golden age of anti-imperialism, secular nationalism, and Third World assertion. Even with the demise of Third Worldism in the early 1980s, Arafat's ideas never strayed far from their original source.

While he was at King Fuad University, Arafat reorganized the Palestinian Students Union. This period is key to understanding later developments because it was at this time that Arafat hit upon the two convictions that would define his approach to building a Palestinian national movement. According to an associate who knew him in the Egypt days,

Yasser Arafat and I knew what was damaging to the Palestinian cause. We were convinced, for example, that the Palestinians could expect nothing from the Arab regimes, [which were in 1951] for the most part corrupt or tied to imperialism, and that they were wrong to bank on any of the political parties in the region. We believed that *the Palestinians could rely only on themselves*.[1]

The principle of maintaining organizational and operational autonomy is not the only attribute the PLO has retained from its early days. Like all organizations, the PLO was very much a product of its time, and that time was the 1960s. During that decade, two events in particular provided inspiration to political activists throughout the Arab Middle East and beyond: the Algerian Revolution (1954–62) and the post-Suez radicalization of Egyptian politics. The first generated the cult of armed struggle; the second, structures of governance emulated throughout the Middle East. Arafat and his associates immersed themselves in both legacies.

The Algerian Revolution was an astonishingly bloody affair that resulted in upwards of one million casualties. French counterinsurgency, which included a liberal dose of torture against captured insurgents,

---

[1] Helena Cobban, *The Palestinian Liberation Organisation: People, Power, and Politics* (Cambridge: Cambridge University Press, 1984), 21–2.

20. Yasir Arafat came to personify the Palestinian national movement and its doctrine of armed struggle. (Source: Popperfoto/Alamy)

provoked an international outcry (including an impassioned denunciation of French actions on the floor of the United States Senate by a young senator from Massachusetts, John F. Kennedy). For their part, the Algerian revolutionaries not only committed acts of violence against soldiers and civilians alike, they embraced and even fetishized those acts. The psychologist and revolutionary theorist Franz Fanon, whom many consider to be the philosopher of the revolution, went so far as to proclaim violence launched by the colonized against the colonizer to have a liberating and cleansing effect. Violence, Fanon wrote, not only demystifies the power of the colonizer (if you cut them, do they not bleed?), it "introduces into each man's consciousness the ideas of a common cause, of a national destiny, and of a collective history."[2]

Like the Algerian insurgents, the guerrilla commanders who eventually formed the leadership of the PLO embraced the theory of armed struggle. According to the PLO Charter (1968),

Armed struggle is the only way to liberate Palestine. Thus it is the overall strategy, not merely a tactical phase.... Commando action constitutes the nucleus of the Palestinian popular liberation war. This requires its escalation, comprehensiveness, and the mobilization of all the Palestinian popular and educational efforts and their organization and involvement in the armed Palestinian revolution. It also requires the achieving of unity for the national struggle among the different groupings of the Palestinian people, and between the Palestinian people and the Arab masses, so as to secure the continuation of the revolution, its escalation, and victory.

That victory has, of course remained elusive, and some observers, including many sympathetic to the Palestinian cause, have laid blame for the failure of the Palestinian national movement on the doorstep of the cult of violence and the embrace of armed struggle. True, violence has played a key role – perhaps the decisive one – in keeping the Palestinian question on the front burner of international politics. Nevertheless, those who question the value of the doctrine of armed struggle argue that rather than mobilizing and liberating the Palestinian population, the fixation on armed struggle has coarsened Palestinian political culture, placed the average Palestinian on the sidelines of the national struggle, and distracted Palestinians from the slow, deliberate spadework

[2] Franz Fanon, *Wretched of the Earth* (New York: Penguin Books, 1967), 73.

essential to nation-building. According to the late Palestinian-American intellectual, Edward Said,

For decades we have relied in our minds on ideas about guns and killing, ideas that from the 1930s until today have brought us plentiful martyrs but have had little real effect either on Zionism or on our own ideas about what to do next. In our case, the fighting is done by a small brave number of people pitted against hopeless odds.... Yet a quick look at other movements – say, the Indian nationalist movement, the South African liberation movement, the American civil rights movement – tell us first of all that only a mass movement employing tactics and strategy that maximizes the popular element ever makes any difference on the occupier and/or oppressor. Second, only a mass movement that has been politicized and imbued with a vision of participating directly in a future of its own making, only such a movement has a historical chance of liberating itself from oppression or military occupation. The future, like the past, is built by human beings. They, and not some distant mediator or savior, provide the agency for change.[3]

Regardless of whether one chooses to believe Fanon or Said, the doctrine of armed struggle sanctioned the dominant role played by the guerrilla groups and their leaders in the Palestinian national struggle, just as the dominant role played by the guerrilla groups and their leaders in the Palestinian national struggle sanctioned the doctrine of armed struggle. Since 1969, representatives of guerrilla groups have dominated the PLO Executive Committee, which, in effect, acted as Yasir Arafat's cabinet.

Arafat founded Fatah in the late 1950s with the help of close friends he had made in Egypt and Kuwait, where he had gone to work after his studies. This group would form the inner circle of Fatah for years to come. Throughout its history, Arafat's Fatah has articulated a straight-forward nationalist message uncluttered by leftist or pan-Arabist jargon or aims: "Fatah ... solemnly proclaims that the final objective of its struggle is the restoration of the independent, democratic state of Palestine, all of whose citizens will enjoy equal rights irrespective of their religion." Compare this easily comprehensible message with the appeals to social revolution and class struggle found in the charter of another guerrilla group, the more ideologically sectarian Popular Front for the Liberation of Palestine (PFLP): "The PFLP's vision for creating a more

[3] Edward Said, *From Oslo to Iraq and the Road Map: Essays* (New York: Pantheon, 2004), 29–30.

just society, free from all forms of exploitation, is guided by . . . Marxist interpretation and dialectical materialism in its understanding and analysis of social reality." Because of the simplicity of its message, and because it has been able to draw from all layers of society, from notables and merchants (whom Marxists would classify as exploiters) to peasants and workers (the exploited), Fatah has always been the largest of the guerrilla groups. It has thus always provided the executive committee with the most members.

The remainder of the seats on the executive committee have gone to the sympathizers and leaders of an entire alphabet soup of other groups: the PFLP, the PDFLP (Popular Democratic Front for the Liberation of Palestine, now simply the DFLP), the PPSF (Palestine Popular Struggle Front), the ALF (Arab Liberation Front), and al-Sa'iqa (the only non-acronym, *al-sa'iqa* is Arabic for "the thunderbolt"). Like the PFLP, some of the guerrilla groups have differentiated themselves from their competitors by claiming adherence to one or another ideology – Marxism-Leninism, Maoism, Pan-Arabism, Ba'thism – although such adherence is, more often than not, a matter of expediency or sponsorship. Since, for example, al-Sa'iqa and the ALF have received support from, respectively, Syria and Iraq, both groups have had to toe the party line laid down by the ruling Ba'thists in the two countries. Other groups were simply founded by independent political entrepreneurs who recruited bands of followers around themselves. It has not been uncommon for some of the smaller groups to include no more than several hundred members. It is enough to make one wonder why such leaders as Ahmad Jibril of the minuscule Popular Front for the Liberation of Palestine–General Command (PFLP-GC) deserve to sit on the executive committee at all.

Nevertheless, sit they do. Seats on the executive committee are determined by a consensus of PLO leaders, usually meeting *in camera*. Their choices are then ratified ("elected") by the Palestine National Council (PNC), the legislative branch of the PLO. Because the PNC consists of representatives of officially recognized organizations – the General Union of Palestinian Students, General Union of Palestinian Workers, General Union of Palestinian Women, General Union of Palestinian Farmers, Higher Council of Palestinian Youth and Sport, and so on – as well as independent delegates, the PLO claims that the PNC is the

Palestinian nation in microcosm. The reality is a bit more complex. Choosing delegates to the PNC is not entirely democratic: Although some independent delegates are elected, for example, others fill seats that are set aside for them. Furthermore, since the Israelis outlawed the PLO and forbade Palestinians living in the occupied territories from participating in its institutions, West Bankers and Gazans lacked direct representation. Even today, more than a decade after Oslo "legalized" the PLO in the eyes of the Israeli government, representatives of diaspora Palestinians to the PNC outnumber representatives of Palestinians living in the territories by more than 4 to 1 (although the population ratio is probably closer to 2.5 to 1).

The structure of the PLO did not emerge by accident. During the 1960s, governing parties throughout the Middle East and, indeed, the Third World regarded themselves as the vanguard of the progressive elements of society. They also regarded the assemblies and party congresses they convened as a means to re-create their societies along more progressive lines. In post-Suez Egypt, for example, Nasser's government recognized five groups as the building blocks of the new order it was constructing: peasants, workers, intellectuals and professionals, national ("good") capitalists, and the army. In 1961, the Egyptian government called on handpicked representatives of these groups (the Alliance of Working Forces) to ratify a new constitution – the Charter for National Action – and to act as intermediaries whose job it was to keep their constituents informed of government decisions. The Egyptian government's efforts had two effects. First, by classifying "social parasites" (coupon-clipping capitalists, "feudal" landowners) as outside the social order, the government was able to promote its image of a classless society united by a common interest. Second, since each of the categories was linked to the others only through the government, it ensured the government alone would define that common interest without interference from a truly unified citizenry.

Nasser and his imitators throughout the Arab world believed that constructing governing institutions in this manner would expand the reach of those institutions throughout society, create the illusion of a nation unified in a common effort, and make it appear that the revolutionary vanguard that stood at the apex of society (such as the Revolutionary Command Council of Egypt) was inextricably linked to the masses it claimed to represent. But even in Egypt, where there is a relatively homogeneous population and where there had been a long history of centralized power long before Nasser, the attempt by the government to impose its vision on society produced mixed results at best. The results were even less impressive when the Egyptian model was transferred to the Palestinians. The reasons are not difficult to discern: The Palestinian population was scattered and divided between a diaspora community and a long-settled population in the occupied territories. And because it was banned by the Israelis, the PLO had no permanent institutional presence in Palestine and had to compete with both the Israelis and Arab governments in the management of day-to-day life for those it claimed to represent. Thus, when the Israelis attempted to organize the Palestinians of the occupied territories into collaborating "village leagues" in the early 1980s, the PLO could only react defensively, assassinating those who collaborated. The sway of the PLO over the Palestinian population was always more emotive than institutional – a factor that undoubtedly contributed to the competitive posturings of the guerrilla groups. Until the official establishment of the Palestinian Authority in 1996 (and even after), the institutional bonds tying the Palestinian population to the PLO leadership remained tenuous. This will become apparent in our discussion of the intifada, when Palestinians in the occupied territories constructed their own sets of institutions, which claimed fidelity to, but were in fact largely autonomous from, those of the PLO.

There was one additional problem that both Nasser and Arafat had to address: how to avoid rifts within the ruling revolutionary vanguard itself. The charismatic Nasser was able to impose his vision through force of personality. Arafat, a bit more challenged in the charisma department, chose a different path: He opted instead for a policy of inclusion and consensus building. In other words, he embraced all manner of Palestinian groups – even those that opposed Fatah's strategies or those that were aligned with one or another outside power – and brought them into the PLO's inner councils. When conflicts arose over policy, he attempted to resolve them through accommodation and negotiation, not confrontation.

Arafat claimed to have derived his policy of inclusiveness from the historical experience of the Palestinian people, particularly the Great Revolt:

[In 1936] our Palestinian leadership was divided and the rival groups fought each other. Because of this internal fighting many of our leaders were assassinated. After studying these matters, I made a vow that my generation would never repeat the mistakes of the past.[4]

In Arafat's view, the policy of inclusion and consensus building would minimize incidents of intergroup violence. It is likely that it did, although these incidents never entirely disappeared. After the Israeli invasion of Lebanon, for example, Syrian-aligned factions within the PLO launched a full-scale civil war within the organization. The wounds they left on the PLO still smart. The policy of inclusion and consensus building also lends credence to the PLO's claim to represent the entirety of the Palestinian nation and, as such, to be the "sole legitimate representative of the Palestinian people" (as Arab governments acknowledged it to be in 1974). Nevertheless, one cannot help but wonder whether the fate of the Palestinian national movement might have been different had Arafat drawn the same line in the sand against troublesome factions that Ben-Gurion did during his confrontation with the Irgun during the S.S. Altalena incident.

Certainly, the policy of inclusion and consensus building has not been without its drawbacks. Critics of the PLO complain that Arafat spent altogether too much time and effort trying to satisfy even the most excessive demands of recalcitrant rivals and political aspirants. This has made it difficult for the PLO to adjust to changing circumstances, take advantage of new openings or time-sensitive possibilities, or alter its course even in the face of disaster. According to one critic, it is easier to get an ocean liner to change direction than the PLO.

This does not mean that the PLO has not changed its policies over the years, of course. It certainly has. But more often than not, change comes only after it seems long overdue and force of circumstances demands it. Take, for example, the PLO's strategic policy. Article 15 of the PLO charter, adopted in 1968, calls for the "elimination of Zionism in Palestine." This remained the goal of the PLO throughout much of the 1970s, in spite of the fact that the 1967 war had already demonstrated that Israel was in the region to stay, that the frontline Arab states themselves had agreed to pursue the less lofty aim of reestablishing the *status quo ante*,

[4] Ted Swedenburg, *Memories of Revolt: The 1936–1939 Rebellion and the Palestinian National Past* (Minneapolis: University of Minnesota Press, 1995), 152.

and that guerrilla attacks against Israel showed no sign of convincing Israelis they should simply give up, pack their bags, and leave. It was not until 1974 that the PLO officially adopted as its goal the establishment of a Palestinian mini-state in the West Bank and in the Gaza Strip. Even then, the PLO initially hedged its bets by declaring that this mini-state would only be temporary, lasting until all Palestine could be liberated. It took slightly more than a decade after this for the PLO to accept (with reservations) the clause in Resolution 242 that acknowledged "the sovereignty, territorial integrity and political independence of every State in the area" – meaning Israel as well as the Arab states.

Throughout this slow reorientation in policy, Arafat consistently refused to lay down the law on an issue as important as the ultimate objective of the Palestinian national movement. Not only was he averse to alienating PLO hardliners, he feared opening up a rift between diaspora Palestinians (whose claims would not be settled by a mini-state) and Palestinians in the occupied territories. Arafat threw his full backing to a "two-state solution" only after the matter had been, for all intents and purposes, decided for him. In 1987, Palestinians in the territories had launched the intifada against the Israeli occupation, and Arafat had to scramble to get in front of their efforts. As critics of Arafat have been quick to assert, the Palestinian national movement found itself led by a politician when what it required was the leadership of a statesman.

In addition to making the Palestinian national movement slow to change course, the fixation on inclusiveness and consensus building has at times allowed one or another guerrilla group to back the organization into a corner. Perhaps the most notorious example of this was an affair Palestinians call "Black September." Before 1970, Jordan provided the main base for the PLO. Nevertheless, the relationship between the PLO leadership and the Jordanian government was rife with friction: PLO leaders suspected the Jordanian government of having its own agenda when it came to Palestine (which it did), while the Jordanian government resented the disregard for Jordanian law and sovereign rights shown by the Palestinian guerrillas resident in the kingdom. The activities of the PFLP were particularly provocative, since the group viewed the installation of a Palestinian government in Jordan as the first step in the campaign to liberate all of Palestine – or, in the words of the PFLP slogan, "The road to Jerusalem begins in Amman." In the summer of 1970, the PFLP and the allied PDFLP set up roadblocks and staged a number of high-profile terrorist incidents to embarrass the Jordanian government and demonstrate where real power in the kingdom lay. They took hostages at tourist hotels in Jordan and hijacked airplanes, which they landed in the desert outside Amman before blowing them up. Although it had been a principle of Fatah not to get embroiled in the internal affairs of Arab states, the actions of the PFLP and the PDFLP fedayeen left Arafat no choice. Whether prompted by loyalty, opportunism, or both, Arafat overcame his initial reluctance to get involved and threw his support behind his Palestinian comrades in arms.

As can be inferred from the epithet "Black September," the results of Arafat's decision were disastrous for the Palestinians. In mid-September, the Jordanian army struck back, crushing the Palestinian guerrillas, inflicting heavy casualties (PLO estimates run as high as thirty thousand) on Palestinian fighters and civilians alike, and expelling the PLO from its safe haven in Jordan. The PLO was forced to set up its primary headquarters in Lebanon. It remained there until the Israeli invasion of that unfortunate country in 1982. Forced to flee again, the PLO leadership ended up in distant Tunisia, hardly a frontline state, where it had to watch events in Palestine unfold from afar.

Black September would not be the last time one or more of the guerrilla groups would force the hand of the PLO. The numerous terrorist incidents that became the stock-in-trade of those groups had the same effect during the 1970s and into the 1980s. To be sure, these incidents kept the Palestine question alive at a time when the world community would just as soon have seen it go away. And the perpetrators of these incidents could always find justification for their missions in the doctrine of armed struggle. But more often than not, there was method to the terrorist madness that transcended the obvious goals of keeping the dream alive, releasing imprisoned Palestinians, and inflicting casualties on the Zionist enemy. As a matter of fact, guerrilla groups frequently launched their strikes against two targets at once: the Zionist enemy and its supporters, on the one hand, and pragmatists within the PLO, their outside allies, and moderate Arab regimes seeking a way out of the never-ending state of war, on the other. Terrorist planners feared that this latter group was all too willing to compromise Palestinian rights in order to reach a settlement.

Thus, many of the most spectacular terrorist incidents coincided with initiatives to reach some sort of accord, whether between Israelis and

Palestinians or between Israelis and their neighbors. For example, in 1974 three fedayeen from the PDFLP slipped over the Israeli border from Lebanon and killed twenty-two students in a high school in the Israeli town of Ma'alot. It was a horrible crime, committed ostensibly to force the release of Palestinian prisoners held in Israeli jails. Their release was not the only motive, however: The PDFLP and its Syrian allies – both members of what was then called the "Rejectionist Front" – were worried lest the Israelis and Egyptians come to a separate agreement on the disengagement of their troops in the Sinai. They were particularly concerned that once the two sides reached an agreement on disengagement, they would enter into negotiations on broader issues. This would leave the Palestinians and Syrians to fend for themselves. The raid was timed to put the Egyptians in a bad spot and discourage horrified Israelis from sitting down with their antagonists. In the end, the Israelis and Egyptians continued their talks despite the bloodshed.

Similarly, there was an upsurge in terrorist attacks in late 1985 that included the hijacking of an Italian cruise ship, the *Achille Lauro* (during which an American, Leon Klinghoffer, was killed) and shooting sprees at the Rome and Vienna airports (organized by Abu Nidal, a PLO renegade). The attacks coincided with an agreement reached between King Hussein of Jordan and Yasir Arafat to unite their efforts to reach a settlement based on United Nations Resolution 242. The Israelis and the Americans signalled that they were open to negotiations on this basis, as did the European Community, which began to play a more active role in the politics of the region. This time, however, the attacks had the anticipated effect. Negotiations broke down amidst bloodshed and mutual recriminations.

All too often, critics of the PLO have looked at incidents like the aforementioned, shaken their heads, and observed derisively that the PLO and Yasir Arafat have "never missed an opportunity to miss an opportunity." One man's opportunity is, however, another man's opportunism, and for all those who have faulted the PLO and Arafat for missing opportunities, there are others who would commend them for not abandoning any part of the national legacy they have been entrusted to preserve. Karl Marx once wrote, "The tradition of all past generations weighs like a nightmare on the brain of the living." The PLO has not been the only nationalist movement to face the problem of just how much of that tradition it can cast aside.

That being said, it should also be clear that the record of PLO achievements has been less than inspiring. The PLO has not brought about the "elimination of Zionism in Palestine," established a viable (or, for that matter, unviable) state, or even improved the lot of the Palestinians under occupation. Sometimes decisions made by the leadership have bordered on the bizarre. Arafat threw the support of the PLO behind Saddam Hussein in 1990 when the Iraqi dictator invaded Kuwait. A year later, he supported a brief, half-hearted coup by communist hardliners against Premier Mikhail Gorbachev of Russia. In both cases, Arafat's decisions alienated longtime financial and diplomatic supporters (the Gulf states and Russia). As we mentioned earlier, after a coalition that included several Arab states liberated Kuwait, the Kuwaitis expelled seventy thousand Palestinians working in their country. The PLO's leadership has been chased from Amman to Beirut to Tunis, only to end up headquartered in a partially demolished structure in Ramallah. Arafat personalized power and purposely refrained from building institutions that would ensure an orderly transition and administrative continuity after his death. And, as we shall see below, the PLO has even managed to squander its greatest asset – its monopoly over the Palestinian national movement – in spite of having earned the epithet "sole legitimate representative of the Palestinian people."

But even its harshest detractors cannot deny that the PLO has had to face conditions that might have crushed a less resilient nationalist organization. The PLO has had to function outside the territories Palestinians claim as their historic homeland. This has made it all the more difficult for it to mobilize its natural constituency, keep it mobilized, and direct resources to the national struggle. It has had to address the concerns of those diaspora Palestinians who hold onto the keys of their ancestral properties in Israel and dream of reclaiming them and of those nondiaspora Palestinians who want nothing more than to lead normal lives where they are. It has had to fend off internal challenges that all too often have been supported by outside powers, as well as external challenges that all to often come from those claiming to be allies. And of course it has had to do all this while facing an enemy that not only fields the second largest per capita army in the world (after North Korea), but has not hesitated to use that army in its efforts to crush the PLO and assassinate its leaders.

21. "Children bearing rocks," 1988. (Source: Peter Turnley/Corbis)

In spite of it all, the PLO has managed to post its share of successes, diplomatic and otherwise. For most of the world, the PLO still remains the "sole legitimate representative of the Palestinian people." Most important, the PLO did manage to salvage Palestinian nationalism in the wake of what very well could have been knockout blows in 1939 and 1948 and has kept it alive through some very rough times. This by itself is no mean achievement.

INTIFADA

In the aftermath of the 1967 war, the Syrian poet Nizar Qabbani (1923–98) wrote a poem called "Footnotes to the Book of Setback."[5] The poem, a harsh indictment of the Arab performance in the war, includes the following lines:

> We want an angry generation
> To plough the sky
> To blow up history
> To blow up our thoughts.

[5] Nizar Qabbani, "Footnotes to the Book of Setback," in *The Chatto Book of Dissent*, ed. Michael Rosen and David Widgery (London: Chatto and Windus, 1994), 101–5.

We want a new generation
That does not forgive mistakes
That does not bend.
We want a generation
Of giants.

Twenty years later, Qabbani got his wish and celebrated it in another poem entitled, "Children Bearing Rocks":[6]

With stones in their hands,
they defy the world
and come to us like good tidings.
They burst with anger and love, and they fall
while we remain a herd of polar bears:
a body armored against weather.

Like clams we sit in cafés,
one hunts for a business venture
one for another billion
and a fourth wife
and breasts polished by civilization.
One stalks London for a lofty mansion
one traffics in arms
one seeks revenge in nightclubs
one plots for a throne, a private army,
and a princedom.
Ah, generation of betrayal,
of surrogate and indecent men,
generation of leftovers,
we'll be swept away –
never mind the slow pace of history –
by children bearing rocks.

The poem is, of course, an ode to the Palestinian intifada and its paradigmatic symbol: unarmed Palestinian children throwing stones at Israeli tanks. The word *intifada* is Arabic for "shaking off." Before it was associated with the Palestinian uprising against Israeli occupation, Palestinians and other Arabic speakers used the word to refer to such mundane phenomena as the actions of a wet dog shaking off the rain. The intifada of 1987–93 was anything but mundane. Like the events of

---

[6] Zachary Lockman and Joel Beinin, eds., *Intifada: The Palestinian Uprising against Israeli Occupation* (Boston: South End Press, 1989), 100.

1936–9, 1948, and 1967, the intifada marked a turning point not only in the history of the Palestinian national movement but in the Israeli–Palestinian conflict as well.

At the time of the outbreak of the intifada, the Palestinian national movement had fallen on hard times. The Israeli occupation of the West Bank and Gaza Strip had entered its third decade. The PLO, crushed in Lebanon and forced to throw itself on the mercy of the United States, found itself headquartered fifteen hundred miles away from the site of the struggle. The flurry of diplomatic activity aimed at resolving the dispute in 1985 collapsed in the wake of a bloody series of attacks and reprisals. In an emotional speech delivered in 1986, King Hussein of Jordan, whose government had been coordinating policy with the PLO, announced that he had had it with both Arafat and the organization he chaired. And King Hussein was not alone in washing his hands of the Palestine problem. By 1987, the rest of the Arab world had turned its attention to a different problem.

In the wake of the peace treaty signed between Israel and Egypt at Camp David in 1979, the Arab League expelled its largest member, accusing it of breaking ranks and betraying the Palestinian and Arab causes. Anwar al-Sadat, president of Egypt, remarked at the time that the Arab world would come crawling back. In 1987, his prediction came true. Seven years earlier, Saddam Hussein's Iraq had launched an attack on Iran, believing that the Iranian Revolution of 1978–9 had so weakened his enemy that victory would be quick and sure. It was not, and by 1987 the Arab states were facing the prospect of an Iranian victory that many felt could endanger them all. In November of that year, Arab leaders met in Amman, Jordan, to discuss what to do. They decided that they had to stand firmly with Iraq, and if that meant exonerating Egypt so they might draw on its resources and support, so be it. The summiteers decided leave it up to each state to determine its own policy toward Egypt. Their willingness to reintegrate Egypt into the inter-Arab balance of power was a clear signal that the Arab world was prepared to place the Palestinian-Israeli issue on the back burner. When Yasir Arafat arrived in Amman to complain, King Hussein sent a subcabinet minister to meet him at the airport. The Palestinian national movement, it appeared, was on its own.

Less than a month later, everything changed. On 8 December 1987, an Israeli military truck hit a carload of Palestinian laborers in the Jabalya refugee camp in Gaza, killing four of them. Since an Israeli businessman had been stabbed to death two days earlier, the rumor spread that the collision was no accident but rather an act of revenge. The Gaza Strip exploded in riots and demonstrations. Rioting soon spread to the West Bank and East Jerusalem. The intifada had begun.

Twice before we have seen how a seemingly minor event such as an assassination of an archduke or a discovery of an arms cache touched off conflagrations far in excess of what a reasonable observer might have expected. Here is a third example. As in the case of World War I and the Great Revolt, a historical accident (literally, in this case) sparked the outbreak of the intifada. As in the case of World War I and the Great Revolt, a historical accident would have passed with little notice had the spark not fallen on dry tinder. The conditions of the occupation provided that dry tinder. Furthermore, as bad as those conditions had been, during the mid-1980s they were getting worse – and there was no end to the occupation in sight.

By 1987, there was no aspect of life in the occupied territories, no sector of the Palestinian economy, no part of the Palestinian landscape that had remained untouched by the occupation. Over the course of twenty years, the Israelis had buried the Palestinian population beneath a mound of regulations that not only were irksome but intruded into all aspects of life in the territories, from land use to employment to travel. The Israelis had expropriated land in the occupied territories for "military training," "public needs," and even nature preserves. They had constructed settlements that dominated the countryside. In the three years preceding the intifada alone, the Israelis built seventeen such settlements in the West Bank and the Gaza Strip and increased the settler population to more than sixty-eight thousand. Israeli agricultural policies had so devastated Palestinian agriculture that less land was under cultivation in 1987 than had been under cultivation in 1947. Israeli labor policies discriminated against Palestinian workers and barred them from enjoying the social benefits and wages granted Israeli workers. Tight-fisted Israeli public investment policies – or disinvestment policies, as many observers called them – wreaked havoc on infrastructure, and after the Israeli economic crisis of 1983, little money went to education and welfare support in the territories. Adding to the volatility of the territories were severe overcrowding (an estimated 3,754 Gazans per square mile), a population that was overwhelmingly young and resentful (more than half the population of the territories was under the age of fifteen, one-third between the ages of fifteen and thirty-four), and a policy of repression known as the "iron fist," which included administrative detentions, house demolitions, deportations, and school closings.

None of this guaranteed that an explosion would occur, of course. Popular uprisings are rare occurrences in history, and populations are just as likely to be cowed or dispirited by repression and impoverishment as they are to rebel. But for some reason, the ten-year period beginning in the late 1970s was a particularly volatile one in world history. Popular uprisings, which previously had been a rare occurrence became almost commonplace as unarmed populations throughout the world – China, Poland, South Africa, Nicaragua, Iran, the Philippines, Czechoslovakia – faced off against heavily armed soldiers to resist entrenched power. The population of the occupied territories did as well.

The intifada lasted for five years. Although it had begun to unravel by the time the Palestinian leadership, heeding the "spirit of Oslo," finally declared it over, it could not have continued for as long as it did without organization and planning. Soon after the initial eruption, the intifada became routinized. It did not take long for the residents of the occupied territories to work out an informal division of labor among themselves. This enabled them to maintain themselves while sustaining the rebellion. Just as important, a leadership and set of institutions soon emerged that acted to guide the rebellion, coordinate the activities of the population, and, when necessary, impose discipline.

On the most fundamental level, the division of labor was generational. Palestinian youths – of which there was a plentiful supply – manned the front lines of the rebellion. They skirmished with Israeli soldiers and tanks, enforced strikes and boycotts called by the leadership, distributed leaflets, and assisted local committees in their day-to-day activities. Perhaps their most important function was their role as actors in a theater of rebellion. Images of unarmed youths confronting Israeli tanks and soldiers with nothing more than stones and slingshots could not fail to strike a chord with an international audience and transform the Israeli David into an Israeli Goliath. Israel's position was hardly enhanced when the architect of the "iron fist" policy in the territories, defense minister Yitzhak Rabin, ordered Israeli soldiers to break the arms of stone-throwing Palestinian children. Since the Palestinians in the territories would have been incapable of defeating the Israeli army in a head-to-head showdown, what better way could there be to force Israeli citizens to confront the nature of the occupation and arouse the international community to pressure Israel to end it? And what stronger message could be sent to Palestinian adults than to remind them of the risks being taken and the sacrifices being made by their children?

Although youths manned the front lines, adults participated in what social scientists call "passive mobilization." Palestinian adults engaged in civil disobedience and organized boycotts of Israeli products and employers. They refused to cooperate with the civil administration or pay taxes, withdrew their money from Israeli banks, organized work gangs to help with the harvest, obeyed commercial and general strikes, and launched self-help initiatives to promote economic self-sufficiency. These activities were planned, coordinated, and monitored through a network of formal and informal grass-roots organizations, such as student and political groups, professional and neighborhood associations, and Islamic charities. Here, for example, is a description by a woman named Sarona who participated in one of the women's committees:

The Intifada began in December 1987. The intifada didn't just happen instantaneously. It came into being because there was a movement building towards it, even though we did not know what it was.

During school I was only introduced to the work that students were able to do. Once I finished school I entered into the women's committee. This gave me more of a bird's-eye look at society and the social problems that society was facing.

We took on several projects. Many women did not know how to read and write . . . so one project was to combat illiteracy.

Another activity of the women's committees was making social visits, having in mind a topic they wanted to discuss with the woman of the household. Our society has been brought up in such a traditional way that women would accept oppression or repression in the household rather than even think or talk about liberating themselves as women. We would attempt to take these women to other areas, to be introduced to many other people. One of the downfalls of a traditional household is that the woman is between four walls. She doesn't see much other than her own experience. So if she were able to go out and see women in other villages, how women who were more developed were working and taking a role in society, this would give her some hope or new insight on what she could possibly become.

The overall strategy of working with women involved two things: first, becoming involved in the social life of the woman, and second, through the involvement in that relationship building a politically conscious woman. The first of these was the primary goal. Women were facing real problems. And, we felt, if we wanted to be active and to gain the confidence of the masses, we needed to make those problems our problems.

Those women who lived on the same street and were active in the women's movement would meet on a regular basis. But the following month, those women would meet with the women on the next street. The goal was that these individuals see themselves as part of a movement of individuals who were related to each other, not to think that the whole movement was themselves. Twice a year there was a conference or a convention of the entire women's movement when we all got together.[7]

Although these groups frequently coordinated their activities on a citywide scale, the intifada initially lacked regional coordination. This problem was resolved in January 1988 when a group calling itself the Unified National Leadership of the Uprising (UNLU) emerged. The UNLU claimed to speak in the name of all the rebels. It issued communiqués (which were distributed as leaflets and read over Syrian and Iraqi radio) urging solidarity and issuing marching orders for the population of the territories. The first communiqué, for example, called for a general strike and warned against breaking ranks: "We warn against the consequences of becoming involved with some occupation authorities' henchmen who will seek to make you open your businesses. We promise you that we will punish such businessmen in the not too distant future."

Interestingly, the first communiqué also placed the UNLU under the authority of the PLO. The relationship between the two bodies was both cooperative and wary. Although the UNLU consisted of local loyalists of the guerrilla groups, the key to understanding its relationship with the PLO resides in the word "local." Distance and lack of local knowledge interfered with the ability of the PLO leadership to supervise their activities closely. So did the fact that the PLO represented the interests of both those Palestinians who resided outside the territories and those inside them. The former naturally sympathized with their brethren, yet, as we have seen, had goals that frequently reflected broader territorial aspirations.

[7] Staughton Lynd, Sam Bahour, and Alice Lynd, *Homeland: Oral Histories of Palestine and Palestinians* (New York: Olive Branch Press, 1994), 85–6.

On the other hand, both the PLO and the local leadership in the territories needed each other. The local leadership sought to exploit the aura of its special relationship with the PLO to prevent the emergence of political rivals. On the one hand, they feared the influence of socially prominent moderates, many of whom hailed from notable families. They understood that these moderates would be more acceptable to the United States and regional powers and more likely to compromise the rebellion's goals. On the other hand, they feared competition from Islamic groups, such as Hamas, that were decidedly less moderate. The UNLU thus sought to derive legitimacy from an association with the PLO and its icon-in-chief, Yasir Arafat. But the question of legitimacy worked both ways. The PLO could not afford to stand on the sidelines while a new leadership scored a rare success against the Zionist enemy. As we shall see in the next chapter, this fear of being made irrelevant played an important role in encouraging the PLO to accept the Oslo Accord.

The fear on the part of local leaders that traditional notables or Islamic radicals would attempt to make an end run around them points to one of the weaknesses of the rebellion that would eventually undermine it. When rebellions such as the intifada erupt, they incorporate all segments of society that harbor grievances against a common enemy. Once rebels begin to make programmatic demands or take measures to enforce revolutionary discipline, calls to unity wear thin and united fronts begin to crumble. The appearance of the UNLU thus did not guarantee unanimity in policy or opinion. Over time, class, gender, and ideological divisions that had festered below the surface of Palestinian society reemerged and the UNLU increasingly had to resort to coercion to maintain discipline. Oftentimes, freelance activists took it upon themselves to enforce "revolutionary discipline." This was particularly the case because the ranks of the uprising drew from lower-class youths who . . . well, acted like lower-class youths. For example, advocates of women's rights complained that in the cities of the West Bank and the Gaza Strip youths harassed and even assaulted women who wore Western dress in an effort to compel them to switch to so-called Islamic dress: headscarf, long coat, and so on. Although many commentators have read this to indicate an "Islamicization" of public space, it is just as probable that many poor youths associated Western dress with the upper classes they bitterly resented. As is the case during other popular rites (Carnivale, Mardi Gras), the uprising provided an opportunity for participants to invert class hierarchies.

If, so far, the description of the intifada sounds familiar, it is because it bore an eerie resemblance to the Great Revolt of the 1930s. Both rebellions began with minor incidents and quickly spread throughout a politically marginalized and increasingly impoverished Palestinian population. Local, popular-based groups sustained both rebellions and assumed responsibility for a wide range of political, social, and economic functions. The emergence of these groups demonstrated the resiliency and democratic potential of Palestinian society, of course. But the competition among these groups and their novelty often led to desperate attempts to extend their influence through force and intimidation. As in the case of the Great Revolt, the intifada soon descended into gang-type violence and hooliganism.

In the end, the intifada demonstrated both the advantages and disadvantages that rebels might gain by employing tactics of noncooperation and resistance to frustrate an occupier or colonial power and make its rule untenable. On the plus side for the Palestinians, the intifada put the international community on notice: The Palestine question was not about to fade away. At the same time, it transformed the occupation from a fact of Israeli life into a financially and morally debilitating problem. Israeli soldiers who had been seen – and, perhaps more important, who had seen themselves – as bulwarks against foreign aggression now spent their tours of duty among a hostile population, breaking up protests and maiming and killing children. During the first seven months of the intifada, about six hundred Israeli soldiers refused to serve in the territories. Others sought exemption because of the onset of previously undiagnosed injuries and illnesses. But in their resistance to the occupation, Palestinians paid a heavy price. Between 1987 and 1993, Israeli soldiers killed 900 to 1,200 Palestinians and injured about 18,000 (another 500 Palestinians died at the hands of Palestinians). About 175,000 Palestinians passed through Israeli jails, and Israeli human rights organizations estimate that about 23,000 Palestinians were subjected to "harsh interrogation" (read: torture). The Israeli army destroyed about two thousand Palestinian houses as punishment. And it is estimated that by the end of the intifada the standard of living in the territories had declined 40 percent.

It is, of course, up to Palestinians to decide whether the intifada was worth the human cost. And with all that has happened since – Oslo, the collapse of Oslo, the second intifada (which began in 2000), the shift in the Israeli position from negotiating a settlement to imposing one, the failure of the Palestinians to achieve sovereignty – there is much to be weighed. However Palestinians may come to regard it, the intifada did convince enough Israelis that the cost of holding onto the occupied territories outweighed the benefits. In 1992, Israelis elected Yitzhak Rabin prime minister. A member of the Labor Party and architect of the "iron fist" policy, Rabin had run for office on a platform that included a pledge to find a way out of the quagmire. That pledge took the Israelis to Oslo. Before we turn to Oslo, however, there is one loose end that must be tied up.

COMPETITION

Among the various organizations that emerged during the intifada were two that continue to challenge the dominance of the PLO over the Palestinian national movement: the Islamic Resistance Movement (better known by its acronym, Hamas) and its counterpart, Islamic Jihad. These organizations are best known for having injected a new lethality into the struggle between Israelis and Palestinians – the tactic of suicide bombings. At the height of the bombing campaign, which lasted from late 2000 through the first half of 2003, there were ninety-five suicide bombings. Although a number of these bombings were carried out by factions associated with the PLO, most can be laid at the doorstep of the Islamic political organizations. Targeting both Israeli soldiers in the occupied territories and civilians in Israel, suicide bombers killed upwards of 366 Israelis during this period.

Like the PLO before them, Hamas and Islamic Jihad proclaim the liberation of Palestine to be their primary political goal. Unlike the PLO, Hamas and Islamic Jihad refused to recognize Israel or support a two-state solution. And these organizations differ from the secular PLO in another way as well: In addition to advocating the liberation of Palestine, these organizations are committed to the reconstruction of Palestinian society according to Islamic principles. Islamic activists in Palestine, like Islamic activists elsewhere, not only demand that the domain of Islamic law be widened, they promote "Islamic norms" of behavior (dress codes for women, bans on alcohol) and have constructed alternative "Islamic institutions" that would act as the building blocks of the new society.

The spread of Islamic politics in the occupied territories during the 1980s might be attributed to a convergence of a number of events. Certainly, the success of Islamic movements in other parts of the Middle East resonated with Palestinians, who had witnessed governments and organizations espousing national unity based on secular principles fail time after time to liberate Palestine or end the occupation. Islamic movements may have come in various shapes and sizes, but they were mutually reinforcing, and the success of Islamic politics in one place showed populations in others just what Islamic politics might accomplish. Palestinians could not help but be impressed by the achievements of Hizbullah, which had emerged in Lebanon after the Israeli invasion of 1982. Many credited the organization, the new form of politics it represented, and the Islamic social solidarity it promoted with scoring the first real victories against the Zionist foe.

However inspiring the example of Hizbullah and other Islamic organizations may have been to Palestinians, Islamic politics would not have taken root in the occupied territories had the ground not been properly prepared for it. The proliferation of Islamic charities and social welfare associations set the stage for the emergence of Islamic political organizations and eventually provided the platform. Over the course of the occupation, the number and reach of these charities and associations expanded enormously, as did their importance in society. A variety of factors contributed to this expansion, but two in particular are noteworthy. First, in the wake of the oil boom of the 1970s, oil-producing countries such as Saudi Arabia and Kuwait increased their Islamic philanthropy in the West Bank and the Gaza Strip, financing a host of Islamic foundations and mosques from which those foundations distributed largesse. In 1967, there were 77 mosques in Gaza; by the outbreak of the intifada, there were 150. Many of these mosques not only provided shelter to Islamic charities and foundations but acted as incubators for Islamic political organizations as well. For their part, the Israelis gave tacit support to the spread of Islamic associations in the territories. The Israeli government believed that by providing relief and services to the population of the territories, Islamic associations would alleviate the direst distress and thus keep Palestinians pacified. In addition, the Israelis thought Islamic associations, which concentrated their focus on charitable works, spiritual renewal, and personal piety, might act as a counterweight to the PLO. Little did they realize they were playing with fire.

By the mid-1970s, Islamic charities and social welfare organizations had assumed responsibility for a number of essential activities in the territories, from dispensing relief to organizing daycare, kindergartens, primary schools, vocational training centers, blood banks, medical clinics, libraries, youth and sporting clubs, and soup kitchens. When the intifada broke out, Islamic activists who had cut their teeth in these organizations sprang into action alongside much of the rest of the population in the occupied territories. Joining them were Islamic activists who had gained political experience in trade unions, educational institutions, and professional syndicates. Five days after the traffic accident that sparked the intifada, Hamas announced itself to the world.

Observers disagree on just how spontaneous the emergence of Hamas actually was. Some argue that the Islamic charities and social welfare organizations established during the 1970s and 1980s were merely fronts that masked the long-term political designs of Islamic militants. They point to the fact that a number of those who established charities and welfare organizations had been members of the Muslim Brotherhood, an organization that had been established in Egypt in 1928 and may have been the first mass-based Islamic organization in the Arab world. Not only had Muslim Brotherhood sent assistance to the rebels fighting in the Great Revolt, Muslim Brotherhood volunteers joined the ranks of the rebels as well. After the Great Revolt, the Muslim Brotherhood established branches in Palestine, and by 1948 there were thirty-eight autonomous branches there. Faced with repression in Egypt and Egyptian-held Gaza (Nasser viewed the Muslim Brotherhood as a threat to his regime and person), the argument goes, members laid low, waiting for the right circumstances to reemerge.

Others acknowledge the Muslim Brotherhood connections of some Hamas leaders but treat the "sleeper cell" theory with skepticism. They point to the fact that the Muslim Brotherhood of Egypt was itself divided on strategy. To be sure, some in the organization had advocated political activism, but others believed that their main priority should be the Islamic renewal of society. What would be the point of taking power, these Muslim Brothers argued, if the society over which they ruled remained corrupt and un-Islamic? Thus, the argument goes, the charities and welfare organizations established in the occupied territories had no other purpose than to provide charity and welfare. Those Palestinians who went on to found Hamas and Islamic Jihad could not help but be swept up by events. They naturally put their extensive networks in service to the cause.

Whatever the case, the synthesis of nationalist aspirations, Islamic renewal, and personal piety pioneered by Islamic political organizations created a potent mixture. As with Islamic political organizations elsewhere, Hamas and Islamic Jihad offer their followers an ideology that appropriates the universal message of Islam for what is, in effect, a nationalist struggle. The "Introductory Memorandum" of Hamas puts it as follows:

Hamas is a popular struggle movement that seeks to liberate Palestine in its entirety from the Mediterranean Sea to the River Jordan. It bases its ideology and policies on the teachings of Islam and its juridical tradition. It welcomes all those who believe in its ideas and stands and who are ready to bear the consequences of sacred struggle for the liberation of Palestine and the establishment in it of an independent Islamic state. . . .

The Palestinian people are the direct target of the Zionist settler occupation. Therefore, they must bear the main burden of resisting the unjust occupation. This is why Hamas seeks to mobilize the full potential of the Palestinian people and channel it into steadfast resistance against the usurper.

Palestine is the terrain for confrontation with the enemy. The Arab and Islamic countries are regions from which our Palestinian people can draw support, particularly political, informational, and financial support; but the bloody confrontation with our Zionist enemy must take place on the sacred soil of Palestine.[8]

It should be evident from this document that Palestinians do not support Hamas and Islamic Jihad because they have given up on nationalism. Rather, they support Hamas and Islamic Jihad because they believe these organizations to represent a more effective means of achieving nationalist goals. And it does not hurt that many perceive the PLO as too corrupt to trust and Hamas and Islamic Jihad as selfless purveyors of charity and social services.

[8] Khaled Hroub, *Hamas: Political Thought and Practice* (Washington, DC: Institute for Palestine Studies, 2000), 295–6.

However much the Israeli government may regret letting the genie out of the bottle, Hamas and Islamic Jihad have certainly proved to be a counterweight to the PLO. Both have studiously avoided diluting their freedom of action and so have avoided joining the PLO, the UNLU, and the Palestinian Authority, the proto-government established in areas of the West Bank and the Gaza Strip under Palestinian control. When the Palestinian Authority tried, at the insistence of the United States and Israel, to clamp down on Hamas and Islamic Jihad, it was met with armed resistance. Although the PLO has officially accepted the two-state solution, Hamas and Islamic Jihad kept the campaign for the liberation of all of historic Palestine alive, declaring Palestine to be an "Islamic trust" that cannot be divided or surrendered. Like various guerrilla groups associated with the PLO, they have used terrorism to sabotage any attempt to arrive at a solution that would compromise the full realization of their territorial demands.

Whether in the future Islamic political organizations will remain a counterweight to the PLO or vice versa is not at all clear. The authority of the PLO and the Palestinian Authority (which is, in effect, the institutional presence of the PLO in the territories) has been undercut by incessant corruption, internal squabbling, institutional fragility, their own authoritarian tendencies, and actions of the Israeli government. Certainly, Israeli military incursions into territory supposedly under PA authority and the expansion of Israeli settlements have done little to demonstrate the ability of the PLO and Palestinian Authority to deliver the goods. To top it all off, the death of Yasir Arafat leaves the PLO without an iconic figure who can command the loyalty of most Palestinians. All these factors have strengthened the hand of the Islamic political organizations. At the same time Arafat's body was being lowered into the ground in Ramallah, public opinion polls in the Gaza put the level of support for Hamas at around 30 percent whereas support for Fatah hovered at around 20.

On the other hand, Islamic political associations face obstacles as well. Although Hamas and Islamic Jihad have attracted widespread support among Palestinians, they have excited widespread fear as well. Many Palestinians – PLO loyalists, secular nationalists, advocates of women's rights, and so on – do not support Islamic politics on principle. After five years of the first intifada and four years of the second, Palestinians are exhausted. The all-or-nothing demands of Islamic

radicals have been effectively countered by the Israeli strategy of imposing Israel's will unilaterally through the construction of the separation
barrier and recurrent military incursions into the occupied territory. And
throughout the Middle East, the wind seems to have been taken out of
the sails of Islamic movements, which have repeatedly had to confront
repression, co-optation, and the limits of their own competence. Certainly, the Israeli campaign of "targeted assassinations" has taken its
toll on the leadership of Hamas and Islamic Jihad. With all the accu-
mulated pressures building on Hamas, the tensions over strategy and
tactics that have long simmered between the organization's West Bank
and Gaza leaders have taken on a new life, fueling speculation about
impending divisions in the ranks.

Perhaps the clearest indicator of the future of Islamic political organizations in the occupied territories might be found in their own history and the history of similar movements elsewhere. As we have seen,
the Islamic tendency in Palestine has exhibited flexibility in the past,
responding to changing circumstances by adopting new tactics, strategies, goals, and organizational forms. Thus, Islamic political organizations in Palestine might very well take a page out of the book of their
counterpart in the north. During the Israeli occupation of Lebanon,
Hizbullah provided the Shi'i Muslim community with social services
while waging a fierce guerrilla campaign against Israel. Although
Hizbullah still lobs the occasional missile in the direction of Israel, it
is, for all intents and purposes, part of the Lebanese political establishment. Hizbullah participates in electoral politics, and soon after it began
contesting elections, it came to control the largest bloc of votes in the
Lebanese parliament. If the Palestinian Authority is able to establish its
credentials as the government of an independent Palestine, Hamas and
kindred organizations may well follow suit. Hamas has already taken
a first step in this direction: In December 2004, shortly after the death
of Yasir Arafat and the announcement of elections for his successor, the
West Bank leader of Hamas announced for the first time that it would
accept a two-state solution.

SUGGESTIONS FOR FURTHER READING

Abu-Amr, Ziad. "Hamas: A Historical and Political Background." *Journal of Palestine Studies* 22 (Summer 1993): 5–19. Concise but informative article on the origins of the Islamic group.

Christison, Kathleen. *Perceptions of Palestine: Their Influence on U.S. Middle East Policy*. Berkeley: University of California Press, 1999. A history of official American attitudes toward the Palestinians, president by president.

Cobban, Helena. *The Palestinian Liberation Organization: People, Power, and Politics*. Cambridge: Cambridge University Press, 1984. Excellent, if a bit dated, introduction to the PLO.

Hroub, Khaled. *Hamas: Political Thought and Practice*. Washington, DC: Institute for Palestine Studies, 2000. Hroub presents an impressive array of documents in his account of the movement's ideological origins and evolution.

Lockman, Zachary, and Joel Beinin, eds. *Intifada: The Palestinian Uprising against Israeli Occupation*. Boston: South End Press, 1989. Selection of articles from the periodical *MERIP Reports*, along with supplementary materials.

Peteet, Julie. *Gender in Crisis: Women and the Palestinian Resistance Movement*. New York: Columbia University Press, 1991. Analysis of contemporary Palestinian nationalism using gender as a framework for analysis.

Said, Edward, and Christopher Hitchens, eds. *Blaming the Victims: Spurious Scholarship and the Palestine Question*. London: Verso, 1988. Collection of provocative essays on Palestinians and the Palestine question and how they are viewed in the West.

Sayigh, Yezid. *Armed Struggle and the Search for State: The Palestinian National Movement, 1949–1993*. Oxford: Clarendon Press, 1997. Similar in nature to Cobban's book but more expansive and current.

Stein, Kenneth. The Intifada and the 1936–1939 Uprising: A Comparison." *Journal of Palestine Studies* 19, no. 4 (1990): 64–85. Underscores the continuity in the Palestinian national struggle and situates the intifada in its historic context.

10

THE RISE AND FALL OF
THE OSLO ACCORD

From December 1992 through August 1993, an unofficial delegation of Israelis (acting with the knowledge of their foreign ministry) met with a delegation of Palestinians in Oslo, Norway. In talks hosted by the Norwegian foreign minister and his wife, they hammered out a formula for peace between Israelis and Palestinians, known ever since as the Oslo Accord. Once the negotiators had put together a general framework, they presented it for official consideration.

From Rhodes in 1949 to Madrid in 1991, the path leading to peace had been littered with the remains of failed attempts to bring about a settlement. What made the Oslo negotiations revolutionary was their configuration: Rather than engaging Israel and its neighbors through either the Rhodes or conference formats, the Oslo format brought together Israelis and Palestinians in face-to-face negotiations for the first time. By reducing the conflict to its most elemental level – a conflict between the two peoples, both of which claimed the right to inhabit and control some or all of Palestine – the Oslo negotiations brought the century-old struggle full circle.

It was no coincidence that the Arab-Israeli phase of the conflict began at the dawn of the Cold War and ended soon after American president George H. W. Bush and Soviet president Mikhail Gorbachev pronounced the Cold War over. Although the Arab-Israeli conflict certainly played itself out according to its own internal logic, just as certainly the Cold War rivalry between the two superpowers played a significant role in driving and sustaining the conflict.

Beginning in 1948, when both the United States and the Soviet Union weighed the Cold War costs and benefits before granting recognition to Israel, the two superpowers never for a moment forgot the global implications of their policies in the region. For forty years, American policymakers approached or justified their intervention in the conflict in terms of containing the Soviet Union or rolling back its influence in the region. Thus, Henry Kissinger designed his shuttle diplomacy to marginalize the role of the Soviet Union and make the United States indispensable to all parties in the conflict, and President Reagan pronounced Israel a strategic asset in the struggle against international communism. For forty years, the Soviet Union exploited the conflict in an effort to break containment and gain a regional advantage over its antagonist, hoping that it might translate a regional advantage into a global one. Hence, for example, the Soviet Union deliberately escalated tensions on the eve of the 1967 war to energize an anti-Israel, pro-Soviet Arab alliance, and it restocked the arsenals of its allies in the aftermath of the war. Then, abruptly, the Soviet Union imploded, leaving statesmen and politicians to deal with an entirely new problem: how to define the post–Cold War world order.

The immediate post–Cold War period was a period of extraordinary optimism. There is perhaps no better example of this optimism than an article written in 1989 by Francis Fukuyama in the periodical *National Interest*. The article, entitled "The End of History," predicted that the demise of the last of the great totalitarian systems of the twentieth century and the end of the Cold War heralded the beginning of a new international order in which regional conflagrations and nationalist violence would vanish before the onward march of democracy and freedom. The killing fields of Bosnia, Kosovo, Somalia, and Rwanda and of course the attacks of 9/11 soon demonstrated just how clouded Fukuyama's crystal ball was. Nevertheless, Fukuyama did capture the spirit of the day. The same optimism that drove Fukuyama's argument found expression in George H. W. Bush's "New World Order."

The New World Order was the first practical attempt to come to grips with the changed circumstances of the post–Cold War era. While at best a vague concept, the New World Order seemed to rest on two pillars: multilateralism and globalization. Although the United States was the sole remaining superpower, American statesmen had learned a powerful lesson from the usefulness of NATO and other multilateral institutions in winning the Cold War. Applying this lesson, they argued that the United States could be most effective in the post–Cold War world if it did not attempt to impose the American will unilaterally on the world (a lesson neoconservatives in the administration of George W. Bush have shunned). True, America would take the lead in international affairs, but it would marshal the strength of the international community behind it through diplomacy and consensus building. The new multilateralism got its first test in the Gulf War of 1991, when the Security Council of the United Nations, which includes Russia and China as members, sanctioned the American-led effort to drive Iraq out of Kuwait.

Globalization was the economic correlate of the new multilateralism. It promised prosperity to all members of the international community if only they would tear down the barriers that impeded the global exchange of goods. Globalization enthusiasts were quick to assert that, with the end of the Cold War, economics had replaced ideology as the common currency of world affairs (ignoring the fact that the neoliberal economics touted by globalization enthusiasts – free trade, open markets, invisible hands, etc. – was, of course, just another ideology). To paraphrase Calvin Coolidge, in the post–Cold War world, the chief business of *all* people would be business.

History may very well judge the short-lived New World Order to have been as naive as Woodrow Wilson's Fourteen Points – which, by the way, also rested on the twin pillars of multilateralism and globalization. Nevertheless, for a brief shining moment, it was the only game in town.

The optimism of the moment appealed to many Israelis who had become tired of the constant grind of the intifada and who looked forward to the economic benefits of peace in the new global economy. For them – and here we are referring to the almost 60 percent of Israelis who supported the Oslo Accord when it was first presented – stubbornly holding onto the occupied territories and expanding settlements there had become more of a burden than an asset, particularly since these policies represented *the* stumbling block to Israel's full integration into the regional and world communities. If the intifada and its diplomatic fallout did not provide proof enough of this, there was the Gulf War, which did much to persuade Israelis that the highly touted defensive value of the territories had been overstated. After all, while the Israeli army was preoccupied with putting down a Palestinian insurgency provoked by the occupation, Scud missiles from Iraq rained down on Israel from afar. Just as disturbing, Israel's erstwhile ally, the United States, kept its "strategic asset" at arm's length lest it alienate the Arab members of the grand coalition.

It was during this period that some Israelis began promoting the notion of a "post-Zionist" future. If Israelis were to forego the ideological obligations imposed by Zionism, they claimed, and accept the fact that Israel was just another small state in a world community that included many other small states, they could begin to live "normal" lives like the citizens of those other states: They could be at peace with their neighbors, they could trade with them, they could curtail the huge outlays for defense and restructure their economy to make it more efficient. This would enable Israelis to compete more effectively in the global marketplace. Although the doctrine of post-Zionism never gained more than a limited following, a majority of the electorate did respond to the new circumstances by electing a Labor Party candidate, Yitzhak Rabin, prime minister in June 1992. No one could accuse Rabin of being "soft" on military and defense issues: He was not only the architect of the "iron fist" policy in the territories but had been responsible for the expulsion of fifty thousand Palestinians from the towns of Lydda and Ramle in the 1948 war. Rabin's candidacy further benefitted from the intransigence of his Likud opposition on the issue of settlements and territorial expansion, as well as from the post–Gulf War aspirations of many Israelis. The platform on which he ran promised to reverse Likud policy in the occupied territories by freezing settlement activity for one year. It also promised to negotiate an interim agreement on Palestinian autonomy in six months.

The PLO also responded to the new circumstances, although, it appears, more from apprehension about the future than out of hope. We have already discussed some of the factors that generated this apprehension. Headquartered in far-off Tunis, the PLO had been caught unawares at the outbreak of the intifada and, over the course of the insurgency, faced challenges to its leadership from a new generation of homegrown activists, including Islamic activists. The disintegration of the Soviet Union had eliminated the PLO's most important diplomatic patron, and Arafat's diplomatic bungling did little to endear him to Moscow (which rubbed salt into Arafat's wounds by restoring diplomatic relations with Israel, broken since 1967). As the Soviet Union disintegrated, tens of thousands of Soviet Jews – 175,000 alone in 1990 – who had previously been barred from leaving the country emigrated to Israel. The Likud government of Israel expanded the construction of settlements in the occupied territories to house these new immigrants and encouraged

Israeli employers to hire them to replace Palestinian workers. All the while, conditions in the territories continued their decline as the intifada spun out of control and as the Arab Gulf states, piqued at Arafat's pro-Iraq stance, cut off financial assistance to Palestinians. Adding insult to injury, the PLO was not even invited to the Madrid Conference held at the end of the Gulf War (although unaffiliated Palestinians were allowed to attend). If being the "sole, legitimate representative of the Palestinian people" was to continue to mean anything at all, the PLO would have to do something it had never done before: get ahead of events and shape their course.

The Oslo Accord signed by the Israeli government and the PLO actually includes two separate protocols. The first consists of an exchange of letters of mutual recognition between the two parties. Arafat's letter to Yitzhak Rabin reads as follows:

Mr. Prime Minister,

The signing of the Declaration of Principles marks a new era in the history of the Middle East. In firm conviction thereof, I would like to confirm the following PLO commitments:

The PLO recognizes the right of the State of Israel to exist in peace and security.

The PLO accepts United Nations Security Council Resolution 242 and 338.

The PLO commits itself to the Middle East peace process and to a peaceful resolution of the conflict between the two sides and declares that all outstanding issues relating to permanent status will be resolved through negotiations.

The PLO considers that the signing of the Declaration of Principles constitutes a historic event, inaugurating a new epoch of peaceful coexistence, free from violence and all other acts which will endanger peace and stability. Accordingly, the PLO renounces the use of terrorism and other acts of violence and will assume responsibility over all PLO elements and personnel in order to assure their compliance, prevent violations and discipline violators.

In view of the promise of a new era and the signing of the Declaration of Principles and based on Palestinian acceptance of Security Council Resolutions 242 and 338, the PLO affirms that those articles of the Palestinian Covenant which deny Israel's right to exist, and the provisions of the Covenant which are inconsistent with the commitments of this letter are now inoperative and no longer valid. Consequently, the PLO undertakes to submit to the Palestinian National Council for formal approval the necessary changes in regard to the Palestinian Covenant.

Rabin's letter to Arafat reads as follows:

Mr. Chairman,

In response to your letter of September 9, 1993, I wish to inform you that, in light of the PLO commitments included in your letter, the Government of Israel has decided to recognize the PLO as the representative of the Palestinian people and commence negotiations with the PLO within the Middle East peace process.

The exchange of recognitions seems straightforward, but it is not. Palestinian skeptics and opponents of Oslo point out that although Arafat's letter to Rabin recognizes the State of Israel, nowhere in his letter to Arafat did Rabin ever recognize the right of Palestinians to establish a sovereign state of their own. Furthermore, by recognizing Israel, Palestinians conceded that close to 80 percent of historic Palestine – the territory within the pre-1967 boundaries of Israel – would forever remain off the bargaining table. This meant that all future territorial adjustments would come from the West Bank and the Gaza Strip. The territory controlled by Israel could only get larger; the territory controlled by the Palestinians could only get smaller. Palestinian skeptics and opponents of Oslo thus accused Arafat of throwing away the only real bargaining chip the Palestinians had at the outset of negotiations. This is why Mahmoud Darwish responded to Oslo by writing, "Who will strike our flags, us or them?" and sarcastically put the following words in Arafat's mouth: "We could not raise the siege / So let us surrender the keys of our Paradise to the Minister of Peace, and be saved." This is also why many Palestinians have treated Israeli demands for further territorial concessions with such resentment.

The second protocol signed by Arafat and Rabin is called the Declaration of Principles. The declaration stipulated that Israel and the PLO would negotiate the withdrawal or redeployment of Israeli forces from the Gaza Strip and the Jericho area within three months. (Although the geographic extent of Gaza is obvious, just what the "Jericho area" comprised immediately became a subject of dispute. The Israelis claimed it consists of the town of Jericho, a territory of about 15 square kilometers. The PLO claimed it comprises Jericho and its environs, a territory of about 150 square kilometers. Whatever the case, this was not a propitious beginning to a "partnership for peace.") Both Gaza (excluding the Israeli settlements) and Jericho would then be granted self-governing status; Israelis and Palestinians would negotiate an "interim agreement," which would define and authorize the creation of a Palestinian representative council; and the council would, in turn, draft a blueprint for an "interim self-governing authority": the Palestinian Authority. After Palestinian elections, the two sides would enter into "permanent status negotiations." These would be concluded no later than July 1997 and would resolve the few small remaining outstanding issues: Jerusalem. Right of return. Refugees. Settlements. Security.

The Declaration of Principles thus took a form long familiar to observers of Middle East negotiations – a form that stressed "process" over "content." As we have seen, in the immediate aftermath of the 1967 war, the United States attempted to broker a permanent settlement between Israel and Egypt known as the Rogers Plan. American Secretary of State William Rogers journeyed to the Middle East carrying with him a prepackaged agreement that merely required the assent of the two governments. According to the Rogers Plan, Israel was to withdraw from all the territory it had taken from Egypt, and Egypt was to sign a peace treaty with the Israelis. What could be simpler? But the terms of the Rogers Plan were too far-reaching for either side to swallow right off the bat, the plan failed, and peace negotiators learned a valuable lesson for the future: Rather than presenting two sides with the final terms of an agreement at the outset, Middle East negotiators should begin with small confidence-building steps. Only after confidence was built could the big-ticket items be put on the table. Supporters of this strategy point to its successful application in the aftermath of the 1973 war, when the United States brokered negotiations between Israel and Egypt leading to the Camp David peace agreement of 1978. Skeptics, on the other hand, contend that Anwar al-Sadat's desperation to get the Sinai back, not the strategy of the negotiators, was the key factor in reaching an agreement.

The underlying idea of the aforementioned strategy is that small steps lead inevitably to larger ones, particularly since the two sides in negotiations get into the habit of talking and compromising. This makes it easier for negotiators to reach successive interim agreements and build momentum. It also makes it easier for negotiators to sell the compromises reached along the way, as well as the final treaty, to their governments and publics. Nevertheless, there are a number of problems associated with the strategy as well. Confidence is an elusive concept at best, and to rest a diplomatic strategy on confidence building may be putting too many eggs in a pop-psychology basket. A process-driven formula also encourages both sides to haggle over small issues so that they might be in a better position when the next round of negotiations begins. As the issues under negotiation become increasingly complex or the compromises demanded become increasingly onerous, negotiators and mediators must expend increasing amounts of their political capital to keep the process going and sell their decisions to increasingly skeptical governments and publics. Finally, why would anyone assume that agreements on relatively trivial issues will lead to agreements on more significant ones? For example, just because Israel promises to dismantle illegal settlements and the PLO promises to erase clauses from its charter advocating the destruction of Israel, this does not mean that either side would ever be prepared to compromise on Jerusalem or the settlements authorized by the Israeli government. Compromising on either would likely lead to the downfall of whatever government that signed on to it. Little wonder, then, that neither Israelis nor Palestinians retained their enthusiasm for the Oslo process for long.

The deadline for the "interim agreement" came and went. Finally, in September 1995, Arafat and Rabin signed Oslo 2 (as the interim agreement came to be called) in a ceremony on the White House lawn. The agreement outlined the powers and duties of the Palestinian Authority, and as stipulated in the Declaration of Principles, elections were held in January 1996. As might be expected, Palestinians chose Yasir Arafat to be the first president of the Palestinian Authority. In addition, the agreement divided up the West Bank into areas of varying Israeli control: Zones A, B, and C. Israeli forces were to withdraw from each area according to a preestablished timetable, and as they did, the Palestinian Authority would assume control. Although Israeli withdrawal from Zones A and B would take place almost immediately, the agreement linked withdrawal from Zone C to the permanent status negotiations. In other words, the agreement held Palestinian Authority control over approximately 70 percent of the West Bank hostage to negotiations over Jerusalem, refugees, settlements, and security. Rubbing salt into Palestinian wounds, Oslo 2 also allowed for an expansion of "bypass roads" to link the settlements with each other and with Israel. No matter how much of Zone C eventually came under the control of the Palestinian Authority, those roads would act as dividers preventing free movement of Palestinians from one "canton" to another.

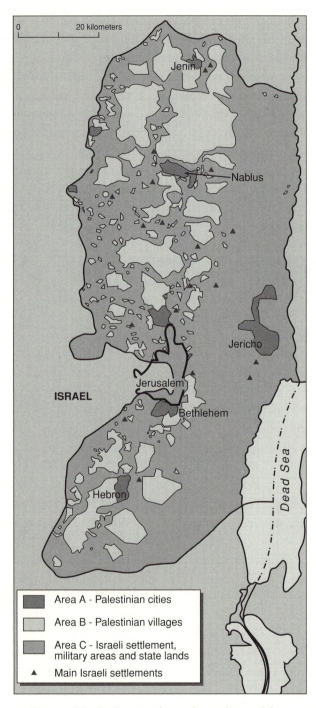

Map 10. West Bank zones of control according to Oslo 2.

Clearly, the Israelis had negotiated with greater skill. Nevertheless, Rabin's opposition at home, including the Likud and Gush Emunim, charged the prime minister with giving away the store. A little more than a month after Rabin signed Oslo 2, a Jewish religious extremist shot him dead. At his trial, the assassin testified that he shot Rabin because the prime minister wanted "to give our country to the Arabs." Six months later, Israelis elected a Likud candidate and Oslo opponent, Benjamin Netanyahu, prime minister.

THE DECLINE AND FALL OF THE OSLO PROCESS

About a decade after the signing of the Oslo Accord, the Associated Press ran the following story:

JERUSALEM (AP) – Despite a new US push for a truce, Israel raided Palestinian towns and refugee camps Friday, killing at least 36 Palestinians on the deadliest day in 17 months of fighting. Five Israeli teenagers and a soldier were killed by Palestinians.

Hours-long battles raged in a Gaza village and two West Bank refugee camps, with Palestinians coming under heavy machine-gun fire from Israeli tanks and helicopters....

In the West Bank refugee camp of Tulkarm, dozens of Palestinian gunmen were pinned down in alleys and in homes, surrounded on all sides by Israeli forces, including helicopter gunships firing from above. Israeli troops called on the gunmen over loudspeakers to surrender. About 250 Palestinians were rounded up in a local school.

Israeli troops barred Palestinian ambulances from entering the camp to retrieve casualties, and a count of six Palestinians killed in the camp – including a 9-year-old-boy – was expected to climb....

In the Jewish settlement of Atzmona in Gaza, a Palestinian gunman killed five Israeli teenagers during a 15 minute rampage that began just before midnight, Thursday. The assailant, a 19-year-old member of the Islamic militant group Hamas, emptied nine ammunition clips and threw six grenades before he was shot dead by Israeli troops. Four of the teenagers were killed while studying religious texts, and the fifth was burned to death by a grenade hurled into his dormitory.[1]

How did things get so bad so quickly?

[1] Karin Laub, "Middle East Violence Intensifies," Associated Press, 8 March 2002.

Oslo 2 was not the last agreement signed by Palestinians and Israelis. In January 1997 the two sides agreed to divide the West Bank city of Hebron into exclusive zones of control, and in October 1998 they signed the "Wye Memorandum," which addressed some of the issues unresolved by the previous two agreements. Nevertheless, it was apparent that it did not take long for the so-called spirit of Oslo to evaporate. The Hebron and Wye agreements were only reached after extensive American prodding, and subsequent attempts to speed up the Oslo process, bring it to completion, or even get the two sides to fulfill their commitments were stillborn.

Earlier we compared nationalist movements to a "house of many mansions." Although both parties to the Oslo negotiations included those who, for reasons noble or ignoble, placed a premium on reaching a settlement, both camps also included those who felt the agreements represented a betrayal of principle. These dissenters threw up roadblocks at every juncture. The Israelis had their Likud Party and Gush Emunim, the Palestinians had their rejectionists and Hamas. But while there was an ironic symmetry between the Likudniks and the rejectionists and between Gush Emunim and Hamas, there was also a significant difference between the two camps as well: Arafat had staked his reputation on Oslo and remained committed to the process. Nevertheless, from force of habit or weakness, he failed to bring the opponents of Oslo in line and allowed himself to be carried along by events rather than shaping them. Those opponents also fell into a familiar pattern by committing acts of violence against Israelis designed to sabotage the process. As for Israel, the assassination of Rabin brought a government to power that was committed to resisting any further concessions and minimizing the impact of concessions already granted. Palestinian violence played into its hands. For three crucial years a Likud-dominated government, citing security concerns, attempted to mitigate the effects of Oslo. When a Labor-dominated government returned to power, it attempted to turn the Palestinian flank by first reaching a settlement with Syria before refocusing its attention on its Palestinian partner for peace. By that time, the damage had been done.

Between 1993 and the beginning of the second intifada in 2000, Palestinian grievances continued to grow and support for the Oslo process among Palestinians continued to diminish. Although the Oslo process had continued for seven years, the Palestinian Authority was never able to acquire full control over more than 18 percent of the West Bank. Israel expropriated 200 square kilometers of land, added thirty new settlements and expanded those already in place, ordered the construction of almost 500 kilometers of bypass roads to link those settlements to Israel, and constructed ninety thousand new housing units in the settlements and in East Jerusalem. Between 1993 and 2000, the number of Israeli settlers in the occupied territories had doubled. At the same time, Israel began regularly barring Palestinian workers from entering Israel. The Israeli government cited security concerns, but Palestinians were not entirely convinced. Israel had begun replacing Palestinian workers with about two hundred thousand East and South Asians, eastern Europeans, and Africans while the ink was still fresh on the initial accord. To many Palestinians, withholding employment while maintaining control over vital resources such as water seemed to be a strange way of ushering in the era of "two states living side by side in peace and security" and might even be considered the height of bad faith.

The patience of Palestinians in the territories with the Oslo process thus wore thin. So did their patience with the incompetence and corruption of the PLO, whose members controlled the Palestinian Authority. The PLO leadership, jealous of its prerogatives, dismantled the grassroots organizations that had emerged during the intifada, imposed censorship on news outlets, and constructed nine different agencies to police the population. The "Tunisians," as the returned PLO exiles were called, built lavish villas for themselves and their families, granted monopolies to their friends and took kickbacks for doing so, and squandered much of the billion dollars of yearly assistance granted the Palestinian Authority by the United States and the European Union. Although Arafat himself lived frugally, Arafat's wife lived in Paris on a Palestinian Authority subsidy of a hundred thousand dollars a month – this at a time when Palestinians had been reduced to poverty (according to a World Bank report, by 2004 one half of Palestinians in the territories lived on less than two dollars a day). And Arafat's habit of personalizing power had disastrous consequences: When he died in November 2004, the secret of where several billion dollars of Palestinian Authority money was died with him.

Thus, by July 2000, the Oslo process seemed to have reached an impasse. To break that impasse, American president Bill Clinton summoned Israeli prime minister Ehud Barak and Yasir Arafat to Camp

David for one last go at revitalizing it. Anxious not to squander his limited political capital on interim agreements, Barak decided to abandon the piecemeal approach that had been the hallmark of the Oslo process until then. In its place, he took a page out of William Rogers's book. Staking everything on one last throw of the dice, he made Arafat a nonnegotiable, take-it-or-leave-it offer that covered everything, from the final disposition of territory to the final status of Jerusalem. Given the choice of taking it or leaving it, Arafat left it. Although Arafat was never known for decisiveness under the best of circumstances, there was a logic to his decision. Palestinian negotiators noted that Israel had not lived up to its previous commitments to redeploy its forces or halt settlement growth. Now Palestinians were asked to set aside what they had already negotiated and accept Israeli assurances of good faith. And Barak's refusal to put his offer on paper (lest it give ammunition to his opponents at home) certainly did little to reassure Palestinians. Rightly or wrongly, the Palestinian negotiators smelled a rat. Much to the chagrin of Bill Clinton, they refused to make a counteroffer and simply walked away.

A cruel irony undermined the Camp David negotiations. Barak made his offer because he feared the continued erosion of Israeli support for Oslo if the process continued to drag on. Arafat and his associates rejected Barak's offer because they feared the continued erosion of Palestinian support for Oslo if they returned home having compromised all of what they considered to be their historic legacy at one fell swoop. Things took a definite turn for the worse two months later, when Ariel Sharon paid a provocative visit to the Temple Mount/Haram al-Sharif in Jerusalem. Palestinians reacted with a second, bloodier intifada.

FROM THE IRON WALL TO THE SEPARATION FENCE

In a marvelous study of Israel's policy toward its neighbors, historian Avi Shlaim takes as his central metaphor an image first applied by Vladimir Jabotinsky in a 1923 essay, "On the Iron Wall (We and the Arabs)." The "Arabs," according to Jabotinsky, will never accept the Zionist project in Palestine and will never willingly make peace with a Jewish state. Thus, Jabotinsky wrote, if Zionists were serious about building a state, they would have to erect an "iron wall" of military strength and impose their presence unilaterally on their neighbors. Shlaim views the iron wall approach as an invariable default position in Israeli politics, not limited to one or another party. It was, after all, the first Labor prime minister of Israel, David Ben-Gurion, who initiated the policy of launching reprisal raids against those states from which Palestinian infiltrators entered Israel. Nevertheless, no Israeli leader has taken Jabotinsky's vision more to heart than Ariel Sharon, who became Israel's prime minister in 2001.

Ariel Sharon was born in 1928 on a moshav about ten miles distant from Tel Aviv. His military career began at the age of fourteen when he joined the Palmach, an elite unit of the Haganah. He fought in all the Arab-Israel wars (1948, 1956, 1967, and 1973) and was commander of Unit 101, which was formed to carry out Ben-Gurion's reprisal raids. It was Unit 101 that staged the bloody and politically destabilizing incursions into Jordan in 1953 and into Gaza in 1955, described in Chapter 8. As the fortunes of the Likud rose in the 1970s, so did Sharon's. In 1977, Prime Minister Menachem Begin appointed him defense minister. It was in this role that he crafted Israel's invasion of Lebanon in 1982 – an escapade that almost derailed his career.

Sharon presented the invasion of Lebanon as a military necessity to clear the southern part of that country of PLO guerrillas. To accomplish this objective, Begin announced that the Israeli army would strike into no more than forty kilometers of Lebanese territory. The Israeli army soon occupied more than 50 percent of Lebanon and even laid siege to Beirut. The depth of Israel's invasion pointed to other reasons for its launching. After Israel and Egypt had signed their peace treaty in 1978, Israel began establishing collaborationist "village leagues" in the West Bank to undercut the power of the PLO there. As we have seen, the PLO, being the PLO, reacted by ordering Palestinians not to comply and by assassinating those who did. To impose its will unilaterally on the occupied territories, the Israeli government needed to eliminate the only organized group that stood in its way, and if that meant hunting down and killing the PLO in Lebanon, so be it.

Unfortunately for Sharon, Lebanon proved to be for Israel what Vietnam had been for the United States: a bloody quagmire. The last Israeli troops left Lebanon only in 2000. Sharon himself was implicated in one of the great atrocities of the war: the massacre of between 700 (the official Israeli tally) and 2,750 (the Red Cross tally) unarmed Palestinian refugees by a right-wing Christian militia in the Sabra and

Shatila camps. The official Israeli report of the massacre, issued by the Kahan Commission, held Sharon indirectly responsible for the massacre. "Indirect responsibility" is an odd way of putting it: The Israeli army fired signal flares the night of the massacre to light the way for the killers. Equally damaging to Sharon's reputation, the invasion failed to accomplish any of its goals: The world was horrified at Israeli tactics (including the indiscriminate shelling of Beirut during the eighty-eight–day siege) and condemned it, the United States rebuffed its ally by calling for full Palestinian autonomy (presumably under Jordanian rule) for the first time and by overseeing the evacuation of the PLO leadership to Tunis, and the president-elect of Lebanon installed by the Israelis was assassinated. About a year after the invasion, Menachem Begin resigned as prime minister, convinced, the story goes, that he had been deceived by his defense minister. Although Sharon spent the next few years in the wilderness, he refused to give up on his iron wall approach to imposing a unilateral solution to the Palestinian problem.

Sharon's political rehabilitation began under Prime Minister Yitzhak Shamir, who succeeded Begin. Appointed housing minister in the early 1990s, Sharon oversaw the biggest expansion of Israeli settlements – facts on the ground – in the occupied territories to date. Beginning in 1998 he served as foreign minister in the cabinet of political rival Benjamin Netanyahu, and after Ehud Barak became prime minister a year later (elected in no small part because he promised to finally extricate Israel from the Lebanon quagmire), he began a campaign to outmaneuver his political rivals in Likud while restoring that party to power.

On 28 September 2000, Ariel Sharon, accompanied by more than a thousand security guards, paid a visit to a site called by Jews the "Temple Mount" and by Muslims the "Haram al-Sharif" (the noble sanctuary). As we saw in Chapter 1, Jews regard the Temple Mount as hallowed ground because it marks the spot where they believe the first and second temples once stood. Muslims regard the Haram al-Sharif as hallowed ground because it marks the location of the al-Aqsa Mosque, which was built on the site from which Muhammad made his night journey to heaven. According to the report commissioned by the United States government – the Mitchell Report – Sharon went to the site for no other reason than to enhance his political fortunes: By visiting the site, he hoped to embarrass the government of Ehud Barak, which would be forced to decide whether to permit Sharon access to a Jerusalem religious site, and he would upstage his Likud opponents. Whether he anticipated its effects or not, Sharon's visit had consequences that far transcended his job status. The following day, Palestinians held a demonstration that was broken up by Israeli police using live ammunition. Four demonstrators were killed. Protests spread throughout the territories. Although the Israeli government was quick to place the blame for the protests and the ensuing violence on the Palestinian Authority and Yasir Arafat, the Mitchell Report thought otherwise:

We have no basis on which to conclude that there was a deliberate plan by the Palestinian Authority to initiate a campaign of violence at the first opportunity, or to conclude that there was a deliberate plan by the GOI [government of Israel] to respond with lethal force.

However, there is also no evidence on which to conclude that the Palestinian Authority made a consistent effort to contain the demonstrations and control the violence once it began, or that the GOI made a consistent effort to use non-lethal means to control demonstrations of unarmed Palestinians. Amid rising anger, fear, and mistrust, each side assumed the worst about the other and acted accordingly.

The violence that exploded in the wake of Sharon's visit to the Temple Mount/Haram al-Sharif catapulted the ambitious general – who had earned the nickname "the bulldozer" not only for his girth but for his ability to plow through his adversaries without hesitation (or for that matter, subtlety) – into the position of prime minister of Israel.

The particular events that have taken place since the outbreak of what has become known as the "second" or "al-Aqsa intifada" are too depressing to recount in detail. With the onset of the second intifada, the suicide bombing campaign undertaken by Hamas, Islamic Jihad, and PLO militants who feared that they were being upstaged by their Islamist rivals began in earnest. In March 2001, a Palestinian suicide bomber killed three Israeli women in Netanya, a small city between Tel Aviv and Haifa. In May, a suicide bomber killed ten Israelis and wounded another hundred at a shopping mall. In August, a suicide bomber blew himself up along with eighteen Israelis in a pizza parlor in Jerusalem. Six of the eighteen Israelis were children. Five bombs went off in Jerusalem on 5 September.

The object of terrorism is to terrorize, and it was doing the trick. During the first three months of the second intifada, about three-quarters of all "incidents" recorded by the Israel Defense Forces pit Israeli soldiers against unarmed Palestinian civilians, and since the outbreak of the second intifada, about three Palestinians have died for every Israeli: Of the approximately four thousand deaths attributable to the second intifada, three thousand were Palestinian and over five hundred of these were Palestinian children under the age of eighteen. These numbers, and the Palestinian grievances that sparked the second intifada in the first place, were drowned out by the horror roused by the terrorist outrages. The Israeli government responded to the wave of suicide bombings by ordering the extrajudicial assassinations of those whom they blamed for carrying out or inciting the campaign, by launching reprisal raids into Palestinian towns, by destroying the homes and orchards of families of accused terrorists, by imposing checkpoints outside every population center and refugee camp throughout the territories, and by closing off the economic links between the territories and Israel.

Then came 11 September. The al-Qaida attack on the United States finished off the New World Order, which had been languishing anyway under the drift of the Clinton administration and its uneven response to the horrors of Rwanda, Bosnia, and Kosovo. Ten days after the attack, President George W. Bush announced a new doctrine that the United States would use to define the international order: the War on Terrorism.

We will pursue nations that provide aid or safe haven to terrorism. Every nation, in every region, now has a decision to make. Either you are with us or you are with the terrorists. From this day forward, any nation that continues to harbor or support terrorism will be regarded by the United States as a hostile regime....

This is not, however, just America's fight. And what is at stake is not just America's freedom. This is the world's fight. This is civilization's fight. This is the fight of all who believe in progress and pluralism, tolerance and freedom. We ask every nation to join us....

This country will define our times, not be defined by them.

If the New World Order provided the context in which Oslo could emerge, the War on Terrorism provided the context in which Israel could pursue a policy of imposing a unilateral solution on its Palestinian problem.

It should have been a no-brainer for Ariel Sharon to place Israel on the side of angels in the War on Terrorism. Ever the bulldozer, however, Sharon first misstepped. Recalling American efforts to put together the Gulf War coalition, Sharon warned the United States not to repeat Neville Chamberlain's Munich policy: "Do not try to appease the Arabs at our expense." But Sharon had more than one ace in the hole: He could count on the support of the neoconservative policy planners in the Bush administration, some of whom had worked with the Likud Party in the past, and he could count on the blundering of the Palestinian leadership, which seemed oblivious to the new dispensation. By April 2002, George W. Bush was calling Sharon a "man of peace," in effect granting the Israeli leader carte blanche as an ally in the War on Terrorism.

If the Palestinians appeared oblivious to the new dispensation, Sharon soon took to it like a duck to water. In the wake of a suicide bombing that left thirty dead in March 2002, Sharon ordered "Operation Defensive Shield," the largest post-Oslo Israeli incursion into Palestinian territories to date. Israeli forces reoccupied Palestinian towns and cities in all three zones – A, B, and C – including Bethlehem, Hebron, Ramallah, Nablus, Jenin, and Gaza. In their effort to "route out the terrorist infrastructure," Israelis waged gun battles with armed Palestinians, blew up houses, made mass arrests, and deployed helicopter gunships, tanks, and bulldozers to reduce whole city blocks to rubble. In the process, about five hundred Palestinians died. When a United Nations envoy arrived in Jenin, he called what he saw "horrific beyond belief" and compared the effects of Israel's action in the city to an earthquake. In Ramallah, the Israeli army left Arafat's compound in ruins and kept the president of the Palestinian Authority under virtual house arrest until his last days. Updating the well-worn cliché "We don't negotiate with terrorists" for the War on Terrorism, Sharon ended contacts with the Palestinian Authority, declaring there was no one to talk to.

Sharon's lament that there was no one to talk to on the Palestinian side – a lament seconded by an American administration consumed by the War on Terrorism – effectively sidelined the Oslo process. This doesn't mean that various parties didn't continue trying to keep the process limping along. They did, and by the beginning of 2003 there were a number of plans on the table. These plans were both official (the Roadmap for Peace, underwritten by the United States, Russia, the European Union, and the United Nations) and nonofficial (the so-called Geneva Accord and People's Voice Initiative, fashioned by independent

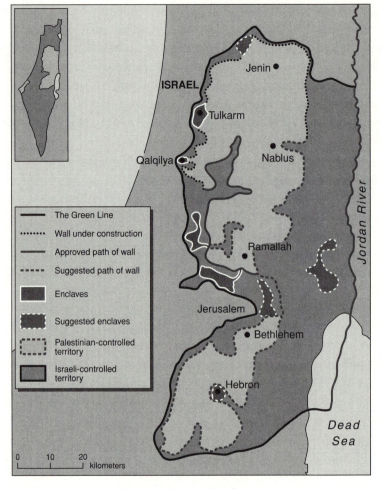

Map 11. The separation barrier.

Palestinians and Israelis who sought to recapture the magic of 1993). The Roadmap followed a step-by-step strategy; the others put everything on the table at once. Not that it much mattered anymore: Times had changed and Sharon had a strategy of his own. If he could impose this strategy under the figleaf of one or another plan, so much the better; if not, he would impose it anyway.

In April 2002, the Israeli government had announced that it would begin construction of a barrier to prevent suicide bombers from infiltrating into Israel from the West Bank. Called by the Israelis a security fence and by Palestinians a separation wall, the barrier follows a rather

22. In 1948, the western half of the West Bank town of Baqa was integrated into Israel while the eastern part of town remained outside. The barrier now separates one part of the town from the other. (Source: Reinhard Krause/Reuters/Corbis)

circuitous route. Instead of adhering to the 1949 armistice lines that had served as Israel's unofficial border for over half a century, the barrier – which will eventually consist of a 450-mile stretch of concrete walls, electronic fences, barbed-wire fences, and trenches – sometimes cuts deeply into the occupied areas and incorporates the largest of the West Bank settlement blocs as well as Jerusalem.

Palestinians, human rights groups, and most of the international community have condemned the construction of the barrier for a number of reasons. To begin with, the barrier establishes new facts on the ground that, if the diplomatic process should ever recommence, would mark a revised starting point for Israeli negotiators. Furthermore, building the fence requires the uprooting of Palestinians, the confiscation of their lands, and the division of villages from the lands under cultivation. The path of the fence encircles whole towns, like Qalqiya and Tulkarm, and surrounds East Jerusalem, in effect cutting off the populations that live in those places from the rest of the West Bank. According to the World Bank, about 150,000 Palestinians have had their lives disrupted so far by the barrier and, if and when it is completed, another 150,000 will be in the same boat. Once the barrier is complete, 200,000 more

Palestinians will find themselves living in territory under direct Israeli jurisdiction. Their choice: live under Israeli rule or leave and move to territory under Palestinian jurisdiction. Thus, for many Palestinians, human rights groups, and members of the international community, the barrier represents the first step to a kinder, gentler form of ethnic cleansing.

The Israeli government, on the other hand, touts the effectiveness of the barrier in stopping infiltrators and cites a 90 percent drop in suicide bombings since construction of the barrier began in earnest. Perhaps so. But suicide bombing is a tactic, and tactics are easily modified to fit new circumstances. In October 2004, suicide bombers attacked a hotel and tourist camp in the Sinai packed with vacationing Israelis, killing thirty-four. In December 2004, "Palestinian militants" set off an explosion in a tunnel dug underneath an Israeli checkpoint in Gaza, killing five Israeli soldiers. The barrier was, of course, not at all effective in preventing these attacks.

Building the barrier was not the only unilateral action initiated by the Sharon government in its quest to reshuffle the post-Oslo deck. In February 2004, the Sharon government announced that it planned to withdraw all Israeli settlements from Gaza. This was not the first time someone in the Israeli government floated the idea of "disengaging" from Gaza. To many in Israel, Gaza has hardly been worth holding onto. Although the most zealous members of the settler movement oppose withdrawing from *any* conquered territory, other Israelis have argued that there is little reason to retain an overcrowded, impoverished, and hostile territory to which 50,000 soldiers have to be deployed to protect 7,500 Israeli settlers. The idea of disengaging from Gaza has floated around Israeli ministries since shortly after the 1967 war, and "Gaza First" withdrawal proposals were part of the 1993 Declaration of Principles and a 2002 attempt to arrange a ceasefire during the second intifada. (Because Palestinian negotiators were afraid that "Gaza First" might become "Gaza First and Last," they insisted Israeli withdrawals from Gaza be accompanied by at least token Israeli withdrawals from the West Bank. Hence, in 1993 "Gaza First" became "Gaza and Jericho First," and in 2002 "Gaza First" became "Gaza and Bethlehem First.")

Although the settler movement balked, the Israeli Left and the United States government rallied around Sharon's proposal, arguing that the leopard had changed his spots. In 1958, French president Charles de Gaulle had proclaimed, "Vive Algérie française" (long live French Algeria); in 1959, de Gaulle reversed himself and called for Algerian self-determination. The old cold warrior Richard Nixon went to China in 1972. Now it appeared that Ariel Sharon, formerly the patron saint of the settler movement, had become an Israeli de Gaulle or Nixon by likewise reversing himself: Rather than expanding the territory under Israeli control, he was actually diminishing the territory under Israeli control. Could this be a first step to further disengagements, this time from the West Bank? Indeed, Sharon had already announced that he was prepared to abandon some northern settlements that lay outside the barrier and move 50,000 to 70,000 settlers to settlements encircled by the barrier.

Others are more skeptical. They point out that under the disengagement plan Israel would continue to control Gaza's borders, airspace, trade, and electrical grid, as well as the flow of workers in and out of the territory. The fact that Israel has decided to take this step with or without the consent of the Palestinian Authority, they maintain, means that Israel is prepared to walk away from the bargaining table, possibly for good. As a matter of fact, they view the withdrawal from Gaza as part of a diplomatic strategy aimed at thwarting the latest peace proposal on the table – the Roadmap for Peace – and easing any pressure on Israel to make further concessions. With the disengagement, Sharon can boast that Israel has done its part – now its up to the Palestinians to do theirs. A top aide to Sharon, Dov Weisglass, said as much in an interview published in the Israeli newspaper *Haaretz*:

The significance of our disengagement plan is the freezing of the peace process.... It supplies the formaldehyde necessary so there is no political process with the Palestinians.... When you freeze the process, you prevent the establishment of a Palestinian state, and you prevent a discussion on the refugees, the borders, and Jerusalem. All with [an American] presidential blessing and the ratification of both houses of Congress.[2]

It is, of course, impossible to know whether Weisglass was boasting or merely trying to calm the Likud's political base. Whatever the case,

---

[2] Ari Shavit, "Top PM Aide: Gaza Plan Aims to Freeze the Peace Process," *Haaretz*, 6 October 2004.

many Israelis and much of the outside world are resigned to what is now being called a "long-term interim process."

It is impossible to predict just how long a long-term interim process will last. It could be six months, six years, or forever. As far as the Sharon government is concerned, the ball is in the Palestinian court, and whatever the Palestinians choose to do behind the iron wall is up to them. But Israeli policy is not made or implemented in a vacuum, and there are a number of variables that have recently been introduced into the Israeli–Palestinian equation. These variables include the death of Arafat, Palestinian Authority elections, Hamas's strategic flip-flop, and the American reengagement in the peace process in tandem with its awkwardly named "Partnership for Progress and a Common Future with the Region of the Broader Middle East and North Africa" policy. Then there is always the matter of the volatility of the Israeli political scene, the fragility of its coalition governments, and the question of the day: Will the settler movement mount an effective resistance to the Gaza withdrawal and, if it does, will other Israelis have the stomach to take the settlers on? Regardless of the uncertain prospects for a settlement, however, it remains significant that no statesman, no diplomat, no pundit is even suggesting that a resolution to the conflict might be achieved by, for example, brokering a deal between Israel and Syria. All would agree that any resolution to the conflict, if there is to be one, ultimately lies in the hands of the two principals, the Israelis and the Palestinians. This remains the legacy of Oslo.

SUGGESTIONS FOR FURTHER READING

Makovsky, David. *Making Peace with the P.L.O.: The Rabin Government's Road to the Oslo Accord.* Boulder, CO: Westview Press, 1999. A detailed account of Israeli motivations for entering into the Oslo process.

Malley, Robert, and Hussein Agha. "Camp David: The Tragedy of Errors," *New York Review of Books*, 9 August 2001, 59–65. Revisionist insider account of the Camp David negotiations. In subsequent issues there are rebuttals by Ehud Barak and Benny Morris and replies by Malley and Agha.

Said, Edward W. *From Oslo to Iraq and the Road Map: Essays.* New York: Pantheon, 2004. The last political essays by the man whom many considered the foremost Palestinian public intellectual of his time.

Schiff, Ze'ev, and Ehud Ya'ari. *Israel's Lebanon War.* New York: Simon and Schuster, 1984. First popular account of war, told by two journalists.

Shlaim, Avi. *The Iron Wall: Israel and the Arab World.* New York: W. W. Norton, 2001. Shlaim uses Jabotinsky's metaphor of an "iron wall" to explain Israel's policies toward its neighbors.

Siegman, Henry. "Sharon and the Future of Palestine," *New York Review of Books*, 2 December 2004, 7–14. Skeptical view of Sharon's policy initiatives toward the conflict.

Silberstein, Laurence J. *The Postzionism Debates: Knowledge and Power in Israeli Culture*. New York: Routledge, 1999. A look at both sides of the debate over what might be either a major ideological shift in Israeli public life or a tempest in a teapot.

EPILOGUE

Yasir Arafat died on 11 November 2004. Within hours, the PLO chose Mahmud Abbas as its new leader. Almost two months later, Palestinians residing in the West Bank and Gaza Strip went to the polls and elected Abbas president of the Palestinian Authority.

Although Mahmud Abbas (Abu Mazen) had been a founding member of Fatah and a long-time crony of Arafat, he had, over the years, developed a reputation different from that of his boss. During the 1970s, he was among the first PLO leaders to advocate negotiating with Israelis, and by 1977 he openly endorsed a two-state solution to the conflict. Abbas led the Palestinian delegation in Oslo in 1993, and during the 2005 campaign for the presidency of the Palestinian Authority, he promised to restart talks with Israel. He also called the violence of the al-Aqsa intifada "counterproductive" – a far cry from calling it "wrong" but, considering the atmosphere in the occupied territories, certainly not something to be scoffed at. The day after his election, he received a congratulatory telephone call from Ariel Sharon. For the first time in years, diplomats and pundits began to speak with cautious optimism about the promise of the "post-Arafat era."

During Arafat's last years, the Israeli and the American governments had charged that the ailing leader was the chief obstacle to peace. To be sure, Arafat only sporadically challenged factions inside and outside the PLO that were responsible for the violence of the al-Aqsa intifada. More often than not, he opted for the time-tested but ineffective policy of accommodation and negotiation, treating Islamic Jihad of 2000 as if it were the PFLP of 1970 and as if the circumstances and the stakes were the same. And to be sure, Arafat was responsible for the corruption endemic to the PA. After all, even though the man may not have been personally corrupt, the buck certainly stopped there. Not only did Arafat temporize as his associates enriched themselves, their families, and their clients at public expense, he blocked the institutional development of the Palestinian Authority that might have frustrated their worst excesses.

Whatever Arafat's sins of omission or commission, however, it might also be argued that declaring Arafat the chief obstacle to peace was a self-fulfilling prophecy. By asserting there was no one to talk to, the Israelis and their American backers personalized the conflict at a time when their entire diplomatic strategy was based on the assumption that the momentum created by the process itself would be sufficient to overcome any obstacles placed in its way. By asserting there was no one to talk to, the Israelis and their American backers effectively granted the gunmen and bombers veto power over the peace process, undercut moderates on both sides who could have used progress in negotiations to isolate those gunmen and bombers, and relegated all issues save Israeli security to secondary importance.

With the election of Abbas, there was no longer no one to talk to. And after an initial period of uncertainty, marked by the sort of tit-for-tat violence that had become commonplace over the course of the previous five years, both sides began to take a number of small concilia-tory steps in rapid succession: the Palestinian Authority deployed police on the Gazan border with Israel to stop mortar and rocket attacks; Ariel Sharon and Mahmud Abbas met in person in the Egyptian resort of Sharm al-Shaykh and agreed to a ceasefire; and Israel announced a limited release of Palestinians held in its jails (about 12 percent of its Palestinian prisoners), began negotiations to withdraw its forces from some Palestinian towns, and ended its policy of destroying the homes of terrorists and purported terrorists. Even a bloody suicide bombing in Tel Aviv in February 2005 that killed four and wounded thirty others – an event that surely would have provoked a severe Israeli military response had it occurred under Arafat's watch – effected only a temporary set-back to the newly found spirit of cooperation between the two sides. In an uncharacteristically magnanimous gesture, Sharon even chose to blame the attack, launched by Islamic Jihad, on Syria, which housed offices of Islamic Jihad and had recently taken Iraq's place as a charter member of the axis of evil.

Neither Sharon nor Abbas could afford to let the attack or any other issue get in the way of their budding "partnership for peace." Both have risked their political careers on a smooth Israeli disengagement from the Gaza Strip and from northern settlements in the West Bank. Following weeks of political bloodletting, Sharon finally got Knesset approval for the withdrawal and for a compensation package for settlers. He could not allow his opponents to charge that the planned withdrawal was emboldening Palestinian militants, just as they had charged that Israel's withdrawal from Lebanon had emboldened Hamas. Abbas, too, has a stake in ensuring a successful Israeli withdrawal from Gaza. Although Arafat may have lacked the charisma of a Nasser, he had, over the years, achieved an iconic stature. A lifelong apparatchnik, Abbas has neither charisma nor an iconic stature. Abbas had been elected president of the Palestinian Authority with a little over 62 percent of the Palestinian vote, and because about half of all eligible Palestinians had neglected to vote (Hamas had called for a boycott of the elections), his highly touted mandate was not really much of a mandate at all. Abbas thus needs the Israeli withdrawal as much as Sharon. He needs it to take the wind out of the sails of his opponents and potential opponents, and he needs it to demonstrate that his strategy of reopening negotiations with Israel will yield results.

So here we are as this book goes to press: a budding "partnership for peace" (or, if you are a cynic, marriage of convenience) between Sharon and Abbas, overwhelming Israeli power that enables Israel to remain secure behind defensible borders with or without a negotiated settlement, and an international climate favorable to delivering a final resolution of the conflict. Could it be that historians of the future will look back on the period from 2002 to 2005 – the years of the barrier, Arafat's death, the "freest and fairest elections in the Arab world" (as George W. Bush has called them), and (possibly) the Gaza withdrawal – and declare it to be the period in which the Israeli–Palestinian struggle at long last entered its endgame?

It could be. But even though the end might well be in sight, there are a number of reasons to be wary. First, as alluded to before, the two sides have entered the post-Arafat period with what might prove to be widely divergent expectations. Take the issue of the Gaza withdrawal. Mahmud Abbas and his associates want to believe that the withdrawal, if it takes place, will represent the first step down the road to a comprehensive, negotiated settlement – a settlement that will sanction the establishment of a Palestinian state in an undivided West Bank and Gaza. Although it is impossible to know exactly what is going on in Ariel Sharon's mind, we saw in the last chapter that a close associate has already pronounced the Gaza withdrawal to be a line in the sand, a take-it-or-leave-it challenge to the Palestinians, who could now be left to molder behind the barrier. As if to confirm the worst suspicions of the Palestinians, the Israeli government announced in spring 2005 that it would expand the largest of the settlement blocs in the West Bank by over 3,500 housing units. The Israeli government may well intend to impose a unilateral settlement complete with nonnegotiated, nonnegotiable territorial revisions. If so, Palestinian resentments can only fester.

The second reason to be wary is that neither Sharon nor Abbas has garnered anything near unanimous support in their respective communities for their recent acts and pronouncements. Many in Israel view the Gaza withdrawal as an unprecedented assault on those Zionists who continue to regard all of Palestine as a sacred trust or national birthright. In their eyes, this assault is all the more treacherous because it has been engineered by the politician most closely identified with their own diehard commitment to territorial expansion. The boldest among them talk of resistance, revenge, and even civil war. Then there is the Palestinian camp: Although many Palestinians are undoubtedly weary of the incessant conflict and just want to end the occupation so that they might get on with their lives, others are not so languid. The most militant among them reject what they take to be Abbas's willingness to part with any portion of their national legacy. They argue that their fifty-year struggle against Israel warrants a better outcome than any deal Abbas could possibly get. Others bristle at the continued presence of Israeli settlements, the intrusion of the barrier, or the surrender of Jerusalem to Israeli control. It may be that reports of friction within each community are overblown, or that the opposition to Sharon, Abbas, or both is all bluster and that when push comes to shove it will simply melt away. Or there might be a real crisis looming for one or both of the partners for peace.

Finally, we should be wary because we have been down this road before. The diplomats and pundits who express cautious optimism about the post-Arafat era are following in well-worn footsteps. In 1967, diplomats and pundits proclaimed that the Six-Day War had broken the stalemate and that the Israeli capture of Arab territory had set up a "bargaining situation" that would soon bear fruit. In 1993, diplomats and pundits proclaimed that the Oslo Accord all but made a Palestinian state inevitable. Around the corner was a future of "two states living side by side in peace" once Palestinians had realized their national aspirations and Israelis had gotten used to the idea. Thus, if nothing else, a look at the historical record should give us pause.

This is not to say that a resolution to the conflict will always remain elusive. Nor is it to say that the principals will always regard their conflict as a zero-sum game. After all, as the dispute has evolved, so have the criteria for resolving it. Before the collapse of the Soviet Union, the intifada, Yasir Arafat's ghastly diplomacy, and so on, who could have imagined that informal discussions between Israelis and Palestinians over herring and aquavit (my guess) would have set the stage for the famous exchange of recognitions and the reorientation of the conflict to reflect its true nature? Who could have imagined that Ariel Sharon, whose reputation among Palestinians resembles that of General Sherman among American southerners, would undertake what could turn out to be a precedent-setting renunciation of Palestinian territory? And who can imagine what the effects of that renunciation – if indeed there is one – will be in the long term? Although one must always be wary of grasping at straws, it must also be remembered that the dispute is between two rival nationalist movements and that the demands, configuration, and even durability of nationalist movements are not etched in stone. It just might be that the very demands that are held as nonnegotiable today – the ownership of Jerusalem, the Palestinian right of return, the fate of Israeli settlements – will recede in importance tomorrow as the evolution of both the struggle and the international system that enframes that struggle extends the realm of the possible.

GLOSSARY

absolutist state. One of a number of states constructed in Europe during the eighteenth century in which emperors or kings attempted to centralize power in their own hands.

aliyah (pl. aliyot). Wave of Jewish immigration to Palestine.

amir. Military leader or ruler of Middle Eastern principality.

Anglo-American Commission of Inquiry. Established after World War II to resolve problem of displaced persons in Europe; recommended the British allow the emigration of 100,000 Jewish refugees to Palestine.

anti-Semitism. Hatred of Jews.

al-Aqsa intifada. Uprising against Israeli occupation that broke out in 2000 after Ariel Sharon visited the site on which the al-Aqsa mosque stands.

Arab Club. Nationalist society organized in the wake of World War I and based in Damascus.

Arab Executive. Short-lived body organized in 1920 to coordinate the activities of the Muslim-Christian Associations.

Arab Higher Committee. Council established by leading Palestinian notables and their nationalist allies during the Great Revolt of 1936–9; led by the Hajj Amin al-Husayni.

Arab League. Cooperative association of Arab states founded in 1945; regional equivalent of United Nations.

Arab Revolt. Rebellion instigated and financed by the British and led by Amir Faysal against the Ottoman Empire during World War I.

Artamenan movement. Movement among nineteenth-century German youths for the establishment of colonies in Germany's Polish frontier.

al-Azhar. Islamic university in Cairo.

Balfour Declaration. Statement issued by the British government in 1917 that stipulated, among other things, that the British government viewed "with favour" the establishment of a Jewish home in Palestine.

Basel Program. Policies adopted by the First Zionist Congress in 1897; called for the creation of a Jewish home in Palestine to be secured through diplomacy.

Biltmore Program. Issued by the Extraordinary Zionist Congress of 1942; the program called for the immediate establishment of a "Jewish commonwealth" in all of Palestine.

"Black September." The name given to the brutal suppression of PLO guerrillas and their expulsion from Jordan following an aborted insurrection in 1970.

bypass roads. Roads built in the occupied Palestinian territories that connect settlements with each other and with Israel.

Cairo Conference of 1921. Meeting convened by Winston Churchill at which Trans-Jordan, later the Hashemite Kingdom of Jordan, was created.

caliph. Literally, "successor to Muhammad"; leader of Islamic community.

Camp David Accord. Agreement negotiated by Jimmy Carter, Menachem Begin, and Anwar al-Sadat in 1978; it included a framework for peace between Israel and Egypt and a stillborn framework for peace in the region.

Central Powers. One of two main alliances in World War I; the Central Powers included, among others, Germany, the Austro-Hungarian Empire, and the Ottoman Empire.

chalutzim (sing. *chalutz*). Hebrew for "pioneers."

Christian Zionism. An ideology held by Christians and often rooted in Scripture supporting or sympathetic to Jewish aspirations in Palestine.

conquest of labor. Concept popularized during the second and third aliyot; it called on Jews to undertake all vocations in order to reconstitute themselves as a true nation.

conquest of land. Concept popularized during the second and third aliyot; it called on Jews to spread colonies throughout Palestine to make their imprint on the land.

Constantinople Agreement. Precedent-setting treaty signed in 1915 by Britain, France, and Russia outlining the division of Ottoman territories after World War I.

containment policy. America's grand strategy during the Cold War for preventing Soviet expansion.

cotton principalities. Autonomous domains in eighteenth-century Ottoman Palestine; their name derives from their main export and source of revenue.

Crimean War (1853–6). War between Russia, on the one hand, and Britain, France, Piedmont (in contemporary Italy), and the Ottoman Empire, on the other; name derives from the principal site of the conflict.

dawra. Literally, "circle"; refers to the circuit undertaken by the Ottoman governor or his agents to collect taxes.

diaspora. The scattering of a people of common origin, beliefs, etc., such as the Jews; the places where such people settled.

diaspora nationalism. The theory that all Jews worldwide represented a single subject nationality and were entitled to the same political rights as other subject nationalities.

Dreyfus Affair (1894). The accusation and trial of Captain Alfred Dreyfus, a Jewish-French military officer accused of passing military secrets to Germany.

entente powers. The second main alliance in World War I; the entente consisted of, among others, Great Britain, France, Russia, and eventually the United States.

Eretz Israel. Hebrew for "land of Israel."

"facts on the ground." Israeli term for settlements in the occupied territories.

Fatah. Guerrilla group founded by Yasir Arafat in the late 1950s.

fida'iyyun (fedayeen). Literally, "self-sacrificers"; guerrilla fighters.

firman. A ruling issued by the Ottoman sultan.

Fourteen Points. Entente war aims drawn up by Woodrow Wilson; called for "self-determination" of peoples and the establishment of a League of Nations, among other things.

"*Gegenwartsarbeit.*" Literally, "backwards work"; a doctrine held by some Zionists that advocated stimulating a Jewish national revival among Jews living in the diaspora.

ghetto. Parts of cities to which Jews were restricted.

Greater Syria. Territory comprising present-day Syria, Lebanon, Jordan, Israel, the occupied territories, and far western Iraq.

Gush Emunim. Literally, "bloc of the faithful"; organization of Jewish religious nationalists founded in 1974; noted for founding settlements in the occupied territories.

Hagana. During the mandate period, Jewish military force.

hajj. Annual pilgrimage undertaken by Muslims.

Hamas. Acronym for the "Islamic Resistance Movement"; Islamist organization founded in the occupied territories during the intifada.

hamula (**pl.** *hama'il*). Clan.

Haram al-Sharif (see also Temple Mount). Site in Jerusalem of al-Aqsa mosque and Dome of the Rock.

Haskala. Intellectual movement among Jews that spread during the late eighteenth and nineteenth centuries; also called the "Jewish Enlightenment."

Hatt-i Sharif of Gulhane (1839). Ottoman decree promising equality and rights to all Ottoman citizens.

Higher National Committee. Damascus-based popular nationalist organization, established in the wake of World War I, with branches in Palestine.

Hijaz Railway. Railroad constructed in late nineteenth century to connect Istanbul and Arabia.

Histadrut. Yishuv/Israeli trade union federation.

Hizbullah. Lebanese Islamist organization.

Intergovernmental Committee on Refugees. Established by the Allies at the end of World War II to find a solution to the problem presented by large numbers of displaced persons in Europe.

intifada. The Palestinian uprisings against Israeli occupation; the first intifada lasted from 1987 to 1993; the second intifada (the al-Aqsa intifada) broke out in 2000.

Irgun Zvai Leumi (Irgun). Underground militia established by followers of Vladimir Jabotinsky.

Islahat Fermani (1856). Decree promulgated by the Ottoman government that reaffirmed the rights granted to Ottoman citizens under the Hatt-i Sharif of Gulhane.

Islamic Jihad. Islamist organization that emerged during the first intifada as an offshoot of Hamas.

Jaffa orange. Fruit first cultivated in late nineteenth century Palestine; it is characterized by a thick skin.

Jewish Agency. Governing body of the Yishuv; established in 1929.

Jewish emancipation. The process whereby western European states integrated Jews into their body politic.

Jewish National Fund. Body established in 1901 to buy land for the Jewish community in Palestine.

Jewish Pale of Settlement. Territory in western part of the Russian Empire set aside for Jewish habitation; established in 1791.

jihad. Literally, "struggle"; jihad sometimes connotes an "inner struggle" against sin, sometimes "holy war."

Judea and Samaria. Terms used by Israelis for the occupied West Bank; derived from Biblical names of the territory.

kanun. In Ottoman Empire, law derived from imperial decree.

khirba (**pl.** *khirab*). Satellite villages established by the indigenous inhabitants of Palestine for seasonal agricultural activities.

kibbutz (**pl.** *kibbutzim*). Yishuv/Israeli communal farm; the first kibbutz was established in 1909–10.

kibbutzniks. Inhabitants of kibbutzim.

Kishinev pogrom. Pogrom in Moldavan town of Kishinev, 1903.

Knesset. Israeli parliament.

Labor Zionism. Branch of Zionism associated with the Israeli Labor Party and its forebears; it promotes an ideology grounded in socialist principles.

"land for peace." Formula stipulated by United Nations Resolution 242, calling for Israel to surrender occupied territory to Arab states in return for those states ending their "states of belligerency"; the foundation for every serious peace initiative undertaken by the world community since 1967.

Lavon Affair. The plot organized in 1954 by the Israeli defense minister to blow up American and British installations in Egypt and blame the Egyptians.

Law of Return. Israeli law, passed in 1950, that grants all Jews the right to citizenship.

Literary Society. Nationalist society, similar to the Arab Club, with branches throughout Greater Syria.

"long nineteenth century." Term used by historians to refer to the period between 1789 and 1914.

"Lovers of Zion" committees. Committees established in Romania and Russia after the pogroms of 1881 to assist Jewish emigration to Palestine.

mamlachtiyut. Literally, "statism"; doctrine advanced by David Ben-Gurion to wrest power from the voluntary organizations active during the Yishuv period and place it in the hands of the state.

mandates system. An administrative system established by the League of Nations whereby more "advanced" states were delegated to supervise the development of less advanced peoples to prepare them to face "the strenuous conditions of the modern world."

mandatory power. A nation that assumed control over mandated territories; Great Britain was the mandatory power that assumed control over Palestine.

Mapai. Yishuv/Israeli Labor Party.

market economy. Economy in which people produce mainly for exchange, not consumption.

marketplace economy. Economy in which people produce mainly for their own consumption and depend on markets only for those goods they cannot produce themselves.

maskilim. Devotees of the Jewish Enlightenment (Haskala).

Middle East Supply Center. Originally established by the Allies in World War II to allocate cargo space on Mediterranean-bound freighters; the supply center came to plan and regulate national economies in the Middle East region.

miri. Category of land in Ottoman law; arable fields, meadows, pastures, and woodlands over which the state retained the right of ownership.

mixed farming. The practice of diversifying the agricultural goods produced on a farm, as opposed to monoculture.

Mizrahi. Religious Zionist party; precursor of contemporary National Religious Party.

mizrahi. Jew who immigrated to Israel from Arab lands after the establishment of the State of Israel or the descendant of such a Jew.

moshav (**pl.** *moshavim*). Mixed farming cooperative farms established in the Yishuv.

moshava (pl. *moshavot*). Early Zionist agricultural settlement that borrowed many of its practices from the indigenous inhabitants of Palestine.

mufti. Muslim judicial official who interprets Islamic law.

mujahid (pl. *mujahidin*). An individual who participates in jihad.

Muslim Brotherhood. Founded in 1928 in Egypt, the Muslim Brotherhood was perhaps the first modern, mass-based Islamic political association in the Arab world; it established branches in Palestine in the wake of the Great Revolt.

Muslim-Christian Associations. Nationalist associations founded in Palestine at the tail end of World War I; called for Palestine to be part of a federated, independent Syria.

nakba. Literally, "disaster"; word used by Palestinians to refer to the 1948 war.

negation of exile. Idea held among many Zionists that Jews had to renounce the culture and values of the postexilic Jewish community to become a true nation.

New Historians. Group of Israeli historians that emerged in the 1980s; the New Historians offered a reassessment of Zionist historiography by taking advantage of newly released documents.

New World Order. America's first post-Cold War strategy, built on the assumption that the United States could maintain its position in international affairs best by applying the principles of multilateralism and economic globalization.

"open bridges." Israeli policy, adopted after the 1967 war, that allowed residents of the occupied West Bank to continue to cross over into Jordan.

Operation Hiram. During the 1948 war, Zionist military campaign in the Galilee region of Palestine to remove the Palestinian population.

Oslo Accord. The 1993 agreement reached between Israel and the Palestinians; it included an exchange of letters in which each side recognized the other and it established a framework for further negotiations.

Oslo 2. Interim territorial agreement negotiated between Israelis and Palestinians that established zones under various degrees of Palestinian control.

osmanlilik. Ottoman consciousness or nationalism.

Ostjude. Eastern European Jew.

Palestine Foundation Fund. Body governed by Jewish Agency that underwrote immigration and settlement activities.

Palestine General Congress. Assembly convened in February 1920; called for Syrian independence and elimination of Zionism from Palestine.

Palestine Liberation Organization (PLO). Founded in 1964, the PLO is commonly recognized as the "sole legitimate representative of the Palestinian people."

Palestine National Council (PNC). The legislative branch of the PLO.

Palestinian Authority (PA). The "interim self-governing authority" that, according to the Oslo Accord, is to administer those areas of the West Bank and Gaza Strip not under direct Israeli rule.

Palmach. Yishuv "strike force" organized during the Great Palestine Revolt.

Peel Commission. Commission established by the British in 1937 to investigate the unrest in the Palestine mandate and propose remedial measures; the commission declared the mandate unworkable and proposed division of Palestine between communities.

plantation. Large-scale agricultural unit usually distinguished by monoculture; the immigrants of the first aliyah attempted to establish an economy based on plantations.

pogrom. Anti-Semitic riot, increasingly common in the Russian Empire in the last decades of the nineteenth century.

post-Zionism. The idea that Israel could or should overcome the burden of its Zionist past and become a "normal" state.

primitive rebellion. Prenationalist or nonnationist rebellion, characterized by its brevity, spontaneity, limited reach, and defensive nature.

rent. State income derived from sources other than internal taxation.

Revisionist Zionism. Branch of Zionism that seeks the establishment of a Jewish state on both sides of the Jordan River and rejects the socialist tenets of Labor Zionism.

"Rhodes format." Negotiating formula that avoids bringing together Israel and the Arab states in face-to-face negotiations; instead, a mediator arbitrates the dispute between the parties, who do not meet to negotiate.

right of return. The right, claimed by many Palestinians, to return to their homes inside the Green line that they left during the nakba of 1948.

St. James Conference. Conference called by the British during the Great Revolt; because attendees included Egypt, Iraq, Saudi Arabia, Trans-Jordan, and Yemen, the conference in effect internationalized the conflict in Palestine.

shari'a. Islamic law.

shtetl. Jewish village in the pale.

shuhada' (sing. *shahid*). martyr.

shuttle diplomacy. The diplomatic strategy carried out by Henry Kissinger, whereby he mediated the disengagement of Israeli and Arab forces by flying from capital to capital after the 1973 war.

Stern Gang. Terrorist spin-off of the Irgun.

Suez War. Invasion of Egypt in 1956 by Israel, Britain, and France; known in Egypt as the "Tripartite Aggression."

Sufism. Popular Islam, sometimes mystically inclined, in which followers of a pious founder organize themselves into networks.

sultan. Title adopted by rulers, such as the head of the Ottoman Empire, in the Middle East.

Supreme Muslim Council. Body established by the British during the mandate period to administer Islamic courts and endowments.

Sykes-Picot Agreement. Secret treaty negotiated by France, Britain, and Russia in 1916; it divided up the Ottoman Empire into zones of direct and indirect control and placed Jerusalem under international control.

Syrian General Congress. Parliament elected in the aftermath of World War I; called for independence and unity of "Greater Syria."

Templars. Group of German Protestant settlers who established colonies in Palestine beginning in the late 1860s.

Temple Mount (see also Haram al-Sharif). Site in Jerusalem that, according to many Jews, was the site of the first and second temples.

Third Worldism. A loose doctrine that combined anti-imperialism, non-alignment, and state-guided economic development and was popular among governments of the developing world from the 1950s to the beginning of the 1970s.

Trans-Jordan. The territory to the east of the Jordan River; currently the Hashemite Kingdom of Jordan.

umma. Originally, the community of Muslims; has come to refer to nation.

United Arab Republic. Union of Egypt and Syria that lasted from 1958 to 1961.

United Nations Relief and Works Agency (UNRWA). Successor organization to United Nations Relief for Palestine.

United Nations Relief for Palestine. First apparatus set up by the United Nations to deal with the plight of Palestinian refugees.

United Nations Resolution 242. Resolution passed by the Security Council of the United Nations after the 1967 war; it established the "land-for-peace" formula.

United Nations Resolution 338. Resolution passed by the Security Council of the United Nations after the 1973 war; it fundamentally reiterated United Nations Resolution 242.

United Nations Special Committee on Palestine (UNSCOP). General Assembly committee established in 1947 to investigate the Palestine problem and make recommendations; majority report recommended partition.

utopian socialism. Belief that a harmonious and egalitarian society free of exploitation, competition, and class divisions could be built through voluntary, cooperative efforts.

viticulture. Cultivation of grapes.

Yiddish. Lingua franca of Jews of eastern Europe; derived mostly from German and Hebrew, with some Slavic and Old French.

Yishuv. The pre-state Jewish community in Palestine.

War of Attrition. Launched by Egypt in the wake of the 1967 war, the War of Attrition began with artillery duels between Egypt and Israel on opposite sides of the Suez Canal before escalating into a major international crisis.

War on Terrorism. The second United States strategy in the post-Cold War era; it was sparked by the events of September 11.

White Paper of 1939. Report issued by British government on eve of World War II recommending no partition of Palestine, eventual independence for Palestine once the situation had calmed, limitations on Jewish immigration, and restrictions on land sales; the report was official British policy during the war.

World Zionist Organization. Organization established in 1897 at the First Zionist Congress "to create for the Jewish people a home in Palestine secured by Public Law"; the W.Z.O. has been the central institutional expression of the international Zionist movement.

Zionism. The belief that Jews represent a national community entitled to their own independent state; Zionists have usually (but not always) viewed Palestine as the ideal location for such a state.

TIME LINE OF EVENTS

1516 Ottomans incorporate Palestine into their emerging empire.

1772 First division of Poland among Russia, Austria, and Prussia; the Russian Empire becomes home to large number of Jews.

1791 France becomes first European country to emancipate its Jews; Russian Empire establishes Jewish Pale of Settlement.

1831–41 Egyptian occupation of Palestine.

1839 Ottoman government issues the Hatt-i Sharif of Gulhane, marking the beginning of the Ottoman "reform" period.

1858 Ottoman government issues new land code, granting official recognition to private ownership of land in the empire.

1873 Onset of first real international depression.

1881 With assassination of Tsar Alexander II, widespread pogroms erupt in Russia; "Lovers of Zion" committees founded in Russia and Romania.

1882 Ottoman sultan officially sanctions Jewish immigration to the Ottoman Empire in regions outside Palestine.

1882–1903 First aliyah.

1896 Theodor Herzl publishes *The Jewish State*.

1897 The World Zionist Organization formed.

1901 Jewish National Fund established to coordinate Zionist land purchases in Palestine.

1903 Kishinev pogrom.

1904–5 Russo-Japanese War.

1905 Failed revolution in Russia.

1904–14 Second aliyah.

1909 Establishment of first kibbutz in Degania, Palestine; founding of Tel Aviv as Jewish suburb of Jaffa.

1914–18 World War I; end of the Ottoman Empire.

1917 Revolution in Russia; the British government issues the Balfour Declaration.

1918 Woodrow Wilson announces his Fourteen Points.

1919–23 Third aliyah.

1920 The League of Nations founded; First Palestine Congress; Arab Executive founded; first large-scale Zionist-Palestinian clashes.

1921 The British sever Trans-Jordan (later Jordan) from the territory of Palestine; the United States applies quotas to European immigration for the first time.

1922 The League of Nations ratifies the draft "instrument" that defines the terms of the Palestine mandate.

1923 Vladimir Jabotinsky founds Betar.

1924–8 Fourth aliyah.

1929 Onset of Great Depression; Jewish Agency organized; "Wailing Wall" riots.

1929–39 Fifth aliyah brings close to 200,000 Jewish immigrants to Palestine.

1930 Labor Party (Mapai) founded.

1931 Irgun founded.

1935 Death of 'Izz al-Din al-Qassam.

1936–9 Great Palestine Revolt; founding of the Arab Higher Committee.

1937 British government issues Peel Commission report proposing division of Palestine between Zionists and Palestinians.

1939 British government issues White Paper rescinding call for partition and restricting Jewish immigration and land purchases.

1939–45 World War II.

1942 World Zionist organization issues "Biltmore Program" calling for the immediate establishment of a Jewish commonwealth in all of Palestine.

1946 Irgun terrorists blow up the King David Hotel, the British headquarters in Palestine.

1947 Britain submits Palestine question to the United Nations; United Nations votes for partition of Palestine; civil war breaks out in Palestine between Jewish and Palestinian communities.

1948 State of Israel proclaimed; Arab states invade Palestine.

1949 Ralph Bunche mediates armistice agreements between Israel and its neighbors.

1952 Free Officers take power in Egypt.

1954–62 Algerian Revolution.

1956 Suez War ("Tripartite Aggression"); Israel, Britain, and France invade Egypt.

1957 (?) Founding of Fatah.

1958–61 Egypt and Syria united in the United Arab Republic.

1964 Palestine Liberation Organization founded.

1966 Israel lifts martial law restrictions on Arab citizens.

1967 Six-Day War; United Nations adopts Resolution 242; Khartoum Summit Conference.

1969 Yasir Arafat assumes leadership of PLO.

1970 "Black September": Jordanian government confronts PLO and drives it to Beirut.

1973 The October War; United Nations reaffirms Resolution 242 in Resolution 338.

1974 Arab states recognize PLO as the "sole legitimate representative of the Palestinian people"; PLO calls for the establishment of a Palestinian mini-state on the West Bank and Gaza Strip; Gush Emunim founded.

1977 First Likud prime minister, Menachem Begin, assumes power; Egyptian President Anwar al-Sadat flies to Jerusalem.

1978 Camp David negotiations between Israel and Egypt.

1978–9 Iranian Revolution leads to the establishment of an "Islamic republic."

1979 Israel-Egypt peace treaty.

1982 Israel invades Lebanon; Phalange militiamen massacre Palestinians in Sabra and Shatila.

1987 Outbreak of intifada in occupied Gaza and the West Bank; Hamas founded.

1988 Yasir Arafat agrees to United Nations Resolutions 242 and 338 as basis for negotiations with Israel.

1989 Soviet bloc begins unraveling; United States President George H. W. Bush and Soviet President Mikhail Gorbachev declare end of Cold War.

1991 Gulf War.

1992 Israelis elect Labor Party candidate Yitzhak Rabin prime minister.

1993 Oslo Accord establishes framework for future negotiations between Palestinians and Israelis.

1994 Palestinian self-rule in Gaza and Jericho area begins; Israeli-Jordanian peace treaty.

1995 Oslo 2 signed.

1996 Palestinian Authority elected.

2000 "All or nothing at all" summit held at Camp David; Ariel Sharon visits the Temple Mount/Haram al-Sharif; outbreak of second (al-Aqsa) intifada.

2001 Al-Qaida attacks the United States; President George W. Bush announces "War on Terrorism."

2002 Israeli Prime Minister Ariel Sharon launches "Operation Defensive Shield"; Israelis begin construction of separation barrier.

2004 Israeli Prime Minister Ariel Sharon announces unilateral Israeli withdrawal from Gaza and some West Bank settlements.

BIOGRAPHICAL SKETCHES

'Abd al-Nasser, Gamal (1918–70). Leader of Free Officers Movement that took power in Egypt in 1952; president of Egypt during 1956 Suez War ("Tripartite Aggression") and 1967 war with Israel.

'Abdullah (1882–1951). Son of Sharif Husayn of Mecca; installed by British as amir of Trans-Jordan; first king of Jordan; Jordanian leader during 1948 war.

Arafat, Yasir (1929–2004). Guerrilla leader and chairman of PLO from 1969 to 2004; first president of the Palestinian Authority.

Barak, Ehud (1942–). Labor Party leader; elected prime minister of Israel in 1999; presented all-or-nothing offer at Camp David Summit, 2000.

Begin, Menachem (1913–92). First Likud prime minister of Israel; negotiated Camp David Treaty with Egypt (1979) and authorized Israeli invasion of Lebanon (1982).

Ben-Gurion, David (1886–1973). Second aliyah immigrant to Palestine; leader of Palestine Zionist Executive, the Palestinian branch of the World Zionist Organization; first prime minister of Israel.

Bunche, Ralph (1904–71). American diplomat with United Nations; arranged armistice agreements at end of 1948 war; invented "Rhodes format."

Catherine the Great (1729–96). Tsarina of Russia; established Jewish Pale of Settlement in 1791.

Darwish, Mahmoud (1942–). Palestinian poet; considered by many to be the Palestinian national poet.

Herzl, Theodor (1860–1904). Viennese journalist; Zionist pioneer; organized First Zionist Congress in Basel, Switzerland, at which World Zionist Organization was founded.

al-Husayni, Hajj Amin (1897–1974). Scion of prominent notable family of Jerusalem; mufti of Jerusalem, president of Supreme Muslim Council, founder and leader of Arab Higher Committee during the 1930s and 1940s.

Hussein (1935–99). King of Jordan; grandson of 'Abdullah; expelled PLO from Jordan during Black September (1970); signed peace treaty with Israel (1994).

Ibrahim Pasha (1789–1848). Son of Mehmet Ali; general who led Egyptian invasion and occupation of Palestine (1831–41).

Jabotinsky, Vladimir (1880–1940). Russian-born journalist; founder of paramilitary Betar; emigrated to Palestine, where he organized Irgun; architect of Revisionist Zionism.

al-Jazzar, Ahmad Pasha (1722–1804). Former Egyptian slave, warlord, and Ottoman governor; established principality based in Sidon; nicknamed "*al-saffah*" ("the butcher").

Mehmet Ali (1769–1849). Leader of Albanian contingent of Ottoman army sent to Egypt to oust Napoleon; recognized by Ottomans as viceroy of Egypt; sent Ibrahim Pasha to Palestine.

Pinsker, Leo (1821–91). Russian physician and early Zionist; author of *Autoemancipation*; president of Lovers of Zion movement and moving spirit behind first aliyah.

al-Qassam, 'Izz al-Din (1880–1935). Syrian-born preacher; resistance fighter against French (1919–20); organized guerrillas to fight British and Zionists; death at the hands of British was one of the events that incited the Great Revolt; first true Palestinian national hero.

Rabin, Yitzhak (1922–95). Israeli military leader, politician, and prime minister (1992–5); committed Israel to Oslo Accord; assassinated by religious zealot.

de Rothschild, Baron Edmond (1845–1934). Philanthropist and heir to Rothschild family banking fortune; invested in first-aliyah plantations in Palestine but withdrew support in 1900.

al-Sadat, Anwar (1918–81). Member of Free Officers Movement that took over Egypt in 1952; vice-president of Egypt under Nasser; president of Egypt after Nasser's death; signed peace treaty with Israel (1979).

Sharon, Ariel (1928–). Israeli general, Likud politician, and prime minister (2001–); chief architect of Israeli settlement program; visit to Temple Mount/Haram al-Sharif in 2000 provoked second intifada;

initiated construction of separation barrier and proposed Gaza withdrawal.

Shuqairy, Ahmad (1907–80). Diplomat who worked in the service of various Arab states; first chairman of PLO (1964–9).

al-ʿUmar, Zahir (1749–75). Warlord of bedouin origin; founded cotton principality based in Acre; deposed by Ottomans and Ahmad al-Jazzar.

INDEX